FEMINIST IMAGINATION

Theory, Culture & Society

Theory, Culture & Society caters for the resurgence of interest in culture within contemporary social science and the humanities. Building on the heritage of classical social theory, the book series examines ways in which this tradition has been reshaped by a new generation of theorists. It also publishes theoretically informed analyses of everyday life, popular culture, and new intellectual movements.

EDITOR: Mike Featherstone, *Nottingham Trent University*

SERIES EDITORIAL BOARD
Roy Boyne, *University of Durham*
Mike Hepworth, *University of Aberdeen*
Scott Lash, *Goldsmiths College, University of London*
Roland Robertson, *University of Pittsburgh*
Bryan S. Turner, *University of Cambridge*

THE TCS CENTRE
The Theory, Culture & Society book series, the journals *Theory, Culture & Society* and *Body & Society*, and related conference, seminar and postgraduate programmes operate from the TCS Centre at Nottingham Trent University. For further details of the TCS Centre's activities please contact:

Centre Administrator
The TCS Centre, Room 175
Faculty of Humanities
Nottingham Trent University
Clifton Lane, Nottingham, NG11 8NS, UK
e-mail: tcs@ntu.ac.uk
web: http://tcs@ntu.ac.uk

Recent volumes include:

Radical Conservatism and the Future of Politics
Göran Dahl

Spaces of Culture
Mike Featherstone and Scott Lash

Love and Eroticism
edited by Mike Featherstone

Polar Inertia
Paul Virilio

Performativity and Belonging
edited by Vikki Bell

FEMINIST IMAGINATION

Genealogies in Feminist Theory

Vikki Bell

SAGE Publications

London • Thousand Oaks • New Delhi

First published 1999

Published in association with *Theory, Culture & Society*,
Nottingham Trent University

 SAGE Publications Ltd
6 Bonhill Street
London EC2A 4PU

SAGE Publications Inc.
2455 Teller Road
Thousand Oaks, California 91320

SAGE Publications India Pvt Ltd
32, M-Block Market
Greater Kailash – I
New Delhi 110 048

British Library Cataloguing in Publication data

A catalogue record for this book is available
from the British Library

ISBN 0 8039 7970 3
ISBN 0 8039 7971 1 (pbk)

Library of Congress catalog card number 99–72800

Typeset by Mayhew Typesetting, Rhayader, Powys
Printed and bound in Great Britain by Athenaeum Press,
Gateshead

CONTENTS

Acknowledgements   vii

1 **Affirming Feminism**   **1**
    Outline of the book   13

2 **Phantastic Communities and Dangerous Thinking: Feminist**
   Political Imagination   **17**
    Sculpting feminism   18
    Feminism and figures of finitude   21
    From the first to the third phase with Kristeva: why so
    quarrelsome?   25
    The trouble with being tempted by Nietzsche   30
    Dangerous thinking and the future of feminism   34
    Conclusion: so what if we're phantastic?   38

3 **Suffering: Thinking Politics with Simone de Beauvoir and**
   Richard Wright   **40**
    Wounded attachment? Feminism and ressentiment   40
    Beyond ressentiment: modes of connectivity   53

4 **Appearance: Thinking Difference in the Political Realm with**
   Hannah Arendt   **62**
    'Little Rock'   63
    Appearing in the political realm   67
    Appearance and natality   71
    Difference and/in the public realm   75
    Conclusion   80

5 **Mimesis as Cultural Survival: Judith Butler and Anti-Semitism**   **85**
    Butler, mimesis and imitation: carrying on gender   86
    Judaism, anti-Semitism and mimesis   93
    Mimesis in a new agenda   102
    Conclusion   111

6 **Essentialism and Embodiment: The Politics behind the Paranoia**   **113**
    Essentialism and paranoia   114
    Appealing to the body: re-reading Levinas on the body and
    Hitlerism   119

Emerging bodies, exploding bodies: the work of Frantz
Fanon   124
Embodiment in feminist theory   132
Conclusion   137

7 **Conclusion: Trauma and Temporality in Genealogical Feminist
Critique**   **139**

References   153

Index   161

ACKNOWLEDGEMENTS

The publication of this work owes much to the encouragement of the *Theory, Culture & Society* team, and I am especially grateful to Scott Lash and Mike Featherstone for their initial invitation, and to Stephen Barr of Sage.

I am indebted in many ways to Paul Gilroy, who has co-designed and co-taught several of the courses within which I explored these ideas, but whose generosity has exceeded that role. His thought is truly 'without banisters', as Hannah Arendt put it; and I hope he will see his influence and encouragement reflected in this book. Les Back's work has lived and blossomed across the hall from mine, and I have been delighted to have had the experience of his accompaniment on various – theoretical, personal and musical – journeys. I would like to thank Nikolas Rose for his work, his friendship and support. The 'History of the Present' Network has been a place to discuss issues around the work of Michel Foucault – I am grateful to the group and for the friendship of its members. A big thank you to other colleagues and friends within and outside Goldsmiths College – especially Emilios Christodoulidis, Anne Marie Fortier, Mariam Fraser, Monica Greco, Celia Lury, Maggie O'Neill, Tom Osborne, Colin Perrin, Fran Tonkiss, Vron Ware. My students, graduate and undergraduate, helped me sort out my thoughts more than perhaps they realise.

Judith Butler lent me her office and her inspiration on my term's sabbatical at the Department of Rhetoric, Berkeley, University of California, and gave me the opportunity to have feedback from the scholars gathered there. I thank in particular Dina Al-Kassim for her friendship and careful reading. My time in San Francisco was made special by the generosity of David Eng and the renewed friendships of Marianne Constable, Kum Kum Bhavnani, and Leti and Serena Volpp; also by Tommy Lott, whose considered thoughts and company were much appreciated. Many thanks are due to Lewis Eichele for becoming my cherished friend and for taping *The Simpsons* for me, and to David Goldberg who continues to give me trans-Atlantic encouragement and to share his work generously.

As ever, I thank Sam King – there is no thought without barristers – and Charlotte Pomery, the kindest of friends. Rachel Cottam, Jenny Kent and Pete Jones have been sources of humour and sanity. I acknowledge my family, and especially my nephews: Nathaniel, Vivian, Ashley and Jacob. This book is dedicated to the memory of my granny, Betty Bell, who would have loved to have been able to tease her blue-stocking granddaughter on publication day.

Paul Kerr came back into my life as if to persuade me to fate and faith; my main distraction and my main source of sustenance, I thank him for his love, affection and creativity. Also to Ella, thanks for intermittently reminding me how far past my delivery date this manuscript was, and other stuff besides.

None of the above, of course, bears any responsibility for, nor necessarily concords with, the arguments posited here; these are mine alone.

Vikki Bell
London

1

AFFIRMING FEMINISM

[T]he question of whether or not a position is right, coherent or interesting is, in this case, less informative than why it is that we come to occupy and defend the territory that we do, from what it promises to protect us. (Judith Butler, 1995: 128)

Not 'what can I know?' but rather 'how have my questions been produced?' . . . Not 'what ought I to do?' but rather 'how have I been situated to experience the real? How have exclusions operated in delineating the realm of obligation for me?' Not 'what may I hope for?' but rather 'what are the struggles in which I am engaged? How has my aspiration been defined?' (James Bernauer, 1995: 270–1)

What does it mean to affirm oneself as a feminist? Of what does a 'yes' to feminism consist? The privileged task of writing about one's own political affiliations is one that entails not simply a statement of commitments, and not even that, but a statement of commitment to reworking, genealogically, what one believes. Such a proposition is, of course, a result in turn of a commitment to a particular theoretical stance. And it is one that in a sense I would rather not hold. It would be easier not to have read Foucault, not to place oneself in a position in which every statement is rendered under the scrutiny of Foucault's re-posing of the Kantian questions. In terms of a commitment to feminism, the questions run: How have contemporary concerns about gender been produced? How have feminist aspirations been defined? How have exclusions operated in the realm of feminist obligation? But read Foucault I have, and thus the work presented here has as its initial impulse one that makes wonderous at the same time as it makes worrisome the formation of political 'communities'.

This book is therefore about turning an affirmation of feminism toward the feminist political imagination itself, in contemplation of the very shape and forms of feminist arguments, affiliations and aspirations. Introducing his book *Present Hope*, Andrew Benjamin has written recently 'philosophy is constituted by an act of engagement with its own history. Engagement can take many forms. Here, and in contrast to a simple repetition of the Same, it is present as the process of *reworking*' (1997: 1, emphasis added). Feminism is more than philosophical; feminism has been an articulation, a set of demands, forces and strategies, the successes of which I for one have inherited and benefited from, since it has also been a generational gift. But when I say 'I am a feminist' I am fully aware that any statement of belonging, of aspiration and of commitment is necessarily a mobilisation of both a political *and* a philosophical imagination. And of what does the gift of feminism consist if not a certain bundle of ways of thinking historically, ways of seeing, ways of hoping? It is of feminist theory that I write in this book, and it is a reworking, genealogically, in the sense of an engagement with the gift of feminist imagination.

Why suggest a mode of engagement that takes a genealogical form? Why consider that a commitment to feminism involves a commitment to genealogical thought?

Genealogy, in Nietzsche's sense, was meant to help one understand the nature of one's commitment to the value that motivates inquiry into that same value. Giving one's commitment a history does not necessarily dislodge that commitment, but it gives some insight into its formation, its disparity, contingencies, its becoming, into what has defined it, and hence, in part, defines oneself. For Nietzsche, genealogy is tragic in that the hold that certain commitments (especially, for him, certain religious truths) have upon us are in some ways fateful to who we are (Havas, 1995: 179); while we innocently assume them to be achievements, they can be given histories that are not only contingent developments but also are infused with the will to power (Nilson, 1998; Havas, 1995). In terms of feminist commitment, my engagement with the development of a body of feminist theorising is motivated less by an attempt to reveal the machinations of a will to power, and more in general terms by a commitment to understand the 'yes'. I am writing less along Nietzschean lines, to trace the 'will to power', and more attempting to follow in Foucault's genealogical footsteps, but in a direction that begins from my interest in feminist theory and its genealogical connections. The ensuing questions are such as those posed by the opening quotations of this chapter. What is it that motivates that affirmation? What is the resultant realm of obligation? From what does it protect? How have I been situated by that affirmation?

Thus genealogy is an attempt to historicise values, sentiments and modes of argument in the sense of seeking their relationship to past events and concerns. In this work, I am not attempting a comprehensive genealogy of feminist commitment, a task that would be beyond my scope, and which would be an ambitious task indeed. What I consider in the essays that constitute this book relates to specific aspects of debates that have taken place within feminist theory, or to specific thinkers. Nor am I engaged in autobiography, which would be a genealogy of my particular 'yes'. There is, nevertheless, a 'politics of location' involved in the specific ways in which I have reflected upon feminist debates and theory. My location – British academic feminism – is certainly an important factor in directing my attention. Moreover, the direction in which I pursue the genealogies, the links I follow and connections I make, are also informed by my location and concerns.

And while there is a certain naivety in explaining, or excusing, one's writing according to identity or location – as Gillian Rose has written, *apropos* the suggestion that she might write 'as a woman' or 'as a Jew', 'if I knew who or what I was I would not write' (1993: ix) – still my attention is no doubt channelled to certain issues and problematics (in particular, I have been concerned to think about the connections between feminist theory and racism) that are correlated with where I write from. Exploring certain genealogical paths which are biased toward that concern has taken me to other unfamiliar locations, but in the main the focus has been biased to the links and connections between Europe and the United States. Furthermore, the way in which I argue for a form of genealogical understanding of feminist debates is not *determined* by my location, but that is necessarily shaped by the space that I inhabit, so that I would tend to agree with Spivak when she suggests that 'no one can articulate the space she herself inhabits. My attempt has been to describe this relatively ungraspable space in terms of what might be its history' (1990: 68). I have become interested, as will become clear, in how the development of 'second wave' feminist theory has been shaped by the concerns with thinking racism in the post-Second World War period, when the reverberations of articulating belongings have the shadow of fascism and racist destruction cast over them.[1] The affirmation of feminism, therefore, is reworked as a series of specific genealogies that seek to show how 'race' and questions of racism have been placed within the feminist imagination as it has developed in feminist theory. I have kept my investigations relatively specific and they are, in the main, based around relatively close readings of particular texts. They are, therefore, partial in many senses of the term.

* * *

One has to maintain a certain humility whenever one speaks of political communities, of any community for that matter, as an academic theoretician. Such humility is one that resists the temptation to close the text with statements that assume the position of greater political insight simply by virtue of reflection. The tenability of that assumption has long gone. Theoreticians, like politicians, cease to be interesting, or to offer any hope for the future, whenever they imagine their ideas to encapsulate all that there is to say. Foucault made a statement to this effect (in relation to the Iran–Iraq war):

> There are more ideas on earth than intellectuals imagine. And these ideas are more active, stronger, more resistant, more passionate than 'politicians' think . . .

---

1 I certainly did not intend this book to become 'about' fascism, and, indeed, I still would wish to assert that no part of it is, in any real sense, analytic of such political formations. The focus is always on feminism, and particularly a rumination on the areality of the political imagination that enables and informs feminist thought. However, it is the case that in writing a book which addresses the above problematics, I became more and more drawn into a discussion of theorists from a certain era, the post-Second World War period, who were involved and influenced, some profoundly, some less clearly, by the changing nature of the political contexts in which they wrote. How are we to imagine feminism as a movement of the twentieth century if we do not see its relation and response to other political visions that have animated this century's political movements and moments?

Ideas do not rule the world. But it is because the world has ideas (and because it constantly produces them) that it is not passively ruled by those who are its leaders or those who would like to teach it, once and for all, what it must think. (in Eribon, 1991: 282)

This book begins from the premise that such a position should not be feared; indeed, any sense of danger conjured up by intellectual engagement without the possibility of political solutions must be confronted and understood, rather than altering one's theoretical stance to make it more 'practically' productive. Several debates have surrounded the work of Foucault on this point, for many have found cause to argue that Foucault disappoints. In a search for something more, for a prophetic moment, for some form of guidance, the term 'political' is frequently served (up) as the final accusation: What are the political implications? How are we to become political, remain political, be effectively political? Even, where is the political? Noting that Foucault's refusal to engage with such questions in his written intellectual texts did not prevent him from engaging with politics through other activities in his life – witness the 'humanist' impulses, the roles of reluctant mentor as well as the 'mistakes' of that life – some have sought to sketch the implicit political trajectory of Foucault. I am not convinced that such a route promises much. I am more interested in why genealogical modes of investigation have become cast either as apolitical or as nihilistic. Genealogy is not passive; its engagement is one that is attentive, and attentive to the detail of the present in a way that more straightforwardly 'political' perspectives are not, seeing only the same struggles reproduced in every location. A history of the present suggests a commitment, broadly speaking, to a present that surrounds the commentator, a commitment that is also a decision to be alive to the historical. Agnes Heller has made such a point:

In the absence of historical consciousness, one can live in the present without choosing it. But then, one does not live historically, or rather, one's historical existence remains (or becomes) unconscious. Ever since historical existence became a matter of reflection, the philosopher's scorn turned against the man who lived only in the present, and justly so. (1993: 223)

One of the most controversial aspects of Foucault's work was the sense in which his genealogical reflections on the present avoided the impulse to locate, judge and denounce the political enemy. Frequently, Foucault's attention was on the modes of argumentation that surround and contest the chimerical source of power. His concern with monitoring the ways in which the politics of resistance are enunciated and practised on the 'inside' of power relations – a statement in danger of slipping into the most banal and least constructive of academic exchanges – needs to be kept close to the sheer historical and contemporary weight that such a statement carries. In addressing what follows from this argument, one begins a commentary on those political issues which are our most pressing. Thus the string of questions: Why do we argue like *that*? What are the connotations of imagining that our world functions in *this* way? How are we imagining the *target* of our political struggles? From whence did the imagination of our utopias arise? Such questions pull into the frame a set of questions that have been, and are being, debated and fought around the world over. What notion of citizenship should one mobilise around in the contemporary world, given the genealogies of the concept 'citizen'? What mode of democracy, given its display of imperfections? What ethical criterion, given their crisis? Which affinities?

The invitation to assess critically one's own political affiliations, the modes of constitution and compromise, the forms of rhetoric and argument that are deployed in the name of resistance, is also an invitation to consider the ways in which political imagination is presented, is 'made present'. Denise Riley has written: 'The question of the politics of identity could be rephrased as a question of rhetoric. Not so much of whether there was for a particular moment any truthful underlying rendition of "women" or not, but of what the proliferations of addresses, descriptions and attributions were doing' (1992: 122). The assessment that this book represents is an attempt to take up this approach in its specific context; to consider moments in the feminist imagination with an attentiveness to the modes of address and argument, rather than as it were simply entering into the debates in order to push specific political or theoretical points.

There is nothing obvious about the form and formulations that are practised as politics. The tracing of what counts as, feels or looks like resistance – the logic, calculations, and aporias of its operations – is an attempt to open up for examination the conditions of possibility of the political landscape. Some of the most imaginative and complicated strategies of resistance are performed in times of war amidst violence and uncertainty. But equally there are styles of contestation that are enacted in the most mundane and routine situations of everyday lives, and these too are both political and imaginative. Between the bloody and the everyday, moreover, there are all the various ways in which political involvement is articulated and put to work. Attentive to the historical twists and turns that enable these articulations, the exercise of questioning the political present is not necessarily searching for a telos that will enable a movement and moment beyond that present. The study of conceptions of the political and of utopian visions does not in itself require the offering of a critique that stems from a different alternative imagination; that would be a different exercise, one that battles at the same level of abstraction as the focus of one's attention.

The alternative vision of feminism is a display of an imaginative faculty; but while it is 'about' the future, it is in the present, and, therefore, open to historical and genealogical understanding. Feminism has been made present, in both the sense of gifted and actualised, in my life, in my work, in this book. It offers a way of thinking that is, certainly, political. But it is not merely directive, and it involves all kinds of modes of understandings, often conflictual, about how the world works. One of the tasks of this book is to think longer about some parts of that understanding, because in saying 'yes' to feminism, I commit myself to a form of political awareness, while at the same time I am intellectually obligated to ponder my 'yes' and to think genealogically about that political commitment, for partaking in feminism involves a partaking in marking out boundaries. In the course of his discussion of Derridean thought, Jeff Bennington argues that a 'yes' is not a simple affirmation, but is '*already* a promise of its own repetition, in anticipated memory of itself, divided in its act just as was the signature (itself a way of saying yes to what one signs and to the fact of appending one's name to it) . . . "Yes" opens a future in which one will again say "yes"' (Bennington and Derrida, 1993: 199). Feminists might disagree with such a statement taken out of its context, given the history of sexual violence against women, but declaring oneself feminist is, within 'our' own ranks, considered an affiliation that has a constancy about it. Declaring oneself a feminist is a risky manoeuvre because all statements of affiliation are just that. In the 'yes' to the appellation 'feminist', what does one sign up to repeat?

I am suggesting, therefore, that the repetition that one engages in is a process of involvement in feminism 'becoming historical', and that being alive to how feminist thought sits in relation to past ways of thinking about the phenomena that constitute feminism's concerns is not merely an exercise in thinking about the past, but is simultaneously an indication of a contemporary commitment. It is both 'historical' and futural, for the commitment is to a continuity that operates against time. that battles with the possibility that these commitments may evaporate, and that time will let them be forgotten. In thinking about how the present political imagi-nation might sit within the concerns of this century that has belonged to it, and to 'us' – that is, in thinking genealogically – I am attempting to consider the relationship of the feminist imagination not mundanely to 'its history', but rather to its temporality. Jean-Luc Nancy, whose provocative work I employ in the next chapter, has put the point succinctly: 'History, in its happening, is what we are never able to be present to, and *this* is our existence and our "we". Our "we" is constituted by this nonpresence, which is not a presence at all, but which is the happening as such' (1993a: 160). Feminism is becoming historic, and this both in the sense that it has been a significant force of the twentieth century *and*, more profoundly, in the sense that in its happening it cannot be grasped, giving 'feminists' the enunciative ground for saying 'we', even as the historic quality of what occurs is never present, and never appears as such. The 'we' of feminism here, therefore, is used ironically, referring not to a real, felt sentiment of belonging that is shared by any person declaring themselves 'feminist', but being used more in the sense that feminism is 'becoming historic', that 'we' are becoming constituted by it, and our engagement with 'feminism' is one that necessarily takes the form of an engagement with a non-presence. And this is not to be bemoaned, for to pretend that feminism were simply and merely 'of' the present would be just that, a pretence. The choice to think genealogically – with the attitude of the genealogist – about the feminist political imagination, therefore, emerges out of this conviction that the present feminist political imagination in the specificity of its presentness is formed and informed by the past, by the traces of the past that remain within feminist theory, conceptually, or as motivations to think in certain ways, as well as by the way in which the past is remembered, the connections that are deemed relevant and irrelevant. It is with these issues that this book is concerned.

Sometimes, including in Nancy's work, there is a suggestion that a commitment to political community involves forms of violence, in the sense of the textual violence of excluding or refusing some modes of participation, but also in the sense of the violence that is and has been perpetrated in the name of communities. I would not wish to suggest that a commitment to the imagined political community of feminism should be abandoned simply because it can be thought of as 'community', since I would not wish to assert that all communities can be simply understood as, by definition, exclusionary and therefore to be dispensed with.[2] However, the appearance of several philosophical attempts to unravel the complicities that praise of solidarity and communities has, and has had, with violent events does give pause for thought. And, indeed, one of the main themes of this book is how boundaries have been placed within the feminist political imagination, affecting the way in which the necessary exclusivity of a political imagination has been shaped.

The task of mapping the feminist political imagination, as I am thinking it here, is thus deeply entwined with this concern with the violence of making 'community'. Much recent feminist work has shown how, historically, the centrepiece of feminism – Woman – cannot be posited as simply a matter of bodily difference; for 'Woman' is a discursive construction, entrance to which has been a matter of conflict as the boundaries of the feminine have been, often fiercely, erected and defended. Woman, as an enunciative position and as an ontological basis of community, has been violently policed, exactly because its boundaries are mobile and contestable, and this is the case even within feminism itself (as the much-discussed work of Riley (1988), hooks (1982) and Mohanty (1993) illustrate). It is no longer news that the 'feminist community' itself can operate, and has done so, along certain lines of exclusion. There is a growing literature which confirms that the feminist political imagination is one which has, even with its ostensibly expansive vision and ambitions, been no stranger to exclusions.

The possibility of an inclusive feminist imagination is confronted with the history of exclusions that have operated between women and within feminism. Historical investigations have illustrated how women have been differently placed in various power constellations, in colonial settings, for example, or in contemporary societies, such that the representation of 'women's interests' strains to accommodate the different – if 'intertwined',

---

2 Boyarin and Boyarin (1993), whose work is discussed in Chapter 5, make a similar point. They argue that Jews seem to be denied, because any existing community seems to be denied, positivity by Nancy.

as Said (1994) phrases it – histories of all women (Ware, 1992; Caraway, 1991; Jayawardena, 1995). The now classic *Ain't I a Woman?* (bell hooks, 1982), raised these issues in relation to the history of feminist movements in the United States, illustrating the sense in which feminism deployed an imagination which could not encompass all subjects who were nevertheless positioned in relation to it (see also Sanchez-Eppeler, 1988). In *Feminist Theory: From Margin to Centre*, moreover, hooks wrote explicitly about the 'exclusionary' aspects of contemporary feminist thought and practice that operate on several different levels; she argued the dangers of the reification of feminist thought into an ideology, one that worked against its intentions, to stifle discussion and different modes of seeing the world (1984: 9–10). There, hooks explored the notion that feminist thought must confront the risk it runs of becoming ideological and thereby limiting the fields of obligation for feminism, suggesting that struggle against patriarchal modes of thought and sexist modes of oppression might be better understood and confronted by maintaining an openness of conviction, a 'radical openness', in voicing critique and in forming communities of resistance (1984: 149).

The tasks of representing 'women' and of knowing who the community is that feminism represents have become, and rightly so, vexed questions for feminist theory (see, e.g., Grewal and Kaplan, 1994; Spivak, 1988, 1990). The impact of feminist historical investigations, as well as the feminist involvement in debates crudely gathered under the rubrics of 'post-structuralism' and postmodernism,[3] has meant that the interrogation of the meaning of feminism has taken place on the historical and organisational level as well as on the level of epistemological and philosophical considerations. Elizabeth Spelman's *Inessential Woman* (1988) and Diana Fuss' *Essentially Speaking* (1989) are examples of the kind of interrogation that feminists have made of the epistemological and philosophical questions that arise when one confronts the exclusions that can operate within the feminist political imagination. These influential works focus on the concept of essentialism, the notion that in some way there is something essential about womanhood that unites all women,[4] in detailing the dangers of the assumption that sexual difference can override the differences *between* women.

In short, as a result of various factors, feminist theory has come to the 'end of innocence', to employ the words of Jane Flax (1993), wherever the subject position of 'woman' or the existence of a commonality is concerned. Feminist attempts to develop 'innocent knowledge' have predominantly been attempts to pursue models inherited from elsewhere – be they Marxist, social scientific or liberal political – in the belief that it is possible to discover 'some sort of truth which can tell us how to act in the world in ways that benefit or are for the (at least ultimate) good of all' (Flax, 1993:

3 To speak of the impact of post-structuralism or postmodernism on feminism here is to enter a conceit that 'forgets' the sense in which feminism has been instrumental in bringing about the condition of 'postmodernity' (see Huyssen, 1990).

4 There are several different versions of essentialism (see Fuss, 1989; Fergusson, 1993: 81–91).

133). This desire, however, will no longer hold, for the Enlightenment dream
it presents has been unsettled. Flax, and others, have posed this point as a
'crisis' in which it becomes encumbant upon feminists to see feminism itself
as *within* the constellation under analysis, never as merely and innocently
voicing resistance from 'outside' or 'below' power/knowledge formations.
Thus feminism can be regarded as a political movement with its own
triumphant and troubled past, with its own epistemological, philosophical
and political issues to address, and with its own participation in networks of
power and of knowledge. Indeed, it has been argued that feminism instigates
a counter-discourse in Foucault's sense that relies upon the very terms
which entangle it within the complex relations it is attempting to change. In
Donna Haraway's words, for example, if gender can be considered a
consciousness, it is one 'forced on us by the terrible historical experience of
the contradictory social realities of patriarchy, colonialism and capitalism'
(1991: 179). Such a debate complicates further the status of the term
'woman' and the notion of gender.

There is, I believe, something liberatory in adopting a stance which
surrenders the notion that feminism is located outside the nexus of power,
for such a stance enables the passion that accompanies feminist thought
and practice to be acknowledged as an integral part of what feminism is.
Flax has suggested that feminist thought should regard itself as engaged in
politics rather than epistemology, where sentiment is both necessary and
expected:

> A belief in the connections between truth and knowledge at this point in Western
> history seems far more likely to encourage a dangerously blind innocence rather
> than to prepare the ways for freedom and justice. We should take responsibility
> for our desire in such cases: what we really want is power in the world, not
> innocent truth. (1993: 144)

From a different angle, Wendy Brown (1995) has argued that it should
come as no surprise, *pace* Nietzsche, that sentiment and political argument
work together. Desire and wanting are centre stage in her discussion and
'deconstruction' of identity politics; she writes:

> If every 'I am' is something of a resolution of a movement of desire into fixed
> and sovereign identity, then this project might involve not only to speak but to
> *read* 'I am' this way: as potentially in motion, as temporal, as not-I, as
> deconstructable according to a genealogy of want rather than as fixed interests or
> experiences. (1995: 75)

And a genealogy of want is one that would imply that feminism is composed not just of abstract political analysis but also of sentiment. The
possibility that democracy operates rationally above the level of social
identities, moralism and emotional attachments is an ideal that political
philosophies need to abandon.

The work that I am presenting in this book has been inspired by each of
the intersecting debates that I have been glossing here, although it is not

'about' them. What the reiteration of the varieties of crisis – in 'the subject', 'the political', 'the community' – sets up is a train of thought which contemplates the fate of feminist politics under the weight of these debates. My route here is to take up the concerns of the exclusions, boundaries and histories of feminism through a focus on the formation of feminist theory. Indeed, I begin from the position which I have been describing above insofar as I am regarding the feminist imagination as embedded within the power/knowledge networks within which it emerged, in terms of its passions, formulations and articulations. Historicising feminist commitment (and feminist sentiments) means subjecting it to genealogical analysis that, in turn, opens it to other concerns – concerns that are not discretely or specifically feminist.

Feminist political imagination, as I am using the phrase, is a deployment that clears a space, by opening up ways of seeing and speaking. The modes by which this imagination and this opening emerge are practices that sustain the lines along which the deployment of feminism takes place and that create a political landscape by and within which feminism comes to understand itself. One could say that there is an *areality* to the feminist political imagination, a term that conveys both the sense of spatiality or area (which also entails a sense of temporality) and a sense of the *a*real or imaginary.[5] In this book, I am concerned not to 'map' the feminist political landscape, as if it were a ground to be surveyed, but to follow some of the lines that have contributed to its complex constitution and therefore to the possibility of a feminist imagination. By using the term 'areality', the emphasis is on the imaginative space that emerges. In particular, I am interested in the co-ordinates that are created within this areality, in how the distances and the horizons are imagined and how political and affective relationships are constituted in relation to them. For within a political landscape, there are horizons by which one judges one's location, without being able to know the co-ordinates of that location, since a horizon, maintaining its distance, can never really be approached or 'known'. There are also limits in the landscape, which are distant figures that one can approach, can investigate and which mark a sense of scale.[6] Both horizons and limits are located politically and philosophically, and both are similarly emotionally charged; they can be amazing, inviting, awesome, fearful or impressive. Thus the political landscape is constituted politically, philosophically and affectively.

5 Here I am borrowing again from Jean-Luc Nancy, although I am unfaithful in my adoption, taking this term 'areality' out of context, which was a discussion of communism and compearance (1992). I should also be clear that I am not referring to the Lacanian imaginary in my use of the term imagination.

6 I am attempting to pull out two different terms here – horizons and limits – in a way that differentiates what I say here from Ernesto Laclau's definition of horizons, which for him does both jobs. He writes: 'We call horizon that which establishes, at one and the same time, the limits and the terrain of constitution of any possible object – and that, as a result, makes impossible any beyond' (1996: 102).

I wish to place the feminist political imagination within the twentieth century, as it has been formed in the passage of the twentieth century. This intention comes not merely from a notion that it 'makes sense' to do so, and is surprisingly infrequently explicitly attempted in conceptual work, but also as a response to the dynamics present within current feminist debates. As I argue in Chapter 2, the fears that are articulated in the current debates about the 'crises' are fears about the location of feminist argument in relation to the figures, horizons and limits of the wider political landscape. In pursuing such lines of thought, I mean to argue that feminist concerns are not narrowly 'about women', even if the subject 'Woman' unites them, because feminism is *of* this century; not that there weren't feminist movements prior to it, but, in terms of its cultural presence and continued development, feminism's political imagination has been constituted and developed within this century, and its 'happening' has occurred within the 'happening' of the twentieth century. No doubt this century will be remembered in many ways, but I have become intrigued by the questions that are raised in the space between Kristeva's comment that this century will be remembered as the century of women, and Foucault's comment to the effect that one can speak about 'the proof' of the twentieth century: how do we know it happened? In writing this book, my attention has been drawn to the ways in which the feminist political imagination, as evidenced in feminist theory and philosophy, is placed in relation to struggles and events that have occurred in the history of this century.[7]

I am interested in attempting to read feminist theory against the grain, not for its focus on women and femininity, but with attention to the unexpected characters – the feared fascist in both the debates on the directionlessness of contemporary feminist theory and in debates on essentialism and embodiment, the downtrodden and resentful young black man in Simone de Beauvoir, the totalitarian character in Hannah Arendt, the 'mimetic Jew' shadowing Judith Butler's use of the concept of mimesis. My approach is led, therefore, by the feminist debates themselves, by reading them for the figures that are sometimes suprisingly drawn and positioned within those debates and within the landscape imagined there.

In pursuing the specific genealogies that constitute the substantial chapters here, I am laying out the suggestion that the feminist political imagination has a strong correlation with other attempts to think the specificity of

---

7 The intention is not to become caught up in the debates that take place around the question of whether there is a generic fascism, nor those about causality, psychology or morality in relation to fascistic movements. Closer are those arguments that seek to place women in relation to fascist movements in terms of participation or policies (see, e.g., Durham, 1998) but still these are outside my remit. The intention is much more to consider how the feminist political imagination has sculpted itself in relation to a figure of fascism that has been formed this century, leaving aside, somewhat, the question of whether or not that figure is an accurate one that truly 'represents' all the different fascisms. This is not because that is my primary interest in reading feminist theory, but because I have become convinced that there is a sense in which feminism has an underexplored relation to this figure, on political, philosophical and affective levels.

the twentieth century, and, especially, the racial trials of the twentieth century. I mean to treat these questions only as they arise in relation to the feminist political imagination, in order to understand their place there as reflecting very real concerns about feminist politics. There is indeed something amazing about the events of this century, but it is with the more sober, gentle approach of the genealogist's attitude that I wish to pursue feminist theory and philosophy's relationship to them. I mean to turn the amazement toward feminist modes of imagining not in order to sit stunned, but in order to signal certain connections that I believe enrich the portrait one can draw of twentieth-century feminism. Thinking philosophically about the political imagination of feminism, therefore, has become for me entwined with the need to think philosophically about the understandings, images and sentiments that the feminist imagination displays.

The approach is not properly historical in the sense of tracing the institutional and organisational relations between different groups or responses and rallies around such issues. My questions stem much more from the genealogical attitude that asks: how did the history of 'race' and racial struggles ever come to be thought of as *parallel* to the history of feminism? How did 'we feminists' manage to emerge with a political landscape that could sustain the enunciation of feminism? The more one sets about answering such questions, however, the more one is drawn to ask: in what way is the question of racism 'within' the feminist political imagination? How are the concepts by which we understand oppression shared outside feminism's boundaries? How do we imagine the enunciative position of feminism differently from other demands? What are the histories of the 'borrowed concepts' in feminist thought?

Such an ambitious task is bound to be incomplete. I am also bound to disappoint. It will disappoint because each of the chapters is what I have termed a specific genealogy, because the book as a whole does not form a complete genealogy; moreover, each of the specific genealogies pursues a particular line of argument with regard to a particular issue that may not be the reader's particular interest in the debate. Further, the book will disappoint in that I have chosen to turn attention to the way in which 'race' and (anti-Semitic/Nazi) fascism are figured in feminist political imagination, whereas there are, of course, several other issues and concerns that could have been highlighted. These are treated in ways that belie, as I have suggested, my politics of location, and may be received as a way that again privileges Europe. Moreover, I am treating them as *figures* in the sense that they appear within the areality of the feminist political landscape, which has meant a focus on the written word, on the styles of rhetoric and modes of argumentation that one finds there. While not 'the feminist imagination' *tout court*, my only defence against such a charge would be that I have considered some key texts from the 'feminist library', some particular voices, debates or issues, and that however incomplete a source of remembrance, one of the principal ways in which the happening of feminism, its becoming historic, is revealed or 'made present', and one of the ways in which the guarding against future forgetting is attempted, is through such a library. Thus we keep certain books and debates on our feminist shelves, literally or metaphorically, and, with them, I am arguing that it is not only a feminist history or library that we keep.

Outline of the book

There is a photograph by Eve Arnold – 'Self portrait in a distorting mirror, 42nd Street, New York' (1950) – in which she stands looking down into her Rolleiflex, composing her self-portrait in the mirror, the warped surface of which refuses an accurate or simple reflection. We see only the bowed head of Arnold as she is preoccupied with her own image and her own image-making. She is the creator of this image, while simultaneously she appears to be engrossed somewhere else, gazing deep into the box that she holds in her hands. Viewing the photograph now, we are in the privileged position of being able to study her while she, eyes downcast, appears shy and studious, avoiding our gaze, intent on framing the peculiarly elongated image with precision. In capturing her own image, Arnold also presents – it could hardly have been accidental, yet one suspects it wasn't exactly planned – the image of a passer-by. A rimmed hat rests, tilted slightly upwards, on his head, his hand raised to his mouth as he draws upon a cigarette. Masculine symbols. He is a shadowy figure, his silhouette merging with the blurred background shapes. He is, seemingly, unaware of the efforts that have preceded the capturing of this moment. Arnold herself stands slightly to the right of centre, the eccentric subject of her own self-portrait.

Even where the ostensible focus is presented as though it were unitary, a self-portrait, there is another caught in the lens. In *Feminist Imagination* I am interested in how a studied gaze at the constitution of a feminist imagination, such as that found within feminist theory, can become an exercise in noticing the figures that have peopled the image, becoming part of the patterns that are formed, and forming part of the overall picture – not always clearly drawn, nor necessarily in focus; but neither incidental nor accidental. Sometimes the figure is caught, sometimes the figure has passed by, not caught, but just off frame, leaving only the trail or the sense of having been there. Noticing and exploring these other figures is a journey, or a series of journeys, in the feminist political imagination. I mean to suggest that the constitution of a feminist subject, a feminist enunciative position, is a form of rhetorical sculpture that creates its form out of a range of discursive and affective materials. We can investigate even as we admire the results of such creativity, tracing the boundaries of the form that emerges, wondering which figure has just passed by that left such peculiar marks, such passions, or who the figure sketched in the corner represents, what histories would she or he lead us to? There is a sense in which the feminist subject is non-identical with herself, and her position is eccentric. Her history is a shared history in which concerns and affiliations other than those ostensibly 'feminist' circulate, touch upon and emerge, creating the movements, the flows and the eddies of her politics.

Feminist Imagination concerns itself with these (e)motions: the connections with the events and the figures, out of focus or just off frame, that create the passions, fears, neuroses that are made central to feminist theory. I am intrigued by the impact that politics outside feminism has had on feminist theory; and, in particular, I am intrigued by the impact that politics around 'race' has had on it, although not in the sense of a rational conversation, necessarily. Arnold's photograph would have a completely different feel to it had she called out to the passer-by and taken a photograph of the two of them face to face, in profile perhaps, considering each other without the mediation of a camera, the distorting mirror and the blur caused by his distance from the point of focus. It is the figures that inhabit feminist theory in this shadowy mode that provide the intrigue here – not just in the sense that sexual difference needs duality, or in the game of finding how what passes for 'feminist theory' is unbeknownst to itself, a 'raced' canon; but in the sense of finding how movements, of real people, of concerns and of concepts, resonate through the motions and emotions of contemporary feminist theory. My questions are bound together in these ways, while they take several different approaches to them.

The next chapter, Chapter 2 – 'Phantastic communities and dangerous thinking: feminist political imagination' – is intended as a recasting of the debate that has taken place over the past decade or so concerning the feminist use of 'post-structuralist' philosophy. In the past, I had tended to think that this debate was based on a series of misreadings of post-structuralism, and that the latter was much less of a threat to feminist theory than those bemoaning its arrival believed. I still hold that there is much that is misconceived about these debates. However, I wanted to try to reposition the debate by asking what it is that those who regard post-structuralism as dangerous actually fear. Taking a route via Julia Kristeva's 'Women's time' (1986), a piece that connects feminist theory explicitly to the concerns I wish to explore, I argue that the fear is for the fate of feminist theory in its relation to a wider political landscape, and to the horizons and figures one finds there. It is not that dangerous thinking is wrong – that has never truly been the way the debate has been articulated – but it is dangerous; it is that which opens the door to dangerous political positions. I argue that the language in which feminists debate this issue betrays these fears and haunting figures. This chapter sets up the book in that it establishes an attitude toward my reading of feminist theory and philosophy, one that attempts to read it in contexts other than its immediate one, to suggest that the sculpting of feminist subjects and the feminist subject has not involved their abstraction from an empty political landscape, but has been very much entwined with other politicised figures.

It is in this vein that I move to the following chapter, Chapter 3 – 'Suffering: thinking politics with Simone de Beauvoir and Richard Wright' – where I consider the work of Simone de Beauvoir in relation to that of

Richard Wright, the African American novelist, as a way to consider recent arguments that have suggested that identity politics is a mode of political argument based upon *ressentiment*. By exploring the intertextuality of de Beauvoir with Richard Wright, I am able to consider and critique the forms of parallel argument that treat 'race' and sex as parallel oppressions, and that come close to a form of *ressentiment* as well as providing a critique of a tendency always to regard feminist politics as identity politics in that sense. A consideration of these two writers that explores their intertextuality can also allow a more nuanced reading, one that finds what I have termed 'modes of connectivity' across raced and gendered boundaries. De Beauvoir was drawn to thinking 'race' even as she had her focus on women, and, likewise, Wright's reputed misogyny can be tempered by reading those moments where the power structures of racism are portrayed as less absolute. Thus feminism can be thought of as a political imagination that reaches beyond itself even as it creates its specific positionality.

Chapter 4 – 'Appearance: thinking difference in the political realm with Hannah Arendt' – takes another figure deeply affected by the Second World War, Hannah Arendt, in order to situate her ambivalent status within feminist theory in the context of this book. I argue that it is of interest that Arendt's distinctions between different 'realms' of life were put to the test when she wrote about the desegregation of schools in the States in the 1950s. For here she forces us to consider what it means to adopt a late twentieth-century feminist version of her thoughts on these realms when she herself made such a controversial intervention at that time. Through a focus on the concept of appearance, I argue that we can understand that Arendt's piece has an integrity with her project as a whole, even as I argue that it is deeply flawed in its treatment of the question of racial difference. It is arguably because of the evils that Arendt wished to avoid, those of totalitarianism, that she treats, paradoxically perhaps, the issue of desegregation in such a peculiar and non-intuitive manner, making her case – as a writer presently being reconstituted as a feminist theorist – an intriguing one for the project of this book.

Chapter 5 – 'Mimesis as cultural survival' – focusses on the work of Judith Butler, presenting a certain specific genealogy of her usage of the concept of mimesis, one which connects her work on mimesis with the writings of Theodor Adorno and Max Horkheimer, and Jean-Paul Sartre, on anti-Semitism. The chapter argues that giving Butler's work this particular genealogical reading enables one to illuminate the concept of 'cultural survival' in her thinking about processes of producing effective gendered identities, effective both in the sense of being effects and of being understood as coherent identities. By connecting Butler's work with her sympathetic contemporary writers on Judaism, furthermore, one is able to begin the difficult exploration of the way in which these writers are presenting the theoretical relationship between racialised and gender identities.

Chapter 6 turns to the issue of essentialism and embodiment, exploring the ability of the term 'essentialism' to kindle a flame that causes much fire

in feminist theoretical circles. I argue that it is possible to push Diana Fuss'
suggestion that essentialism should be regarded as part of various deployments, and as in and of itself a term that need not convey such negative
affect. Why then has it this ability in feminist theory? And how does the
recent interest in pursuing a feminist 'theory' of embodiment relate to it? I
argue that if one puts these questions in the light of the work of Emmanuel
Levinas and Frantz Fanon, both thinkers who were concerned with the
question of embodiment in relation to questions of essentialism, but in
different contexts, the movement of the feminist debate, and the sentiments
that underlie it, can be understood in different light. The need to theorise
the body is not an attempt to reassert the body, to ground a political
philosophy in Truth, but it is an attempt to make a theoretical intervention
that acknowledges that, if identity has a constitutional relation to
embodiment, it is also a site for powerful political appeals, ones which
feminism cannot afford to ignore in pursuit of an anti-essentialism that
leaves no space for talk of 'the body'.

Finally, Chapter 7 concludes the book with some reflections on the mode
of analyses carried out, taking as its route the notion of trauma in relation
to genealogical critique, in order to argue that the book is intended as a
contribution to feminist work which regards the 'subject' of feminism as
one that necessarily brings with it other subjects with other histories.

2

PHANTASTIC COMMUNITIES AND DANGEROUS THINKING: FEMINIST POLITICAL IMAGINATION

Me, myself, who? Today myself, a woman who writes, a woman part of whose identity is therefore caught up in the drama of Writing and the drama of Woman.

Ours is, for me, the era of double temporality: it is the broken-backed century that Mandelstram lamented, the twilight of freedom; and in our grating and jarring present, it is the bitter dawn of liberty, that season of turmoil and anguish, in which the western world in particular is in the throes of dissociation and reorganisation; in which civil wars and nationalist fevour arise from disorder which is both good and bad; and in which a phobia of non-identity has spread, and individuals, and nations like individuals are infected with this neurosis, this pain, this fear of non-recognition . . .

Who is afraid of non-identity, non-recognition? (Helene Cixous, 1993: 19)

[W]hat is today? . . . One can say that the task of philosophy today is and what we are today, but without breast-beating drama and theatricality and maintaining that this moment is the greatest damnation or daybreak of the rising sun. No, it is a day like any other, or much more, a day which is never like another. (Michel Foucault, in Lotringer, 1989: 251)

How is feminism to survive in an era of non-identity? Are we searching to find our way in feminism's twilight? How is feminism to imagine its political horizons at the end of the twentieth century, when so many feminist theorists are engaged in a critique of feminism's past 'mistakes', 'oversights' and misplaced projections? What hope for us when theorists are embracing the idea that identity politics may enable the very problems we critique to persist? If 'we feminists' continue to happen, are we destined to operate in melancholic fashion, carrying our unresolved past with us? If we read post-structuralist philosophy, does the delight[1] that feminism offered dissolve with any decision to be persuaded?

This chapter considers how we might theorise political imagination with regard to feminism. It begins with an exploration of the question of

---

1 Kristeva suggests that feminism, through its questioning of sexual difference, has brought a certain delight to a civilisation which 'outside the stock exchange and wars, is bored to death' (1986: 193).

political imagination, setting forth an argument that the political identification that draws one into such an imagination is a 'cutting through' of
time, and taking as its departure point the suggestion that in a post-
Marxist world the fears associated with non-dialectic conceptions of
politics need to be faced, obliging us to leave behind teleological versions
of history and to embrace the possibilities of thinking feminism as itself
performative. With this move, the terrain extends to the markers which
locate much current social theory, seemingly endlessly and pointlessly
caught up in the postmodernity debate as we stumble, in our dusky
present, over the slumbering figures of modern political thought – identity,
recognition, freedom. Such a position is one that demands that feminism's
attentiveness to the present be ready to see the specificities of our philosophical and political present without rushing to a conclusion that would
put smiles on the wrong faces.

There is, of course, no *one* feminism that belongs to the present. Writing
at the end of the 1970s, Julia Kristeva, in her much-reprinted article
'Women's time', spoke of the differing temporalities articulated by different
but concurrent feminisms. Before exploring some of the tensions of her
article, which is more fraught than it has oftentimes been taken to be, I
want to pause on her use of the term 'temporalities'. Why should we
consider politics through the notion of time, or, put slightly differently,
why should we consider these questions through the prism of the politics of
time?

Sculpting feminism

Such a manoeuvre leads us to consider the ways in which, as Jean-Luc
Nancy has put it, we begin, inaugurate or enter history (1993a: 146).
Nancy's position – which I see as compatible, notwithstanding certain
reservations, with Foucault – treats historicity 'as performance rather than
as knowledge or narrative' (1993a: 144). When theory gives up the notion
of the dialectic, history itself becomes, in a sense, suspended; history itself
is called into question. If our time is the end of History, it is a History
conceived as the movement of a summation by which the self presents
itself to itself, by which the Idea of the self and the Idea itself is revealed
(Nancy, 1993a: 148–9). In the stead of History, then, we are left with the
historicity of history. Nancy's ruminations on this topic become
particularly pertinent to this discussion when he catches himself using a
language of 'our time':

> [T]o be outside history or to enter another history (for which the name 'history'
> no longer perhaps applies) is the 'suspense' specific to our time.
>   But what does 'our time' mean? 'Our time' means precisely, first of all, a
> suspension of time, of time conceived as always flowing. A pure flow of time
> could not be 'ours'. (Nancy, 1993a: 150)

This is where the questions arise concerning being in common and of the link between temporality and space that his use of the term 'community' suggests.

Jean-Luc Nancy's position is suggestive for feminism, given the debates that have been taking place within feminist theory in relation to the possibilities of commonalities in the political, insofar as his argument is premised on the notion that politics is the place of the exposition of community, where community is not a common being but is a matter of existence as it is *in* common. This '*in* common' is not the expression of a common substance that underlies and causes the expression of community, nor is it the absorption of selves into a common that would imply that the exposition of community is a fusion of many bodies into one body, a communion (Nancy, 1991: xxxviii). On the contrary, 'being in common' means, Nancy argues, no longer having in any form, in any empirical or ideal place, a substantial identity. What one has is rather the sharing of 'lack of identity'. Indeed, the community that becomes a unity, and that forms an identity loses the being *in* common, since, for Nancy, the truth of community lies in the retreat of such a being (common identity) (1991: xxxix).

Thus does Nancy suggest that rather than see community as the expression of a common being, which necessitates a political programme that will allow the expression of the essence of that commonality, one ought instead to think of community as a matter of 'existence inasmuch as it is *in* common'. In politics, there is the exposition of finitude, a *shared* lack of infinite identity, and that exposition is community: community 'does not sublate the finitude it exposes. Community itself is nothing but this exposition' (Nancy, 1991: 26). The work[2] of community is therefore repeatedly to expose the shared and strange 'being-the-one-with-the-other' while always retreating from a singular 'being of togetherness' (Nancy, 1991: xxxviii–xxxix). Hence Nancy's formulation that community is definable as the *being-ecstatic* of Being itself (1991: 6, emphasis added). The modern experience of community is not a work to be produced (an ideal future) nor a lost communion (a nostalgia for a past), but 'space itself, and the spacing of the experience of the outside, of the outside-the-self' (Nancy, 1991: 19). And hence his pertinence to the issue of politics 'in an era of nonidentity', where feminism might be thought of as a community in Nancy's terms, not as an expression of shared identity but as the exposition of a shared non-identity with those with whom we, ecstatically, share that finitude.

Community then can be regarded as something that *happens*, and that demands to be considered not as something historical, but as an *event*, a being-in-common that ushers forth a notion of *finite history*: 'history . . .

---

2 In fact, Nancy argues that community cannot be comprehended as a work. Drawing upon Blanchot he suggests that community takes place in the 'unworking', in the sense that community is constituted by the suspension that human beings are, and that it is more pertinent to think about what community withdraws or retreats from, its interruption and fragmentation (1991: 31).

does not belong primarily to time, nor to succession, nor to causality, but to community, or to being-in-common' (Nancy, 1993a: 143). The appropriation signalled by the 'our', the immobilisation or arrest that the 'our' instigates, is the very question, the very making, of temporality. Temporality becomes a space or domain that we make 'our' property:

> It is not that we dominate this time – our time – (indeed, how little we do!). But it is much more that time presents itself to us as this spatiality or 'spacing' [*espacement*] of a certain suspension – which is nothing else than the *epoch*, which of course, means suspension in Greek. (Nancy, 1993a: 150)

If this is the case, then we can follow Nancy to the extent that he gives us an ability to think through the happening that creates the 'our' – a spacing that 'spaces time itself', that cuts through the flow of time in order to enable 'a reciprocity between "our" and "time"' (1993a: 151). By this happening, we are able to say 'we':

> [I]t is a matter of the space of time, of spacing time and/or of spaced time, which gives to 'us' the possibility of saying 'we' – that is, the possibility of being *in common*, and of presenting or representing ourselves as a community – a community that shares or partakes of the same time, for community itself is this space. (Nancy, 1993a: 151)

The metaphor of sculpting that I employ draws upon Nancy's sense of cutting through time, of forming a commonality with and by that cut. Thinking of feminism as a 'community' may be to stretch (or restrict, depending on one's point of view) the definition of community, and likewise the aspiration of feminism, but, on another level, such a supposition is one that is frequently repeated: it is *as if* we feminists were, in some sense, a community. Feminist political imagination is not given, but is formed, it is sculpted, and it is this creative process that I am interested in. If we think of 'feminism' as I have suggested – as the exposition of a shared non-identity with those with whom we, ecstatically, share that finitude – it is necessary to give some content to this creativity. Otherwise, one remains at the level of abstraction that is Nancy's. There must be in this exposition of a shared but absolutely non-identical finitude, an attentiveness to gender, and it is this – the quality and content of the political articulation of feminism – which is necessarily an attempt to cut through time. How do we perform the cutting through of time that makes feminism 'ours' and makes for a feminist 'we'? Moreover, it is necessary to link this notion of sculpting a being *in* common and its attendant notion of *becoming historical* with the notion of political horizons. In the sculpting of the ecstatic feminist 'we', there is a sense in which feminism as a political imagination 'places' itself in relation to the political horizons available. The co-ordinates of this spatial metaphor are, of course, not fixed co-ordinates; political imaginations and, therefore, political horizons, in the sense of imagining different political configurations and possibilities, alter and move as new articulations shift ground. Thus feminism, as the articulation of political imagination, can be, and indeed should be, regarded as inserting itself into a mobile complex of political visions through both the predominantly vertical image of cutting through time and through the predominantly horizontal images of tracing a place for its imagination onto the landscape constituted by available and often conflictual political imaginations. In this way, the spatial and the temporal are entwined in the consideration of political imaginations. In the next section I want to suggest that feminist political imagination is a performative sculpting that takes place, as one would imagine, amidst the wider political horizons of the twentieth century.

Feminism and figures of finitude

The 'proof of the twentieth century',[3] its very specificity, has been one that is associated with the modes of political affiliation it threw up for philosophical and political thought. If 'our time', conceived in the vein adopted by Cixous, remains one of dissociation and reorganisation around the issue of identity, and if, as the quotation from her Amnesty Lectures in 1992 suggests, the issues of belonging and political identification continue to be struggled with and bitterly fought over at the end of the twentieth century, they are so fought over under the spectre of fascist movements of the twentieth century and understood inevitably by persons who are aware of the dangerous possibilities of certain modes of argumentation. Politically speaking, 'we know' we have lived through this century because we understand political imaginations, their hopes and, perhaps more so, their dangers, in relation to the horizon that fascist movements have constructed for political visions.

It is not simply that these movements and regimes were so awful that they form limit cases. Their extremes are not the only reason that they are limit cases; there is something about the articulation of these visions that accords them the position of limit cases. It is certainly the case that fascism, and Hitler's National Socialism in particular, has been positioned not simply as a limit case in our understandings of political visions, but also, as Andrew Hewitt has suggested, it is regarded as the privileged mode of thinking apocalypse:

> [F]ascism seems to have become the privileged modality of the apocalypse, functioning both spatially as a totalitarian model of society's destructive self-completion, and temporally through a rhetoric of 'final' solutions, of ends and of thousand-year regimes without end. (1995: 18)

Nazism, as a limit case political vision, was theatrically concerned with its temporality, imagining itself simultaneously as never-ending and as dying, as a tragedy whose personnel were inevitably to die and leave their

---

3 A term Foucault uses in discussion of the Paris–Berlin exhibition (1996: 294).

task in the hands of future generations.[4] This, together with the coupling of blood and soil, and the spatial dimension expressed in its expansionist ethic, made it the insidious and murderous political movement it was; that is, the particular configuration of temporal and spatial vision it mobilised have made it 'the privileged mode' of apocalypse.

Much has been said and written in film and literary criticism on the impossibilities that follow the Holocaust,[5] on the impossibility of representing it because it takes us to the limits of violence and permissible representation, as well as the impossibility of representation because, before one even begins, one is caught between the risk of representing it as merely 'another topic' and the impossibility of the 'witness testimony' form, unavailable to those who were not there.[6] Yet in representing it as unrepresentable or ineffable, it has also been argued that there is often an act of mystification. Gillian Rose suggested that 'to argue for silence, prayer, the banishment equally of poetry and knowledge, in short, the witness of "ineffability", that is, non-representability, is *to mystify something we dare not understand*, because we fear that it may be all too understandable, all too continuous with what we are – human, all too human' (1996: 43).[7] Moreover, even for those writers who suggest its 'unwritability', such as Blanchot (1986), the Holocaust cannot be ignored: the writer is left with 'the unenviable task of writing on the unwritable, necessarily and guiltily' (Stoekl, 1995:

---

4 There is a sense in which the temporal dimensions of National Socialism were explicitly articulated so as to form a limit case in our twentieth-century notions of political visions. That is, the way in which the Nazis sculpted their 'we' in relation to ideas of the past and the future, placed their political formation 'at the limit'. For Hitlerism tangled race and blood into the myth of the Aryan race in ways which simultaneously figured the 'awakening' of the German people and the imagination of that people's death with the attempt to draw a trajectory between the glory of the ancient Greeks and the German people (Lacoue-Labarthe and Nancy, 1990). Moreover, the architectural projects of Nazi sympathisers imagined their monuments as at some future point indistinguishable from those of the Roman Empire (see architect Speer *Inside the Third Reich*, 1970: 56), and planned necropolises that would honour the dead around the borders of the future *Lebensraum*, to serve as eternal reminders of the unification of Europe carried out by the German people (Wilhelm Kreis, quoted in Michaud, 1993). These suggest the sense in which Nazism attempted to plan the remembering of future generations, forming a stark contrast with the forgetting of the camps and the people there exterminated: 'The gigantic mausoleums imitated from the past and destined for the eternally heroic *Volksgemeinschaft* correspond to the anonymity that was to erase from history even the very name of the Jewish people' (Michaud, 1993: 232). There was therefore a tension in the event of National Socialism, as Michaud argues, because there was an imitation of styles of the past that was an attempt to 'pass something off', to give tangible proof of the power of a community incarnated as past . . . *already there* and *already historical*' (Michaud, 1993: 229).

5 I am aware that objection can be taken to this term, and that alternatives may be preferable. I use it here only because it is employed by much of the so-called 'post-Auschwitz' writing that I am referring to here.

6 In sociology, there has been a different strategy, which perhaps may be understood in the context of such debates in literary criticism, in the sense that there the Holocaust has been placed within the very context of modernity (especially explicitly in Bauman, 1989).

7 Adorno's argument that there can be no poetry after Auschwitz is made in several places, but is referred to in *Negative Dialectics* where he reconsiders his earlier statement (1973: 362–3).

140). Somewhere amidst the ways to proceed – knowing on the one hand the necessity to recognise the Holocaust as, in Blanchot's words, *emblematic*, risks making it historical and thereby complicitly 'work for one', and knowing on the other that while one needs to know, 'the empirical' is impossible – one nevertheless proceeds. In what follows I do not seek to represent the Holocaust, but I do want to suggest that feminist thought and debates have a relationship to the privileged mode of thinking apocalypse, and, in particular, to those ways of arguing that are considered reminiscent of, resonant with, or defenceless against, fascism. This is about the way that a representation, or a 'figure', becomes significant within the political landscape within which one imagines oneself, and the way in which one enters debate, and the forms of argumentation one employs there. It is about what I termed in the last chapter the *areality* of the feminist imagination.

If the twentieth century has witnessed the phenomenon of fascism displayed in most spectacular forms, spectacles that twentieth-century technologies were able to record and repeatedly display, it has also been termed the century 'of women' and of feminism. What does it mean, then, to be a feminist at the end of the century in which the spectrum of political affiliations has been expanded in this sense?

It strikes me as not incidental that Kristeva began her survey of different temporalities of feminism not with reference directly to feminism, but with a comment on the demise of the place of the nation-state in political visions, and with a comment, specifically, about National Socialism:

[T]he Nationalist-Socialist apocalypse demolished the pillars that, according to Marx, were its [the nation's] essence: economic homogeneity, historical tradition, and linguistic unity. (1986: 188)

Underlying Kristeva's piece is a concern with the modes by which feminism deploys its vision of the future, in a world in which the nation-state is no longer the sole focus of political resistance. She writes in a Europe and a context that not only struggles with the possibilities of emancipatory political visions, once Marx has been undermined as the prophet of liberation, but also with the memories and threats of fascism.[8] How do these form a horizon against which feminism operates? For feminism has also contributed to the demise of thought that reaches for the comfort of homogeneity within the nation, of linguistic unity, of one untainted historical trajectory to the present. Does that make feminism allied to fascism? The leap is too simplistic (though I've certainly heard it made, and in crude and reactionary ways), but what it does mean is that there may be within feminist thought a

8 The way in which Kristeva's piece foregrounds issues of violence has frequently been overlooked in commentaries on her piece, which has often been read as a simple tracing of changes in the feminist movement's approach to the issue of sexual difference. Jacqueline Rose's (1993) *Why War?* is an exception here, although her piece takes the consideration in a different direction, into a discussion of particularly problematic female figures for feminism; namely, Margaret Thatcher and Ruth Ellis.

peculiar need to attend to its relation to the horizon that, I am suggesting, twentieth-century fascisms have formed for thinking politics. For any talk of solidarities, and for any political imagination that is, in some way, searching for the realisation of its vision of emancipation, is to be seen within that troubled landscape.

Kristeva emphasises the challenge that feminism represents in its illumination of the simultaneous solidity and fragility of sociocultural ensembles that operate through the forging of common symbolic denominators in order to allow the nation to be imagined. Feminism has in this sense contributed to the breakdown of left politics conceived as focussed on the nation-state, for feminism's political vision is an ambitious one, one that knows no borders, one that ultimately disrespects the very notion of the nation-state and its institutions. Its 'object' – Woman – resides everywhere and nowhere. It is an expansive vision – but one to which an expansionist ethic is both irrelevant and anathema – that feminism deploys. And yet, in terms of the present debates in feminist theory, there remains a certain fraughtness – around the questions: What is the feminist project? What is a woman? A feminist? – that is by no means disentangled from wider debates around nationalism, fascism and patriotism. The wish to hold on to the hope of a feminism that is non-exclusionary, that is transnational and multicultural, is one that is keenly aware of the dangers of enunciating the case poorly. There is a sense in which the debates around the 'state' of feminist theory and of feminism as a movement are conducted in terms that veer close to a vocabulary of apocalyptic endings, and oftentimes employ a vocabulary of fascism and anti-fascism. Witness the mobilisation of rhetoric of ending too soon, coming too late, of an unseeing feminism following doubtful leaders, of the neglect of real violence through a pursuit of mythical feminine or merely textual politics, of the dangers of making feminism an aesthetics rather than a politics.[9] One of the ways in which the dangers of 'post-structuralism' is articulated employs a spatial language in the sense that it is figured as a danger 'about' the loss of *direction* of/in feminism. Less explicitly, perhaps, there is also a sense in which the fraughtness is figured as having a temporal dimension. Will an adoption of post-structuralism make us go too quickly, accelerate feminism to a dissolution for which it is not ready? If we take this path, will the future involve a 'forgetting' of the reasons why that dissolution took place (and reinstitute patriarchy)? Will a lack of a normative stance open the door to those forms of politics we most oppose; that is, to our limit cases, the most fearful forms of politics?

To suggest that it is an important task of feminist reflection to consider how temporal–spatial assertions and insertions operate is to suggest a form of feminist ethics that is attentive to the ways in which feminist argument is sculpted and the feminist political imagination is deployed. Where then to begin this overambitious task, that of attempting to think through the

---

9 Exactly the issue that Walter Benjamin (1992) saw arising in relation to fascism.

temporal–spatial imagination of feminism within a wider landscape of political imaginations? Let us follow Kristeva awhile, for she offers the opportunity to think about the development of feminist thought through time as a series of alterations in the way of imagining the temporal dimensions of feminist politics.

From the first to the third phase with Kristeva: why so quarrelsome?

[I]f we want our prospective guardians to believe that quarrelsomeness is one of the worst evils, we must certainly not let them be told the story of the Battle of the Giants or embroider it on robes, or tell them other tales about many and various quarrels between gods and heroes and their friends and relations. On the contrary, if we are to persuade them that no citizen has ever quarreled with any other, because it is sinful, our old men and women must tell children stories with this end in view from the first. (Plato, 1974: 132–3, *The Republic*, Book III)

There have been attempts in both Britain and the United States through the 1990s to set up a generational tension within feminist thought, in the form of what were predominantly marketing strategies within publishing that sought to set up a series of popular tracts in younger feminist voices in opposition to those of the preceding generations, with the latter depicted as archaic, out of touch and reactionary. Maybe these debates have more to do with commerce than with any significant debates within feminist thought. And yet the idea of a smooth passage of feminism through time is one that refuses to acknowledge the quarrels within feminism, and the different political visions that sit uneasily under that banner. One of the virtues of Kristeva's 'Women's time', and the reason that it is of interest here, is that it challenges an easy commonality of feminist projects, and begins to address the notion of generation, the notion of the feminist 'we', its 'properties' and 'proprietors', and therefore, I would suggest, the temporality of a feminism that is not isolated from other modes of imagining the political. Kristeva draws our attention to the ways in which *different* spacings have occurred in feminist thought, in the sense elucidated above, and in her attention to the temporalities of feminism she circles the philosophical fragility of feminism's 'we'.

Kristeva maps out three different temporalities of the feminist imagination. 'In its beginnings', she suggests, without giving any clues as to when she sees this inauguration of feminism as having occurred, feminism involved an identification with the 'ontological values of a rationality dominant in the nation-state' (1986: 194). This mode of feminist demand universalises the concept of 'woman', but had its focus on the nation-state, where its demands were directed toward issues of recognition and equality. A second phase, however, after May 1968, has drawn upon aesthetic or psychoanalytic experience in order to consider the specificity of woman's 'intra-subjective and corporeal experiences' (1986: 194). This second temporality, Kristeva argues, 'almost totally' refuses the *linear* temporality of the previous generation, exploring a dynamic of signs that relates it to projects of 'aesthetic and religious upheaval' (1986: 194). By attempting to give Woman an identity that meets with no symmetry in Man, this feminism

> situates itself outside the linear time of identities which communicate through projection and revindication. Such a feminism rejoins, on the one hand, the archaic (mythical) memory and, on the other, the cyclical or monumental temporality of marginal movements. (Kristeva, 1986: 194–5)

In a reading of Nietzsche, Kristeva draws a distinction between the time of the nation that is the linear time, cursive time, and the monumental time which 'englobes the supranational, sociocultural ensembles [such as "Europe"] within even larger entities' (1986: 189). Following this phasing of the feminist movement, then, there was an initial engagement with a national problematic, but subsequently feminism became involved in the problematic of the 'symbolic denominator' that expanded to encompass a global domain. In this second feminist vision, in other words, the passing of time is somehow irrelevant; indeed, with its emphasis on the infinite repetition of cycles, gestation, biological rhythms, there is a sense in which it embraces the eternal. This eternal is what Kristeva assimilates to monumental time, and which almost exhausts the notion of temporality altogether, becoming 'all encompassing and infinite like imaginary space' (1986: 191).

Before delineating the third phase, let us pause on the critique that Kristeva makes of this second phase of feminist thought. Kristeva positions herself with respect to the second phase much as Nietzsche positioned himself in relation to Christian morality. In its imag(in)ing of a counter society, one that is 'harmonious, without prohibitions, free and fulfilling' (1986: 202), this feminism imagines an 'a-topia', and, with this fantasy, places feminism dangerously close to becoming a *religion* in an era in which the West is supposedly undergoing secularisation. It is situated in this very crisis of civilisation.

> I call 'religion' this phantasmic necessity on the part of speaking beings to provide themselves with a *representation* (animal, female, male, parental, etc.) in place of what constitutes them as such, in other words, symbolization. (Kristeva, 1986: 208)

This is, Kristeva suggests, a reaction to the constraints of the sociosymbolic contract, but one which exposes us just the same to 'risks of violence and terrorism', challenging as it does 'the very principle of sociality' (1986: 208).

The figure of Nietzsche haunts Kristeva's piece, as if she were engaged in a similar attempt to rid feminism of the moralism that the former despised in Christianity, as if the separatism and fantasies of this phase of feminism exist for her in an analogous relationship with the religious neurosis that Nietzsche abhorred. Writing of the saint in *Beyond Good and Evil* the latter opined:

> Why did they bow to him? In him – and as it were behind the question mark of his fragile and miserable appearance – they sensed the superior force that sought

to test itself in conquest, the strength of will in which they honoured their own strength and delight in dominion . . . it was the 'will to power' that made them stop before the saint. (1989: 65)

As feminism beomes a religion, so feminists become saints, so that, just as Nietzsche asked 'how is the saint possible?' (1989: 61), it is as if Kristeva asks: how is the (this) feminist possible? Are 'women' to recognise themselves in this global Woman of whom feminists write?

With the rejection of this possibility and this quasi-religious mode of feminism, Kristeva implicitly affirms the rejection of religious morality that Nietzsche attempts. Nietzsche's critique of religion, one that reverberates on some level with Marx's critique, is one that stresses the sense in which there is a temporality at work in religion, one that offers an attitude to the present that fantasises a future higher realm:

> To ordinary human beings . . . religion gives an inestimable contentment with their situation and type . . . Religion and religious significance spread the splendour of the sun over such ever-toiling human beings and make them tolerable to them. Religion has the same effect which an Epicurean philosophy has on sufferers of a higher rank: it is refreshing, refining, makes, as it were, the most of suffering, and in the end even sanctifies and justifies. (1989: 73)

It is implicit in Kristeva's critique that if feminism runs too close to becoming a religious faith, its radicalism may have the effect of dissolving into violent and asocial terrorism, not because it justifies suffering exactly, but because its rage at women's victimisation may create a utopian vision – and this she sees in, for example, the elevation of guiltless maternity – which develops a faith in the future that attempts to serve, in the stead of religion, to 'satisfy the anguish, the suffering, and the hopes of mothers' (1986: 206).

But how does the feminism that Kristeva endorses – the third phase – escape the dangers of this second imagination, and how does it alter the temporality of such a feminism? That one might talk of a third generation is not to suggest that there is another group of feminists who 'take the torch passed on from the second' (Kristeva, 1986: 209). Kristeva is explicit that her third generation 'implies less a chronology than a *signifying space*, a both corporeal and desiring space' (1986: 209). In the third attitude, which Kristeva seems to suggest she had only a glimpse of at that time, 'the very dichotomy man/woman as an opposition between two rival entities may be understood as belonging to *metaphysics*' (1986: 209). With a challenge to the very notion of identity, sexual identity is challenged; and in this manoeuvre, Kristeva imagined, there would be the 'demassification of the problematic of *difference*', which would imply a simultaneous 'de-dramatization of the "fight to death" between rival groups and thus between the sexes' (1986: 209). Such an attitude moves the locus of violence from the social contract, where feminist attention has previously been focussed, and where it took up a position now known under the rubric of 'anti-essentialism', on to the place where it operates with greatest 'intransigence': 'in other words, in personal and sexual identity itself' (Kristeva, 1986: 209).

Kristeva's third phase is one that translates into the refusal of a model of powerful/powerless as the predominant mode of social organisation, because with the 'interiorisation' of the sociosymbolic contract comes the analysis of 'the potentialities of the *victim/executioner* which characterise each identity, each subject, each sex' (1986: 210). There can be no idealisation of Woman. Again Kristeva indicates a Nietzschean legacy when she references 'aesthetic practices' in her pondering of how this third phase might avoid becoming a religion:

> It seems to me that the role of what is usually called 'aesthetic practices' must increase not only to counterbalance the storage and uniformity of information by present-day mass media, data-bank systems, and, in particular, modern communications technology, but also demystify, therefore, the *community* of language as a universal and unifying tool, one which totalizes and equalizes. (1986: 210)

The symbolic capacities of any one individual are, this suggests, relative and singular to that person, such that there is a fluidity which demands a responsibility against the threats (Kristeva is unambiguous in suggesting that these are 'threats of death') that are nascent in any attempt to constitute insides and outsides. dualisms between people and groups.

Reading Kristeva's piece with the benefit of nearly two decades more feminist theorising, it seems as if feminism has indeed taken up the issue of the problems of dichotomous thinking and has become involved in wider debates around the possibilities of post-Nietzschean philosophy, with, as a shorthand, the politics left and required by 'post-modernity'. It seems as though feminism has moved quickly in its theorising in order to 'arrive' at the same time as other schools of thought, longer established in theoretical debate, at the door into the problematics of post-structuralism. In a concentrated form, feminism has in its three phases skipped through philosophical problems of the twentieth century to appear, with 'everyone else' at this point. It is as if Kristeva's description is a summary of the philosophy of the twentieth century through the lens of feminism, ending with the third phase that remains, Kristeva is aware, part of a reply to the 'eternal question of morality' (1986: 211). 'Our time', she suggests, is 'about' the demand for a 'new ethics' (1986: 211).

Kristeva's proposal that, according to this third attitude, we are each, regardless of our contingent identities, in some respects 'guilty' and therefore each *responsible*, carrying the burdens of the sociosacrificial order whilst owning the possibility of *jouissance*, mobilises, I would argue, much of the present quarrels within feminist theory. In particular, the deconstructionist (loosely understood) impulse that motivated, with their different philosophical routes, works such as Denise Riley's (1988) *Am I That Name?*, or Judith Butler's (1990) *Gender Trouble*, have energised a debate which has the issue of the politics of a feminist that problematises the man/woman dichotomy at its heart. Moreover, the issue of 'aesthetic practices' has, as Kristeva predicted, become a central issue of thinking feminism.

It is exactly here that worries about the political potentials of a non-directed, allegedly 'post-metaphysic', non-normative feminist philosophy circulate, worries such as those expressed by Tania Modleski:

> [I]nasmuch as radical feminism is frequently called upon to account for its being on the same side of certain issues as the New Right, postmodern feminists might well wish to ponder how they wound up in this new 'alliance' with anti-feminist humanism. (1991: 14)

The quarrels gain momentum here, and the apocalyptic warning against certain modes of 'postmodern' feminism is put with an urgency. Might the dangerous thinking that such a phase of feminism enjoys lead to the demise of feminism? Modleski writes:

> It is not altogether clear to me why women, much more so than any other oppressed groups of people, have been so willing to yield the ground on which to make a stand against their oppression. . . . It is clear to me whose 'real interests' would be served by our ending 'the whole business' of feminism. (1991: 15)

That this is a battle cast within the terms, and employing the accusations, of imperialism and fascism is explicit in Modleski. Who is in a position to call whom by these terms of abuse? Modleski reads Donna Haraway's work as postmodern misplaced 'mistrust': 'so strong is her postmodern mistrust of communicational transparency that . . . she tends to sound at times as if any effort to work toward linguistic commonality is very nearly a fascistic enterprise' (1991: 18). In her retort to 'postmodern feminists', Modleski throws back the insult of imperialism, which she finds in Haraway's discussion of 'the feminist dream of a common language', with her version of new vanguardism (that in some respects she shares with Haraway's 'A cyborg manifesto' that she is critiquing) that places women of colour as its bearers. She suggests that 'white feminists' are becoming sensitive to the way in which 'experience' has operated in exclusionary ways through, in part, 'the work of women of colour like Anzaldua' (1991: 20).[10] The struggles of women 'of various sexualities, classes, ethnicities and races' within feminism who 'have *not* taken up the banner of anti-essentialism' have had to resist the 'efforts of white middle class women to *colonize* them' (Modleski, 1991: 20, emphasis added).

It would be misleading to suggest that Modleski's position is a simple reassertion of Kristeva's second-phase feminism, for she herself embraces the importance of thinking the 'processes' involved in 'defining and constructing the category' Woman (1991: 20). Nor do I wish to set her up as representative of an anti-philosophical nor even an anti-deconstructivist position (indeed, essays such as her 'Cinema and the Dark Continent' are fine examples of tracing the ways in which sex and 'race' are figured, to which many a 'post-structuralist or postmodern feminist' would aspire). Rather, what I mean to call attention to is the modes of argumentation by which 'quarrels' such as this are played out. In general, what I want to

---

10 See the edited volumes Anzaldua (1990) and Moraga and Anzaldua (1983).

do is to push the sense in which these debates are 'about' the political imagination of feminism, its dreams and its aims, its understandings of its past and future: in other words, the way in which the feminist political imagination is formed. In particular, I am suggesting that these arguments about the form that feminism should take are very much about how feminism positions itself in relation to the limit cases of political imaginations: where is feminism in relation to the horizon of fascism, and how are we to safeguard its distance?

The trouble with being tempted by Nietzsche

Present feminist theorists are not grappling with these questions in isolation. Indeed, feminist scholars debate the implications of questions that are central to much present philosophical and social theoretical rumination and in the most ambitious and least obtrusive of ways. Feminist theory is thus part of a more general sociotheoretical attempt to retain a political vision whilst engaging with post-structuralist thought. In this section I want to return to the position that Nietzsche occupies in these debates in order to offer a more sustained answer to the question: 'how did feminist theory get this way?' For the different temporalities of feminism did not simply evolve one out of the other. They were also responding to movements in philosophical thought that are animated themselves by the political fears and possibilities they carry with them. The debates around Nietzsche's legacy illustrate this clearly. Without any pretensions to solving the issues raised by these debates, I want to indicate them in order to suggest that in a world where the violences of all limit cases of political thought remain, feminist theory circulates, as Kristeva predicted, around the questions that are presently posed for those who had demanded and hoped under the banner of freedom. How are we to articulate those demands now? Can we give up our question, which is still perhaps Kant's: what may we hope for?

Because Kristeva's work seems implicitly to 'speak to' Nietzsche's figuring of these questions, because of Foucault's influence on feminist theorising and the latter's indebtedness to Nietzsche, and because of the way in which Nietzsche is frequently positioned as announcing the advent of 'post-modernity', I want to return to his thought in order to sketch in the problematic as he set it up. Nietzsche is widely accepted as the theorist who first considered the conclusions to be drawn for humankind in the sight of nihilism. If a distinction has been drawn between a modern and a postmodern epoch, then Nietzsche's attack on metaphysics has been set up as heralding the moment of philosophical break, because it was he who regarded his work as an attempt to prepare humanity for the approaching war he foresaw with Christian morality (Thiele, 1995: 15). Nietzsche did not see himself as bringing about this state of affairs, however, 'merely' as noticing and pushing it: 'Here is a hero who has done nothing but shake the tree as soon as the fruit was ripe' (in *Human, All Too Human*, 1986: 393). His position is an important one for my argument, because his work has been regarded as potentially, implicitly or explicitly, fascistic, such that his case has resonance with the fears that are articulated in relation to the forms of feminist argumentation.

In the preface to *The Genealogy of Morals* Nietzsche outlines the questions he is pursuing in his polemic; namely, the question of the origin of moral prejudices, of good and evil (1967: 16–17): 'under what conditions did man devise these value judgements good and evil? *and what value do they themselves possess?*' (1967: 17). Such an investigation was entwined, for Nietzsche, with an enquiry into comprehending 'ourselves', and especially in comprehending the elevation of the 'unegoistic'; that is, the 'instincts of pity, self-abnegation, self-sacrifice' (1967: 19), attitudes to the self which Nietzsche saw as crystallised in the figure of the priest, into value-in-itself. For a genealogist of morals, the task is one that refuses to gaze 'haphazardly in the blue' in order instead to be 'gay' in the grey:

> For it must be obvious which colour is a hundred times more vital for a genealogist of morals than blue: namely *gray*, that is, what is documented, what can actually be confirmed and has actually existed, in short the entire long hieroglyphic record, so hard to decipher, of the moral past of mankind! (Nietzsche, 1967: 21)

Nietzsche's attack on morality is born, in part, from a sense that (European) humankind had become weary of man, caught as it was within Christian morality, and that this is what made (Christian?) Europeans not ready for nihilism but *already* within nihilism:

> [P]recisely what has become a fatality for Europe – together with the fear of man we have also lost our love of him, our reverence for him, our hopes for him, even the will to him. The sight of man now makes us weary – what is nihilism today if it is not *that*? – We are weary of man. (1967: 44)

Now ashamed at the cruelty which Christianity finds in life, the sky darkens and pessimism reigns; life has become so repugnant to 'the animal "man"' that 'he sometimes holds his nose in his own presence' (Nietzsche, 1967: 67). Religion, then, has been a way of assimilating those who refuse to 'suffer life as a sickness' (in *Beyond Good and Evil*, Nietzsche, 1989: 74) with unworldliness, breaking the strong and casting suspicion on 'joy in beauty' and bending 'everything haughty, manly, conquering, domineering, all the instincts characteristic of the highest and best-turned-out type of "man", into unsureness, agony of conscience, self-destruction' (in *Beyond Good and Evil*, 1989: 75). The task of the church was to invert love of the earthly and of dominion over the earth into a hatred of the earth and the earthly (1989: 75).

Nietzsche's suggestion that the concept of God is a 'counter-concept of life' leads him to suggest that we 'leave the town' (in *The Gay Science*, 1974: 342) in order to see our morality from a distance, as does the wanderer who wishes to know how high the town's towers are. In taking our distance, we might see 'beyond good and evil' and be instead 'true to the earth'. Against the sense of guilt that Christian morality bequeathed in order to give meaning to the sufferings of earthly life, Nietzsche's proposal was a revaluation of tragic heroism, posed by the figure of the *Ubermensch*. In what he understood to be a Heraclitean world-view, there will be those who flounder in subjectivism, who bemoan the realisation that experience is 'only oneself' (in *Thus Spoke Zarathustra*, 1969: 173); the heroic, on the other hand, will have a different perspective: 'No longer the humble expression, "everything is merely subjective," but "it is also *our work!* – Let us be proud of it!"' (in *The Will to Power*, 1909: 545). The freedom that is given by the proper genealogy of morality, one that reveals the conventions that have taken on the status of truths, is one that requests and requires strength. Thiele summarises Nietzsche's image of the *Ubermensch*, which Thiele sees – not without reason – as also the image Nietzsche had of himself, thus:

> Nietzsche's heroic ideal befits only a wanderer and a solitary. In creating himself, philosophically and biographically, a heroic and hermitic figure, Nietzsche attempts to leap beyond good and evil, beyond political community, social mores, customs, religion, even beyond personal habits and friendships. He shuns his affiliation with humanity, abandons all idols, and spurns any divinities that might accompany him on his odyssey. His is an itinerancy of such isolation that it forbids itself a companion and a resting place both on earth and in the heavens. Nietzsche's individualism amounts to an extreme homelessness. (1995: 21)

Without the comfort of divine guidance, this tragic figure welcomes the struggle that is mortal life, but without himself becoming mimetic of God, and without the comfort of romantic hero worship (Thiele, 1990: 911–12). With his sights set on this earth, and no longer on an after-life, the *Ubermensch* makes of his life an aesthetic project; he is a figure who partakes in life with the greatest of energy, struggling with his existence, his inner self, without understanding that struggle as directed anywhere except to his own inevitably human, but heroically tragic, end.

The debate that takes place under the rubric 'postmodernity' is one that engages with the legacy of Nietzsche's announcement of the end of metaphysics, and many of the worries about the precarious and 'dangerous' positions being adopted within feminist theory can be regarded, similarly, as a series of debates that have arisen in the aftermath of Nietzsche's 'dynamite'. The genealogical impulse that questions the very categories of morality, of all foundational categories, raises the question of how to conceive of, and without, metaphysical categories within feminism. Does that mean the demise of feminist thought and politics? Relatedly, questions are being raised within feminism that surround how to conceive a feminist politics without instituting a new moralism after the demise of 'grand narratives'. There is a fundamental debate that surrounds the question of whether aesthetic practices can be an adequate politics. In short, the danger of Nietzsche's world without metaphysics is seen to be a world without normativity, one that results in an individual quest of struggle, refusing futurity in its adoption of genealogical modes of thought. This is an attitude to the present, a temporality, that is infused with a scepticism that allegedly paralyses attempts to locate the sources of power resistance to which collective forms of politics had mobilised. The worries about this paralysis set an apocalyptic tone to discussions of postmodernism: 'Post-modernism is anticipatory shell-shock. It's as if the bomb has already fallen . . . postmodernist writing confesses (or celebrates) helplessness' (Glittin, quoted in Thiele, 1990: 908). The 'danger' of non-normative genealogical Nietzscheanism is figured as allowing *any* politics, and it is thus that the image of fascism, as our limit case (of right-wing) politics, looms. It is implied that thinking in 'that' way is dangerous because it makes feminist argumentation too open, its boundaries too vulnerable, its vision too opaque. These forms of thought are in danger of blurring into, or allowing access to, the most extreme forms of politics.

Such critiques and such fears are neither simply wrong nor neurotic. It is true that there was within German National Socialism, an attempt to read into Nietzsche's work, support for that political vision. Alfred Baeumler, philosopher of the Third Reich, and professor at the University of Berlin, attempted to claim Nietzsche as a proto-Nazi, stressing his emphasis on responsible heroism as an activism that involves training, his rejection of Enlightenment ideology, his philosophy of the will to power, and his contempt for mediocracy. Baeumler finds in Nietzsche quotations such as the following: 'The species requires the extinction of the misfits, weaklings and degenerates; but Christianity as a conserving force appeals especially to them' and turns such polemics to the case for National Socialism as the politics which understands a heroic 'will to power':

> [I]t takes unexcelled boldness to base a state upon the race. A new order of things is the natural consequence. It is this order which Nietzsche undertook to establish in opposition to the existing one. (Baeumler, 1966, quoted in Mosse, 1966: 100, first published 1937)

Nietzsche's individualism does not preclude the community, race, or people, Baeumler insists, but enables an honouring of the aristocracy of the strong and healthy, whose men 'do not permit their basic instincts to languish in favour of a mediocre average – men who know how to curb and control their passions instead of weakening or negating them' (quoted in Mosse, 1966: 100, first published 1937). The future vision of National Socialism was explicit in its training of youth:

> If today we see German youth on the march under the banner of the swastika, we are reminded of Nietzsche's 'untimely meditations' in which this youth was appealed to for the first time. It is our greatest hope that the state today is wide open to our youth. And if today we shout 'Heil Hitler!' to this youth, at the same time we are also hailing Nietzsche. (in Mosse, 1966: 100–1, first published 1937)

Such a reading of Nietzsche continues into the racist groups of the 1990s, with white supremacists groups still reading into Nietzsche a vision that compares to their own. George Burdi, white supremacist leader of Resistance Records and organiser of internet sites of racist discussion claims Nietzsche as his inspiration: 'I came to understand his discussion of the Superman' (quoted in *The New York Times Magazine*, 25.2.1996, p. 42). Burdi modelled himself, he claims, on the image of the Superman, positioning himself as 'a kind of modern heretic questioning the liberal status quo' (*TNYTM*, 25.2.1996, p. 42).

It is not, however, this sort of reading that leads to present fears of Nietzsche's legacy, one that sees fascism implicit in Nietzsche, for opposite readings of Nietzsche were and are put forcefully.[11] Rather, the fear is that his thought might not have the resources to enable it to respond to such an interpretation. Similar doubts surround the thought of Michel Foucault; there is the fear that genealogical, 'post-metaphysical' thought cannot guard against the most insidious of politics. Thus post-liberal thinkers have sought to reinstate the Enlightenment project as the one with which we should still be involved. Habermas' question to Foucault – 'why fight?' – and Nancy Fraser's critique of the absence of normativity in Foucault, deserve to be taken seriously, and not simply as a way to rethink the debate around the theorising of a peculiarly feminist politics.

In other words, the debates are not advanced by arguments around whose reading of the history of philosophy is 'better' or 'truer'. My argument is that these critiques and the 'fears' that they articulate cannot be answered and debated (at least, not solely) on the level of theoretical fidelity. For the debates are not 'about' truth even as truth is a familiar terrain for their staging. Rather, as they push out to their rhetorical finales, more often than not these positions are about the formation of political horizons and visions. They tell us something about our historical positionality, and about the affective economy of political imagination. If we are tempted by Nietzsche, what hope do we have? In the case of feminism, the finales are about how to maintain a specifically feminist political imagination. How do we give feminist politics some anchorage? Can we do without it? To which horizon are we heading?

Dangerous thinking and the future of feminism

'Our time', conceived in the vein adopted by Cixous, remains one of dissociation and reorganisation around the issue of identity. As the quotation that heads this chapter suggests, at the end of the twentieth century the issues of belonging and political identification continue to be struggled with and bitterly fought over. Not simply because of an accident of the calendar, this present is also one in which the notion of 'the end' is being 'documented', predicted, warned against, and theorised in several arenas.[12] In terms of the feminist political imagination, the task is to refuse the formulation of the predicament in terms of apocalyptic endings.

11 See, for example, Aschheim (1992); and G. Rose (1993).
12 See Dellamora (1995); within feminist theory, see Quinby (1994).

Several different arguments are merged within the debates. Whether we can understand the current feminist debates about the rejection of man/woman as belonging to *metaphysics*, is, I would suggest, a point that is rarely articulated as such. The targets of feminist interrogations of sexual categorisation tend instead to be framed as 'essentialism' or 'Enlightenment dualisms' or, on a slightly different level, a Eurocentrism that collapsed and refused intracategorical differences in the insistence on the sovereignty of the man/woman dichotomy. It is true that these are challenges to certain foundational *faiths* that had purportedly underlain feminist theory, and if these were by definition metaphysical it makes sense insofar as the current debates about finding our way without faith, in nihilism, and the anxieties are about whether we are in denial of the fact that whilst renouncing faith we have set up other leaders (be they Derrida, Foucault or Lacan) who inspire other, possibly more 'dangerous' beliefs. The most dangerous of these, it seems, is when under the very sign 'feminism' women begin to dissolve the foundational moment of feminism: the ability to speak of 'the suffering of women'.

Feminist theorists have arrived at a point at which understandings of political identification and of radical politics place the very project of feminism in question in the sense that attempting to think of the futurity of feminism becomes an arena of contestation. Spivak's important article 'Can the subaltern speak?' (1988) took its point of departure from a challenge to the way in which radical politics is frequently premised on a mode of listening, without adequately theorising the conditions of being heard. Such politics tends to assume a homogeneous group – 'the subaltern' or 'women' or 'subaltern women' – who will be able to articulate a common demand as if from a marginal position. Spivak challenges the sense in which such a politics may be engaged in projects which construct the 'subaltern' who will be heard, as if such a subject position exists somehow 'outside' or 'before' those who ready themselves to hear. In her discussion of the practice of *sati*, Spivak noted the difficulties of wavering between a nostalgia 'before' imperialism, when cultural traditions were 'un-governed', which clearly is not a satisfactory position, and a desire to halt traditional practices that from a perspective 'outside' seem inhumane. The example is a graphic one of how the 'sexed subaltern subject' produces herself as exceptional and absent, through an act of suicide that produces her as, quite literally, unable to speak. Spivak's political response to this problem takes Derrida's lead, since she argues that the texts of the West might be explored for the ways in which they allow or disallow an enunciative space for their conceived 'outside'. Whilst Spivak writes, in part, as a critique of Foucault, and particularly, it seems, of notions such as his 'subjugated knowledges',[13] her

---

13 In an interview collected in *The Post-Colonial Critic*, Spivak suggests that she admires Foucault's work in that he represents 'the texts of the oppressed' and analyses them in a way that 'discloses one's own positionality', while she also objects to how his work leads to the '*theorisation* of letting Pierre Riviere speak for himself, and what the theoretical articulation does for the people who are influenced by Foucault' (1990: 56).

conclusion concurs with his to the extent that it leads us to an interrogation of ways in which speaking positions are constructed discursively through means of subjectification and identification.

Trinh Minh-ha, recognising that 'categories erase the anarchy of differ-ence' suggests that feminism is about taking a certain responsibility: 'to be aware of the established limits and to remove the censure of "non-categorical" thought (Foucault)' (1991: 120). To go on, she suggests, we need to consider the difference between similarity and equality, avoiding the simplification (much as Kristeva critiques the 'second attitude' that splits off 'symbolic language-phallus-man' from 'repressed language-hole-woman'[14]) that 'leads us straight to the criticism of categorization favoured by the "hardware" system' (Trinh Minh-ha, 1991: 128). In a different vein, but a compatible one, the work of Donna Haraway is explicitly about how we might think about the future; her 'cyborg' attempts to offer an emblem of, and for, future struggles without categorisable identities.

Insofar as it involves a rejection of a subjectivity that can be straight-forwardly expressed through language and that is thought to gain recog-nition via demands on behalf of those gathered under the banners that 'represent' it, these versions of feminism pose themselves ambivalently toward the future. Judith Butler states the issue explicitly in her argument that feminism might be addressed not as representation of a constituency – women – but as a representational *claim*:

> The feminist 'we' is always and only a phantasmatic construction, one that has its purposes, but which denies the internal complexity and indeterminacy of the term and constitutes itself only through the exclusion of some part of the con-stituency that it simultaneously seeks to represent. The tenuous or phantasmatic status of the 'we' however, is not a cause for despair, or not *only* a cause for despair. The radical instability of the category sets into question the *foundational* restrictions on feminist political theorizing and opens up other configurations, not only of genders and bodies, but of politics itself. (1990: 142)

In her reading of Foucault, *inter alia*, Butler argues that feminism can no longer argue through a fantasy that ignores the discursive apparatus by which the identification is produced. Rather, locating the problematic within 'practices of signification' results in the notion of 'agency' being rethought as 'a question of how signification and resignification work' (1990: 144) as processes of regulated repetition (1990: 145). Butler argues that identity politics can paradoxically 'presume, fix and constrain' the 'very "subjects" it seeks to represent and liberate' (1990: 148); arguing without foundationalism and notions of 'ready-made subjects' is 'about' the possi-bilities of new 'cultural configurations' that 'expose' the signification prac-tices as such (1990: 149).

Such repositionings of the feminist task have led feminists into debate over the question of politics without identities, without the notion of 'representation', and without the (same) notion of freedom. It is here that

---

14 A formulation she adopts from Gabrielle Fremont.

the apocalyptic tone resounds. These debates have focussed it seems with particular clarity around the feminist utilisation of Foucault; in part, perhaps, because Foucault was frequently pushed himself on this issue.[15] Without wishing to rehearse the debate around Foucault's 'politics' or the political utility of his writings here, suffice it to outline briefly how the politics that his thought bequeaths the feminist reader is indeed a difficult one. Foucault invites us to modes of analyses that attempt to think without 'foundations', to be attentive to the present without imposing the comfort of inherited matrices, to trace the complexities of the *dispositifs* that entangle power and knowledge in our understandings of ourselves. Foucault took much from Nietzsche, and was explicit about the influence of the latter on his work, placing his own oeuvre 'under the sun of Nietzsche's great search' (as he describes it in *The Order of Things*, 1970), stating explicitly that his own analytic tool kit borrowed much from Nietzsche (e.g., in his 'Nietzsche, genealogy, history', 1984a). Although the indebtedness can be too heavily drawn, Foucault certainly took on Nietzschean formulations, especially of 'the nature of genealogical study; the violence of (the origins of) truth; the cruelty, malice, and passion of the will to knowledge; . . . the sacrifice and self-sacrifice of the subject in the endless deployment of the will to truth' (Thiele, 1990: 915). The attempt to think of the self as a 'work of art', to formulate and reformulate our understandings of the self, whilst struggling with Enlightenment, Romantic and psychoanalytic inheritance, is one which follows Nietzsche insofar as it responds to nihilism with an aesthetic perspective (Thiele, 1990: 915). With such a connection, one can comprehend concerns about a feminist use of Foucault. If Nietzsche's work could be appropriated as it was, what hope is there for a feminism that follows his follower?

Foucault's attitude to political imagination and to imagining the future was one that puts its faith in creativity in struggle without defining its purpose or goal. True, the struggle against power relations no longer has the comfort of earlier formulations of the location of power and the power strategies to be opposed, but has to consider, expand and reformulate where these battles take place, which also involves a reflection on the places from and modes by which resistance – in the name of inequality, suffering, and injustices – is allowed to be spoken. This is a stepping back, not a transcendence, but a 'leaving town'. Elsewhere, I have argued (Bell, 1994) that fiction has a place in Foucault's work because it entails just such a distancing; fiction 'puts language on display, disperses it, redivides it and opens it up' (Foucault, quoted by Bellour, 1992: 149). It is this 'opening up' that arguably relates the dream, like fiction, to the wider Foucauldian project, in the sense that it binds the questions of temporality, space and criticism. If the dream is 'the still secret jarring of existence which is taking hold of itself' (Foucault, 1986: 58), a repetition of 'the experience of

---

15 For examples of the ways in which such a 'Foucault and feminism' debate has been staged, see, for example, McNay (1992), Ramazanoglu (1993) or Hekman (1996).

temporality which opens upon the future and constitutes itself as freedom'
(Foucault, 1986: 58–9), one might characterise Foucault's work as an
attempt to provide a waking glimpse of that temporality, a 'jarring' that
reflects on life *as if* one were dead, or, at least, removed? (And yet, like
the dreamer, that simultaneously indicates that one is most alive? 'Dreaming, man . . . "is" "life-function"; "waking" he creates "life-history"'
(Binswanger, 1986: 102)). The 'impasse' within feminism, similarly, might
be framed optimistically as an indication that feminism is 'most alive'.
Feminism's vitality is indicated by the fact that it continues to struggle over
these questions within and outside the academy.

In other words, if we accord with Butler's approach, and with the
formulation of political identity outlined earlier in relation to Nancy, if we
accept the 'radical instability' of our categories and of the 'phantasmatic
"we"', it is not necessarily the case that this accord signals 'the end'.
Against this melancholic position, the feminist task is to remain apocalyptic only in the sense of imagining the end of patriarchal modes of
thought and gendered inequality; genealogical impulses, on the other hand,
need to be seen as anti-foundational and therefore as anti-apocalyptic (as
Quinby, 1994: 36–9 has suggested). If this book is an attempt to look at
the blurred boundaries of the 'being in common' and the blurred nature of
feminist imagination, it is not so that we become melancholic about figures
in our past and possibilities for the future; rather that we 'mourn', in the
sense of Freud's distinction, and incorporate such readings into our present
and mobile identifications. This is a question not just of political but also
of historical positionality.

Conclusion: so what if we're phantastic?

What I have been attempting to argue in this chapter is that it would go
against the genealogical impulse to leave the 'feminism v. post-structuralism'
debate with a point about being anti-apocalyptic. It is as if feminists who are
convinced by Foucault, or by Derrida or by some other 'dangerous thinker',
have become obliged to leave the podium with reassurances that the readings
of the fearful are mistaken and the fears are thereby misplaced. I want to
suggest that the worries surrounding a feminism following Foucault, or
others who take us to similarly feared conclusions, are not without reason;
and the 'dangers' feared of these positions cannot be brushed aside as archaic
or nostalgic modernism. It is possible to take those articulations seriously, to
see them as indications of a political horizon that even genealogical work
needs to work within.

Genealogical investigations have a specific temporality in the sense that
they are attentive to the present and the ways in which the past has made the
present possible, whilst they have an attitude to the future that is at once
closed and wide open, refusing to predict, seemingly refusing to imagine, but
at the same time welcoming of the possibilities of the unknown that is the

future. For even as one might agree that it was precisely in opposition to 'terrorists of theory', the 'bureaucrats of the revolution' and that 'fascism in all of us', that Foucault (1984b) refused to lay out a programme of action, as he argued in his preface to Deleuze and Guattari's *Anti-Oedipus* (1984), that is not to prevent the worry of the unknown. Could not Foucault's art of politics be co-opted, as some attempted with Nietzsche, by 'propagandists of fascist politics interested in such a heroization of struggle?' (Thiele, 1990: 920).

Attempts to 'found' politics that are based on a desire to be rid of the dangers of the future are, in other words, *desires* not based on nor motivated by 'correct analyses', but by the very anxiety that we cannot know the future. But I would suggest that the 'fear' of 'open-ended' genealogical theorising, one that I have suggested might be thought of (in this context, at least) as a fear of 'the end' (of feminism), a fear of extremism, of non-normativity, often explicitly a fear of the ends of democracy, or of fascism, is not necessarily a glib and easy name-calling, nor a debate that is 'about' the truth of the theory in question. It would be more productive to see it as an indication of the awareness of dangers that are not simply somehow 'within' theory. Thus the fears cannot be answered from within a debate about correct analyses.

Fascism in all the varieties it has taken this century *are* limit cases, and it is proper that they should remain 'within' feminist thought and politics, and thought about politics. However, I would not wish that statement to lead to a discussion of feminism that mirrors the discussion that has taken place around Nietzsche's work; that is, one that poses the question in a formulation that sets up a debate around the complicity of certain ways of thinking. Rather, I am suggesting, the tracing of feminist political imagination, its debates and revisions, can be carried out in such a way that the fears are answered through the work itself. The genealogical impulse can be aware of and attentive to the political horizons, and the forms of temporality that I have suggested are intimately tied with political imaginations. Feminism is obliged to revise the ground from which it stands and to consider how its political imaginations have been shaped. The point is not to remove the possibility of political identification with feminism, of speaking feminism, but to pay attention to the manoeuvres by which 'we' do so.

3

SUFFERING: THINKING POLITICS WITH SIMONE DE BEAUVOIR AND RICHARD WRIGHT

[W]here do the historically and culturally specific elements of politicised identity's investments in itself, and especially in its own history of suffering, come into conflict with the need to give up these investments, to engage in something of a Nietzschean 'forgetting' of this history, in the pursuit of an emancipatory democratic project?' (Wendy Brown, 1995: 55)

Wounded attachment? Feminism and ressentiment

In this chapter I want to question how we understand the impulse to politics through an examination of the ways in which feminist argument is made and made to 'work'. In particular, I want to explore the sense in which feminism, as a form of 'identity politics' modelled in modern fashion, might be a candidate for the accusation that its politics is fuelled by a form of ressentiment.[1] An attachment to a political identity as *the* driving force of political argument might be thought of as what Wendy Brown has termed a 'wounded attachment' that, rather than enriching the political field, replays a form of class resentment that 'like all resentments . . . retains the real or imagined holdings of its reviled subject as objects of desire' (1995: 60). Ressentiment, as Nietzsche understood it, relies upon a negative stance that says only 'no'; its only creative deed is to refuse. Moreover, the political vision becomes dominated by an image of suffering that relies upon a particular and owned suffering. There is a 'logics of pain' at work here that depends upon the evidencing of *particular* sufferings that work rhetorically to confer and confirm a politicised identity.

Resentment need not be piously figured as in and of itself disallowable within feminism, as if feminism were too pure for such sentiments; rather, the argument is that a politics, fuelled by a sense of injustice and privation, bases itself upon a privileged figure – the bourgeois white man – whose positionality is evoked as simultaneously coveted and despised. If feminism bases itself upon claims of collective suffering, its efficacy brings with it the

---

1 Such an accusation has been floated implicitly in feminist debate, but also explicitly (see Tapper, 1993).

sustenance of exactly that which liberal democracies allow and depend upon. For such modes of argumentation, ones that rest upon what Brown terms 'claims of injury and exclusion', have proven to be accommodated by liberal democracy, such that, whilst the gains achieved thereby are not to be belittled, the political vision becomes complicit with liberal democracies' need to fashion itself as listening to the demands of groups within its constituency. Moreover, the political vision of feminism becomes dominated by an image of suffering that relies upon a particular and *owned* suffering. Brown has posed the difficult question in terms of democracy, arguing that politicised identities run the risk of investing in a reiteration of their own powerlessness that works to reinscribe that incapacity (1995: 69).

In this chapter I want to question how we understand the impulse to feminist politics. Is *ressentiment* the basis of feminism? Does feminist argument work in that way; that is, by measuring the sufferings of women against a (necessarily imagined) figure who 'has' that which women are denied? I want to argue that interrogating feminism as a mode of political argument cannot begin simply with a rejection of the relevance of this notion of ressentiment – that itself would be an affirmation of the question in hand; rather, an argument has to be advanced that engages with the challenge, before it can be asserted that feminism is not simply a politics fuelled by a sense of injustice and privation that is only and 'merely' reactive.

As an initial starting point, it is safe to say that there is, as a hallmark of identity politics, a rhetorical tendency to ressentiment as Brown suggests. However, there are times when such a reading of feminist texts cannot be sustained, especially now that, with the various recent rewritings of feminism's histories, there is an explicit deconstruction of a languishing model of feminism which would be such a movement. Recent feminist work enables a reconsideration of the political imagination of feminism, and these reflexive rewritings of feminism's histories address, *inter alia*, the sense in which 'feminism' emerges and speaks womanhood. Against the security of a celebratory canonisation, feminist theorists are beginning to question the very logic of feminist argumentation. In this chapter I wish to draw attention to the crafting of feminist politics through a consideration of the way the boundaries of feminism can become blurred, those moments when feminism surrenders the privileged position accorded to female suffering, when gender is not enough, when feminist argumentation makes identifications that shift the subject of feminism outside the bounds of the particularity of that 'wounded attachment'. I do so in order to argue that, at these points, the notion of feminism based on ressentiment falls away, and different rhetorical and political possibilities emerge.

Within this exploration, then, my focus is on the modes of identification that simultaneously carve out and cover over the feminist landscape. I set about this task of exploring the boundaries of feminist argumentation through a focus on a particular connection and alliance of Simone de Beauvoir, possibly the most canonised of feminist writers. In particular, the chapter focusses on the relationship of elements of her work to that of one of her key contemporaries, the black American writer Richard Wright. The chapter reads the work of de Beauvoir and Wright intertextually with a view to understanding the rhetorical figures that operate within the political positions that are drawn there, and the manoeuvres and conflicts that arise through these figures. I want to suggest that the feminist political imagination that de Beauvoir bequeathed younger feminists was one in which, even as she ostensibly focussed on female subjectivity and feminist subjects, was sculpted out of a political landscape within which moved other figures, including the black male figure, my predominant concern here. The chapter reads these moments in de Beauvoir as a site at which to consider the mode of feminist argument, its rhetorical figures and creative manoeuvres.

* * *

The friendship between de Beauvoir and Richard Wright is one that has rarely been commented upon. Yet Wright was 'the only person I'm really fond of here, and whom I see with warm pleasure', wrote de Beauvoir to Sartre during her stay in the United States (1991: 420). There, she spent time with Richard and Ellen Wright, establishing what she imagined as a quasi-familial relationship with them, and their children. De Beauvoir wrote of their eldest daughter, Julia:

> I'd bought a big jar of candies for the little girl, who flung her arms around my neck. She's ravishing, and though I don't usually like children I adore her. Actually all three of them are adorable with me . . . it's like having a real family in New York – I feel at home with them. (1991: 430)

Wright showed her New York, especially the music scene in the city, took her to Harlem, and focussed her no doubt on the question of 'race relations' in the United States, an interest that was also encouraged by her relationship with Nelson Algren, who had, according to de Beauvoir's biographer Deidre Bair, 'first suggested she conduct her study of women in the light of the experience of black Americans in a prejudicial society' (1990: 388). De Beauvoir wrote to Sartre:

> Wright – whom I've come to love with all my heart – came to fetch me and took me to the big Abyssinian church in Harlem, the biggest Gospel Church in the world. We heard the singing and the sermon, and saw how people reacted – they were middle class and pretty restrained, but very impassioned all the same. (1991: 426)[2]

Wright, for his part, was delighted to have the companionship of de Beauvoir on both sides of the Atlantic, as he told an interviewer in Paris (in Kinnamon and Fabre, 1993), and Ellen Wright became de Beauvoir's editor in Paris. Wright had extended conversations with de Beauvoir and Sartre when he first visited Paris, frequently focussing on the concept of

2 See also Gayle (1980: 194) for mention of Wright's hospitality to de Beauvoir in the States.

freedom and the responsibilities that thereby befell the individual (Gayle, 1980: 201). These conversations clearly had a great impact on Wright's thinking; he wrote, for example:

> Sartre is quite of my opinion regarding the possibility of human action today, that it is up to the individual to do what he can to uphold the concept of what it means to be human. The great danger, I told him, in the world today is the very feeling and conception of what is a human might well be lost. He agreed. I feel very close to Sartre and De Beauvoir. (Journal entry, Sept. 1947, quoted in Fabre, 1985: 162)[3]

Clearly, the main point of connection between these two writers is the broad sweep of existentialist thinking, with de Beauvoir's engagement and borrowings, and with Wright's less sustained but sympathetic forays into that philosophical and ethical realm of thought.[4] My interest, however, is more a connection in terms of a shared political dynamic which is concerned with the theorising and politicising that follows once one has declared that the identity of 'object' is an achievement of the imagination.[5]

While neither writer pushed their explorations far into the terrain of the other, there are suggestions enough that this project was not far from their thoughts. De Beauvoir was enraged when implored never to write about 'the Negro problem' whilst she was visiting the States, enjoying as she did the jazz music and clubs, watching 'the marvellous Negro women dance', wandering in the cities and enjoying the racial mix of the States – 'God, I do love New York! It was so mild that by the river's edge there were children sitting, and Negroes, and lots of peaceful people. My eyes and my heart were full of them' (1991: 414). She tells Sartre that she had read a book by John Dollard (1937):

> an excellent book, from which we absolutely must publish huge extracts in *T. M.* It's called *Class and Caste in the South*, by an American sociologist – and the method's as interesting as the content. It's a kind of counterpart to your *Portrait of the Anti-Semite* but on the Blacks – and also scholarly in character. (1991: 431)

Thus it appears that the issue of race and racism was a point of reflection for de Beauvoir, as was the position of women for Wright.

The misogyny of Wright's oeuvre has been critiqued (see, e.g., Decosta-Willis, 1986), and while I do not intend to defend Wright against the charges made by these critiques, I would suggest that there are more sympathetic readings of his characterisations (see, e.g., Gilroy, 1993, 1996).

---

3 According to de Beauvoir's biographer Deirdre Bair, her feelings toward Richard Wright cooled as his marriage with Ellen broke down; de Beauvoir thought that his interest in racial problems had become 'limited to his own' and his marriage was 'a wreck' (1990: 389).

4 *The Outsider* (1953) was a novel very much engaged in exploring existentialist thought. It has generally been thought to be one of the least successful because of it, with reviewers suggesting that Wright had been seduced by Paris and had abandoned his allegiance with black America.

5 As Butler presents Sartre's argument (1987: 108).

Without pretending any centrality to their respective works, my suggestion is that to the extent that issues of 'race' and racism were a concern of de Beauvoir's, gender was one of Wright's. Considering the processes involved in writing *Native Son* (1991, first published 1940), Wright suggests that the position of women arose as something that would require extended exploration:

> The writing of *Native Son* was to me an exciting, enthralling, and even romantic experience. With what I've learned in the writing of this book, with all its blemishes, imperfections, and with all its unrealized potentialities, I am launching out upon another novel, this time about *the status of women in American modern society*. This book, too, goes back to my childhood just as Biggar went, for, while I was storing away impressions of Biggar, I was storing away impressions of many other things that made me think and wonder. (1987: xxxiii–xxxiv, emphasis added)

Despite the fact that this book, also mentioned in an interview conducted with Wright for a magazine in Mexico (see Kinnamon and Fabre, 1993: 31), never materialised, this statement serves as evidence for shared, if unexplored, concerns, and, alongside the friendship, allows one to hear certain resonances and to pursue certain lines of questioning that can be harnessed for the debate I wish to conduct here.[6]

* * *

Recently there has been a closer attention to de Beauvoir as a theoretical writer (see, in particular, Chanter, 1995; Lundgren-Gothlin, 1996; Moi, 1994), drawing attention in particular to her classic work *The Second Sex* (1993, first published 1949) as an ambitious theory of gender development that is produced through an account which draws on a variety of theoretical and philosophical positions. There is, however, another strain to the influences that are registered in her text that are concerned with the issue of 'race', and it is to these that I want to turn in order to prise open the ways in which identity politics operates in de Beauvoir's theoretical writings, taking us into considerations of the way in which her polemics are figured. As I have argued elsewhere (Bell, 1995), there is a sense in which a dynamic between 'race' and gender operates in de Beauvoir's work that offers itself as, on the one hand, evidence of her line of argument, a mode of enhancing that argument, whilst, on the other, it threatens her main thesis, the very notion of *gendered* suffering. Figures of racialised suffering occur at several points in *The Second Sex*, albeit fleetingly, as do direct references to Richard Wright's novels. Tracing these as moments at which de Beauvoir draws parallels and makes comparisons between gender and 'race' enables a consideration of the ways in which her argument illuminates some of the difficulties of fixing certain concepts central to feminist argument as peculiar to the condition of womanhood.

---

6 See Gilroy, *The Black Atlantic* (1993: 186), for the suggestion that there is an intertextuality to be explored.

Let us take a step back to prefigure this discussion of 'race' through de Beauvoir's key argument in terms of the concept of alterity. In the introduction to *The Second Sex*, she writes,

> [Woman] is defined and differentiated with reference to man and not he with reference to her; she is the incidental, the inessential as opposed to the essential. He is subject, he is the Absolute – she is the Other. (1993: xxxix–xl, first published 1949)

There is to this quotation an extended footnote in which de Beauvoir explains the concept of alterity as she reads it in the work of Emmanuel Levinas. De Beauvoir quotes a passage from Levinas in which he is exploring the argument that alterity 'marks the nature of a being' but not simply in terms of the 'opposition of two species of the same genus'. She draws our attention to the passage, in *Time & the Other*, in which he asserts that the feminine is 'le contraire absolutement contraire':

> Sex is not some specific difference . . . Neither is the difference between the sexes a contradiction . . . Neither is the difference between the sexes the duality of two complementary terms, for two complementary terms presuppose a pre-existing whole . . . alterity is accomplished in the feminine. This term is on the same level, but opposed in meaning to, consciousness. (Quotation taken from Levinas, 1987: 85–6, but following abbreviation found in the slightly different translation of de Beauvoir, 1993: xl, first published 1949)

At this point, therefore, de Beauvoir seems to agree with Levinas that the concept of alterity operates for all existents – indeed, she writes in the main text that 'the category of the other is as primordial as consciousness itself' – and yet she is perturbed by the way in which the feminine is figured in Levinas' text, and she halts her borrowings here.[7]

There is something telling in de Beauvoir's allusion to and dismissal of Levinas, for in *Time & the Other* (1987) he is concerned with the way in which alterity had been to his mind reduced back to sameness or *equivalence* in philosophical and political argument, and not least in existentialism, with its emphasis on existents' freedom. His comments on the feminine, flawed as they might be, are part of a more general effort to explore the possibility of theorising the sense of the solitude of being that remains even within an existent's relations with others. This is an account that takes sexual difference and erotic relationships as sites to expand his argument that relationships cannot be understood as struggles of two freedoms where duality is only ever figured either in terms of power contests or as failures in communication. Thus the terrain is one that issues forth similar problematics to those that *The Second Sex* addresses. The problematics of *Time & the Other*, concerned as it is with the encounter,

7 De Beauvoir is attracted to the exploration of alterity, but her footnote comments that Levinas' position is one that 'deliberately takes a man's point of view, disregarding the reciprocity of subject and object . . . his description [which de Beauvoir glosses, against Levinas' text, as 'woman as mystery'] which is intended to be objective, is in fact an assertion of masculine privilege' (1993: xl, first published 1949).

the 'event of alterity' (Levinas, 1987: 87), are echoed in de Beauvoir's own concerns with the psychology of womanhood to the extent that she wishes to work through the specificity of woman's position 'as object' that had been unaddressed in the philosophies that treated all existents as entering encounters, existentially speaking, with an equivalence.[8]

This exposition is not intended to switch the debate on to one concerning Levinas' influence on de Beauvoir, but to suggest that there is a sense in which de Beauvoir avoids an aspect of his argument which resonates with key questions within her own thesis; namely, the interrogation of the conceptual relationship between power and alterity. At their most broad, Levinas' arguments represent a challenge to those who would seek to conceptualise intersubjective events through one theoretical model; erotic relationships are qualitatively different from other relationships (as

8 Levinas' exploration of 'intersubjective space' (1987: 83–4) is premised on the argument that encounters with the other cannot be approached through notions of assimilation, which would be to reduce the relationship to knowledge or bringing 'to light'. Rather, relationships with others are asymmetrical relationships, encounters with absolute alterity as well as the specific alterity of the other. The impossibility of absorbing the other, as one might food or knowledge, maintains the duality of beings and confirms the solitude of existence. The tension between the other 'in front of' and the absolute alterity of futurity that is summoned in the confrontation marks out such solitude. Between existents, existence itself can be spoken about; that is, it can be brought into discourse, but it cannot be shared – this is the pathos of love (1987: 86) in which there is a desire for fusion. In our encounters with one another, Levinas argued, we come 'face to face' with our finite nature in a way that we sense the absolute alterity that we otherwise confront only, perhaps, in suffering, where death is proximate, 'announces itself', and where we are 'backed up against being': 'It is made up of the impossibility of fleeing or retreating. The whole acuity of suffering lies in this impossibility of retreat. It is the fact of being backed up against life and being. In this sense suffering is the impossibility of nothingness' (1987: 69).

When de Beauvoir critiques Levinas' discussion of femininity as 'an assertion of masculine privilege' (1993: xl) she is correct to the extent that he speaks about the feminine as a mystery, thereby betraying the sense in which he speaks as a man. For him, however, femininity is not a mystery because of some romantic or mythical notion of womanhood, but because the erotic relationship has a peculiarly telling place amongst relationships, one that is open to the future without content, and therefore entails 'the very dimension of alterity' (Levinas, 1987: 88–9).

His explorations of eros are offered, it seems, as a way to facilitate a contrast with the face-to-face situation as an ethical relation; for ethics involves a sense of a third party, in a way that the erotic relationship does not. A third party disrupts the intimacy of lovers; the erotic relationship has no social dimension. When he extends his argument to the realm of ethical face-to-face relationships (which are non-erotic), he suggests that these relationships are similarly incomprehensible as power struggles along the lines of Hegel's master-bondsman dialectic; nor are they to be thought of as the coexistence of several freedoms as existentialists would have it, nor even of as moments in which the collective overshadows the particular encounter. The ethical relationship is diminished for Levinas where it is understood in such a way that the subject is identified with the other and 'swallowed up in a collective representation' (1987: 93) (as in social anthropological accounts), and subjects are understood side by side, equivalent and interchangeable. Rather, he suggests, ethics needs to be understood as a face-to-face relationship, as an encounter with alterity, with all the resonance that this statement has for Levinas. The specificity of an ethical relationship is that it remains an exclusive relationship, but one that simultaneously involves reference to a third party, that renders it social and, insofar as that manoeuvre occurs, symmetrical.

are, he suggests, parent–child relationships) because they involve a different – a grasping – relationship with absolute alterity (see Levinas, 1969;
1987).

In this chapter, I wish to explore the issue of equivalence across gendered
and racialised modalities of alterity through a focus on de Beauvoir's use
of racialised figures. How does she employ these figures in *The Second Sex*?
Is she suggesting an equivalence between 'race' and gender? In what sense?

Let us return to de Beauvoir's text. Her introduction to *The Second Sex*
continues:

> [N]o group ever sets itself up as the One without setting up the Other over and
> against itself . . . In small town eyes all persons not belonging to the village are
> 'strangers' and suspect; to the native of a country all who inhabit other countries
> are 'foreigners'; Jews are 'different' for the Anti-Semite, Negroes are 'inferior' for
> American racists, aborigines are 'natives' for colonists, proletarians are the 'lower
> class' for the privileged. (1993: xl–xli, first published 1949)

In making such an extension of the concept of alterity away from the
situation of women, de Beauvoir makes the case that there are some senses
in which the alterity ascribed to women is not a position uniquely suffered
by them. It is this giving up of the position of women as an experience of
gender that intrigues me; what does it mean to suggest that these different
forms of racism illuminate sexual oppression?

One might suggest that de Beauvoir's purpose is to enhance her argument about sexual discrimination through the prism of the racial, that it is
a form of rhetoric that is an argument by association. As an initial position, I want to argue that this is undoubtedly the case. Her rhetorical
position, moreover, read in this vein, is one that does indeed proceed to a
feminist politics that could be characterised by ressentiment. Let me make
this case more fully before I contend, further, that one might also read
these arguments rather differently.

In the passage in which de Beauvoir makes explicit reference to Wright's
Native Son, the sense in which she presents racial oppression as parallel to
gender oppression is made clear. *Apropos* the young girl's development into
the dilemma of objectified subject, the subject who must make herself
object in order to take up her normalised place in the world, she writes that

> it is a strange experience for whoever regards himself as the One to be revealed to
> himself as otherness, alterity. This is what happens to the little girl when, doing
> her apprenticeship for life in the world, she grasps what it means to be a woman
> therein. . . . high as she may raise herself, far as she may venture, there will
> always be a ceiling over her head . . . the little girl lives amongst gods in human
> guise. (1993: 313, first published 1949)

It is at this point that de Beauvoir draws the analogy, suggesting that

> This situation is not unique. The American Negroes know it, being partially
> integrated in a civilization that nevertheless regards them as constituting an
> inferior caste; what Bigger Thomas, in Richard Wright's *Native Son*, feels with
> bitterness at the dawn of his life is this inferiority, this accursed alterity, which is

written in the colour of his skin: he sees airplanes flying by and he knows that because he is black the sky is forbidden to him. Because she is a woman, the little girl knows that she is forbidden the sea and the polar regions, a thousand adventures, a thousand joys: she was born on the wrong side of the line. (1993: 313, first published 1949)

De Beauvoir is explicitly employing the notion of a line that separates girls from things she can witness but not enjoy as a participant. Here then is the coveted figure of the man, free to explore regions forbidden to woman. In this passage, this same figure is watched by Bigger Thomas, and is given a racial identity, as white. De Beauvoir's use of Wright is heuristic not socio-logical, rhetorical not empirical, and it is in this sense that the argument functions to strengthen de Beauvoir's point through an association. The scene from *Native Son* to which she refers occurs near the beginning of the novel, as Bigger and his friend Gus contemplate the passing world. Bigger is meditative, watching the plane high in the sky.

'Them white boys sure can fly,' Gus said.
   'Yeah,' said Bigger wistfully. 'They get a chance at everything.'
   . . .
   'I could fly one of those things if I had a chance,' Bigger mumbled reflectively, as though talking to himself. (1991: 460, first published 1940)

As Houston Baker Jr has commented, the sight of the plane, a sign of the lack of access to mechanical and technological possibilities of the twentieth century, in both Wright and Ralph Ellison's work, does not signify an innocent and pre-industrial state of negritude (1991: 103). What it does set up, however, is a dynamic of ressentiment, since Bigger and Gus articulate their dissatisfaction directed at those they can imitate, but cannot *be*. Bigger and Gus can 'play white', imitating the 'ways and manners of white folks' (Wright, 1991: 461), and laugh at themselves and 'at the vast white world that sprawled and towered in the sun before them' (Wright, 1991: 461). The mimicry however, does not compensate nor does it enable; Bigger positions himself explicitly on one side of a fence, using a perception of relations of privilege as drawn across a line or fence, as had de Beauvoir and as was (and is) common to much discourse on power:

'Goddammit, look!' We live here and they live there. We black and they white. They got things and we ain't. They do things and we can't. It's just like living in jail. Half the time I feel like I'm on the outside of the world peeping in through a knot-hole in the fence . . .' (Wright, 1991: 463)

De Beauvoir's interest was in the social psychology of living as an objectified subject. Woman is obliged to operate in the sexist world in bad faith, for the cultural attempt to make women into objects is one that is doomed to failure. In contrast to Gus and Bigger's play-acting as a way to laugh at those on the 'other side' of the fence, or the 'colour line', for women, play-acting *characterises* feminine subjectivity. As much as Man may imagine her alterity, no existent can really be Other. Thus femininity is an inauthentic state. It is a fantasy, de Beauvoir suggests, of patriarchy; and in order to comply, women presence as other, but could never 'be' other. Thus men demand an inauthentic 'play-acting' and women's existence is sublimated:

> He wants her to be the Other; but all existents remain subjects, try as they will to deny themselves. Man wants woman to be object: she makes herself object; at the very moment when she does that she is exercising a free activity. Therein is her original treason; the most docile, the most passive, is still a conscious being; and sometimes the fact that in giving herself to him she looks at him and judges him is enough to make him feel duped; she is supposed to be something offered, no more than prey. (1993: 295, first published 1949)

De Beauvoir's argument, therefore, is that the complexities of submission and activity in assuming the position of 'other' involve women, therefore, in an inauthenticity. However, she suggests, by contrast, that the relationship that black men have to their 'accursed alterity' is *authentic*, and can therefore become the basis of reaction and rejection of an imposed status as other. The difference is drawn at the level of psychology:

> There is this great difference: the Negroes submit with a feeling of revolt, no privileges compensating for their hard lot, whereas woman is offered inducements to complicity . . . along with the authentic demand of the subject who wants sovereign freedom, there is in the existent an inauthentic longing for resignation and escape; the delights of passivity are made to seem desirable to the young girl. (1993: 313, first published 1949)

Having drawn an image of power as operating across a line and between two groups, therefore, de Beauvoir suggests that there is a difference in the way that two subordinate groups respond to being on the 'wrong side'. In contrast to the clear-sightedness of 'the American Negro', women are made to desire femininity, and therefore to desire their subordination. Women themselves, and the men around women, comply with gendered regimes, such that men are 'duped' into a sense of security that these regimes uphold, whilst women act in bad faith, embracing femininity as an adaption to a situation in which their embodiment places them. Women desire *both* sovereign freedom and resignation. Woman's relationship to her position as 'object' provides no easy route through to political impulse, therefore, because she is faced with a forked road. As de Beauvoir puts it:

> [S]he does not accept the destiny assigned to her by nature and by society; and yet she does not repudiate it completely; she is too much divided against herself to join battle with the world; she limits herself to a flight from reality or a symbolic struggle against it. (1993: 370, first published 1949)

The 'vocation as female' that a woman has is one that is in contradistinction with her 'status as a real human being' (1993: 453, first published 1949).

A peculiar aporia opens in de Beauvoir's argument insofar as the parallel between race and gender has become abstracted away from embodied experiences: all the women are white and all the men are black, again. Such a mode of argumentation has been critiqued before now for its abstractions, historical complicities and sociological compartmentalisations. My interest in this parallel mode of argument in de Beauvoir is as follows: given its 'inaccuracies', what is the significance of this mode of argumentation for thinking in the feminist political imagination? Why does it appear and reappear in de Beauvoir's argument? Is it to be thought of simply as negative – as a mistake or a sloppy mode of argumentation? De Beauvoir's use of the racialised analogy is clearly an attempt to elaborate her argument through association, a rhetorical strategy that does not convince empirically, and it is a mode of argumentation which is extremely problematic, veering close to a psychological essentialism that allows no nuances of gendered and racialised subjectivities, and which, in its abstraction, makes the position of black womanhood an impossible one. Does she submit like a black man, with revolt, or like a woman, with the temptation of complicity? But I want to push the argument beyond a critique on this level, to suggest that the appearance of the figure of a black man within a feminist argument is one that has implications for the way in which the boundaries of the feminist political imagination is being sculpted.

To return to ressentiment, it seems as if de Beauvoir's use of the figure of Bigger Thomas at this point would characterise her feminist political aspiration as one in which and by which women realise their situation and their duplicity *in order to become* revolutionary in the same manner as the 'American Negro'. Her choice to present her argument through the character of Bigger Thomas implies a political imagination which is indeed one of ressentiment, for Bigger has much about him which would justify describing his spirit thus. Wright purposely made Bigger a difficult character to empathise with, unlike his autobiographical figure in *Black Boy*, the story that 'morally responsible Americans' would find 'honest, dreadful' and 'heartbreaking' (as wrote Fisher, in her introduction to the 1945 edition). Distressed to learn that white women were responding to *Black Boy* with pity, and not wanting readers to have the 'consolation of tears' (Gilroy, 1993), Wright made Bigger an uncompromising character whose arrogant masculinism bounces off the page. He is a victim of a racist society, certainly, but a young man whose fear leads him to manslaughter, when in an effort to avoid being discovered in the bedroom of a young white woman, Mary Dalton, he smothers her in a clumsy attempt to silence her alcohol-induced mumblings. His crime gives him a peculiar confidence:

> He had murdered and created a new life for himself . . . it was the first time in his life that he had had anything that others could not take from him . . . Though he had killed by accident, not once did he feel the need to tell himself that it had been an accident. He was black and he had been alone in a room where a white girl had been killed; therefore he had killed her. That was what everybody would say . . . And in a certain sense he knew that the girl's death had not been accidental. He had killed many times before, only on those other times there had been no handy victim or circumstance to make visible or dramatic his will to kill

. . . There was within him a kind of terrified pride in feeling and thinking that some day he would be able to say publicly that he had done it. (Wright, 1991: 542, first published 1940)

If we take the anger of a character such as Bigger Thomas as metonymic of the political impulse behind oppositional movements, we are thinking in terms of a situation of ressentiment. Bigger's hatred of white folk was formed in response to racism, to the 'crime of being black' (Wright, 1991: 721, first published 1940) that he had taken fully upon himself by his actions, and it was such that although he had not raped Mary – in fact, the death scene had begun with a drunken and uneasy but nevertheless sexual excitement between the two of them – he thinks of the event as a rape:

Had he raped her? Yes, he had raped her. Every time he felt as he felt that night, he raped. But rape was not what one did to women. Rape was what one felt when one's back was against a wall and one had to strike out, whether one wanted to or not, to keep the pack from killing one. He committed rape every time he looked into a white face. (1991: 658, first published 1940)

The white men who could fly, the white women who could afford to patronise with their communist politics, the folk who lived in other worlds 'across the line', produced in Bigger Thomas a loathing that was a mixture of hatred and desire, a need to revile but also to *be* the reviled. Nietzsche spoke of an imaginary revenge, a slave morality that begins with a :essentiment that is reactive, that 'says no' to what is 'outside' and different from 'it-self':

'and this No is its creative deed. This inversion of the value-positing eye – this need to direct one's view outward instead of back to oneself – is of the essence of ressentiment: in order to exist, slave morality always first needs a hostile external environment; it needs, physiologically speaking, external stimuli in order to act at all – its action is fundamentally reaction.' (1967: 36–7, first published 1887)

The man of ressentiment conceives his enemy as evil – this is his creation – and from this basic concept he evolves 'as an after thought and pendant, a "good one" – himself!' (Nietzsche, 1967: 39, first published 1887). The spirit of ressentiment, therefore, is one that seeks out enemies and evils in order to consider itself of higher morality; it is a negative reactive spirit that ties its sense of self-morality to its reaction to 'sinners'.

Bigger Thomas makes sense of his manslaughter of Mary in terms of his social relation to the Daltons and their associates. He had now acted, and recreated himself as a being of 'new born strength':

'The shame and fear and hate which Mary and Jan and Mr. Dalton and that huge rich house had made rise so hard and hot in him had now cooled and softened . . . No matter how they laughed at him for his being black and clownlike, he could look them in the eyes and not feel angry.' (Wright, 1991: 584, first published 1940)

Bigger's life becomes further complicated when he decides that he was wrong to have told his girlfriend, Bessie, what had happened. His sense of taking control of his life leads him to his 'second' rape, as he rapes Bessie, and then, deciding she would be a burden to him in his flight from the death sentence, he brutally murders her. His 'queer sense of power' (Wright, 1991: 669, first published 1940) stemmed from the sense of authorship he had: 'He had done this. He had brought this about. In all his life these two murders were the most meaningful things that had ever happened to him' (Wright, 1991: 670, first published 1940). He felt he had finally faced racism – 'this thing' – 'in all its fullness' (Wright, 1991: 670):

> Blind anger had come often and he had either gone behind his curtain or wall, or had quarreled and fought. And yet, whether in running away or in fighting, he had felt the need of the clean satisfaction of facing this thing in all its fullness, of fighting it out in the wind and sunlight, in front of those whose hate for him was so unfathomably deep that, after they had shunted him off into a corner of the city to rot and die, they could turn to him, as Mary had that night in the car and say: 'I'd like to know how your people live.' (Wright, 1991: 670, first published 1940)

* * *

I am not sure that I would be willing to characterise de Beauvoir's 'politics' *in toto* through the character of Bigger Thomas that she invokes. Moreover, his sense of facing the 'mountain of white hate' (Wright, 1991: 712, first published 1940) does show some belated signs of complexity toward the end of the novel, as the theme of hunger, of emptiness and fullness, becomes entwined with the racial politics of the criminal justice system. Bigger Thomas as a figure embodying the spirit of ressentiment, in its simplicity, is not sustained. His will to kill had 'duped' him, 'he knew that hate would not help him' (Wright, 1991: 700, first published 1940) and he flirts with the idea of suicide, in an effort, it seems, to rise above the spirit of ressentiment: 'he hungered for another orbit between two poles that would let him live again; for a new mode of life that would catch him up with the tension of hate and love' (Wright, 1991: 701, first published 1940). But, generally, Bigger Thomas' position is one of suffering, as the preacher who visits him in his cell in the final chapters says to him, 'Tha's whut life is, son. Sufferin'.' (Wright, 1991: 712, first published 1940). Bigger maintains his resistance to the solace of Christianity that the preacher offers him once more, but the feeling he had experienced through his most dangerous of routes, the feeling of taking charge, of making himself *subject*, we might say, is diminished by the end of the novel, where he feels 'emptied' when others defend him (Wright, 1991: 718, first published 1940); he is crushed and defeated, 'so empty and beaten that he slid to the floor . . . He rolled on the floor and sobbed, wondering what it was that had hold of him, why he was there' (Wright, 1991: 735, first published 1940).

At this point all I wish to contend is that there is a sense in which de Beauvoir's use of the unlikely figure of Bigger Thomas serves us particularly poorly as an image of shared modalities of suffering and equally badly as an image of oppositional politics. Her use of Bigger Thomas is employed as a way of suggesting that the suffering of women, the position of being objectified, is one that has been fictionalised by Richard Wright. Her effort to make this rhetorical move becomes highly problematic, and tends toward both a form of essentialist psychologic, positing women and blacks as separate but parallel modes of subjectivity, sexism and racism as comparable modes of oppression, and importantly, suggests an *ought* which has feminism based on revolt in the mode of Bigger Thomas. This is a particularly reactionary and inflammatory stance. It is, indeed, tantamount to a model of ressentiment, with power relations figured as arranged across a dividing line, and identity politics figured as requiring a strive toward authenticity, with the latter modelled, still, upon a figure of a white masculinity. This is not to say that feminism never involves ressentiment,[9] just that what it means for the sense of self mobilised is one that binds feminists to an image of ourselves as only ever sufferers.

Beyond ressentiment: modes of connectivity

I want to suggest, however, a different way to read the coming together of racialised figures with the gendered in de Beauvoir's text, and to elaborate it with reference to Wright's work. This involves tracing a different line of argument, one that posits de Beauvoir's use of racialised figures as a blurring of the boundaries of feminism, a blurring which gives up the spirit of ressentiment precisely because the connection is made. That is, there is a giving up of a purely gendered suffering, and of a politics based on the exclusivity of women's blocked access to power. The social experience of oppression, of being socially designated by discrimination, is what enables – and obliges – de Beauvoir to 'give up' the notion that women's suffering is unique, as she herself argues. Her comments imply a shared alterity in terms of a 'condemned passivity' (1993: 348, first published 1949) between women and, for example, the 'Negroes' of the American South. I want to suggest that in the moments in which suffering is posited as a shared condition, or that empathy is allowed to pass across the lines of identity, there is less a spirit of ressentiment and more the shared hunger that is weary, not of man – it is not nihilistic – but of the categories that so bind us to declaring absolute specificities to our positionalities.

I want to explore the sense of connectivity that de Beauvoir suggests as a way to think of different modes of resisting imposed subjectivities, and hence different modes of politics, differing therefore from the kind of wounded attachment described earlier in terms both of the sense of self mobilised, and the way power is understood.

That it was at the site of music that de Beauvoir interacted with black people in the United States is significant to the extent that Wright was also intrigued by the commonality that music appeared to proffer. In *Twelve*

9 For another view on this, see Marion Tapper (1993), who makes a straightforward argument that ressentiment can be the basis of feminist interventions.

Million Black Voices, a text which accompanied a series of photographs depicting 'a folk history of the Negro in the United States', Wright mused upon the possibility that it was the city that created a common experience or sentiment: 'Why is our music so contagious? Why is it that those who deny us are willing to sing our songs? Perhaps it is because so many of those who live in cities feel deep down just as we do' (1978a: 227, first published 1941). At the same time, however, he was suspicious of an easy moment of connection. The migration north to the cities that he traces in his various works, which he himself undertook, meant that the city music scene was one that had been formed through an experience formed elsewhere and the hunger for a better life that mobilised that movement. The music he writes about is sensual because of the exclusion that black people faced:

> On the plantations our songs carried a strain of other-worldly yearning which people called 'spiritual'; but now our blues, jazz, swing and boogie-woogies are our 'spirituals' of the city pavements, our longing for freedom and opportunity, an expression of our bewilderment and despair in a world whose meaning eludes us. (Wright, 1978a: 227–8)

Thus, whilst 'our music makes the feet of the whole world dance' (1978a: 229), it is exclusion that forms the sentiments expressed there. Wright's understanding of this exclusion is one that he extends beyond the experience of black peoples, suggesting that 'we play in this manner because "all excluded folk play"' (1978a: 228) and the appreciation of white people was understood within the context of black oppression. Wright's understanding of this exclusion is one he sees mirrored in the position of the Irish in relation to the English: 'The English say of the Irish, just as America says of us, that only the Irish can play, that they laugh through their tears' (1978a: 228). The response of white America is one of 'cold disdain' (1978a: 228), when the suggestion is mooted that the thirst expressed in music, which makes the streets of the Black Belts of American cities 'famous the world over' (1978a: 229), might also be channelled into industry, finance and education (1978a: 228).

The connection that Wright makes here between the Irish and the black populations in American cities suggests the sense in which he is understanding the social nature of the psychology of oppression. Wright was clear that it was the experience of struggle in a hostile environment that guided him; in writing his own autobiography *Black Boy*, for example, Joyce's *Portrait of the Artist as a Young Man* was one of several books which shed light for Wright, for the 'double revolt of an Irish youth against the oppressive religious life of Ireland, an Ireland which England was seeking to strangle' reminded him 'of the stifling Negro environment in the South, an environment which is exploited by the whites above it' (Kinnamon and Fabre, 1993: 81). This sense of connection that is not based on racial oppression alone is what could lead Wright to the extraordinary – extraordinary given Bigger Thomas' position – that Bigger was not only black:

Two items of my experience [on moving to Chicago] combined to make me aware of Bigger as a meaningful and prophetic symbol. First being free of the daily pressure of the Dixie environment, I was able to come into possession of my own feelings. Second, my contact with the labor movement and its ideology made me see Bigger clearly and feel what he meant.

I made the discovery that Bigger Thomas was not black all the time; he was white too, and there were literally millions of him, everywhere . . . I became conscious, at first dimly, and then later on with increasing clarity and conviction, of a vast, muddied pool of human life in America. It was as though I had put on a pair of spectacles whose power was that of an x-ray enabling me to see deeper into the lives of men . . . I sensed too that the Southern scheme of oppression was but an appendage of a far vaster and in many respects more ruthless and impersonal commodity-profit machine. (1987: 17, emphasis added)

Wright's connection with sociological thought is not suprising in this context. That the Chicago of sociology, with its emphasis on the conditions of the social and its resulting cartography of discrimination, appealed to Wright, and his writing in turn to them, was due to their shared interest in what such a 'pair of spectacles' did to one's vision of society, and, especially, to one's vision of the city environment.

Robert Bone has traced the connections between Wright and what he terms the 'Chicago Renaissance', a movement of writers, sociologists and their patrons who in the period 1935–1950 collectively formed something akin to the Harlem Renaissance in the preceding 15 years. Bone contends that Wright was a central figure to this movement and, despite the fact that he moved to New York in 1938, he maintained a connection with the city in the sense that he frequently visited family and friends, and conducted research there, but also, more profoundly, because his 'artistic imagination clung to its shaping-place long after he moved to New York' (1986: 449). The city had a lasting effect on him. Wright's autobiographical *American Hunger* opens with a description of his arrival in the city as an experience of unreality, as depressing and full of people moving past each other with indifference: 'each person acted as if no one else existed but himself' (1977: 1, first published 1944). Wright's *Twelve Million Black Voices* echoes this sense of the city as a crowded but alienating place:

We cannot see or know a *man* because of the thousands upon thousands of *men*. The apartments in which we sleep are crowded and noisy, and soon enough we learn that the brisk, clipped men of the North, the Bosses of the Buildings, are not at all indifferent. They are deeply concerned about us, but in a new way. It seems as though we are now living inside of a machine. (1978a: 207, first published 1941)

Wright's explorations of black lives in the city clearly drew upon his own experience as a migrant, and his broad-sweep Marxist perspective gave him some form of analytic through which to view his own and others' experiences; but in writing *Twelve Million Black Voices* he also utilised the files of his friend the sociologist Horace Cayton on the black migrant in Chicago. The spirit of this sociology was documentary, its purpose to see how an impartial mapping of city life would shed light on the standards of living and ways of life found there. Wright's prose tells us of the conditions of life for black migrants, especially in terms of their housing: 'The kitchenette is our prison, our death sentence . . . with its filth and foul air, with its one toilet for thirty or more tenants' (1978a: 212). Such captivity, a different kind now, set up a war of emotions:

> [O]ne part of our feelings tells us that it is good to be in the city, that we have a chance of life here, that we need but turn a corner to become a stranger, that we no longer need bow and dodge at the sight of the Lords of the Land. Another part of our feelings tells us that, in terms of worry and strain, the cost of living in the kitchenette is too high, that the city heaps too much responsibility upon us and gives us too little security in return. (1978a: 211)

The character of Bigger Thomas in *Native Son* is one that is formed from such an experience of the city. The novel opens with an account of him killing a rat in the family's kitchenette, and with the whole family having to get dressed in the one room.[10] The lack of privacy, the poverty and physical strain of such a way of life was to be fully documented in Drake and Cayton's sociological study *Black Metropolis*, to which Wright wrote a preface where he emphasised that the work 'pictures the environment from which the Bigger Thomases of our nation come' (1945: xviii).

The Chicago School approached the urban environment from a roughly speaking evolutionary perspective. Bone highlights the educational lineage of Robert Park that involved, *inter alia*, the influence of evolutionary thought. This influenced Park's sociology of the city, especially in terms of tracing the progression from simple to complex, from homogeneous to heterogeneous, agrarian to industrial, static to dynamic, rural to urban; the freedom that the city afforded as ties became associational (Gesellschaft) rather than communal (Gemeinschaft) is an anxious freedom, but the loss of moral rules governing life is compensated by the increased freedom for individuality. There was an optimism about Parkian sociology. The city was a higher evolutionary stage, a liberation and a source for great cultures; those that suffered there were suffering a process of conflict that would become accommodated as a process of assimiliation took place (Bone, 1986).

The tone of Wright's preface to *Black Metropolis* was less optimistic than Parks' race relations cycle of contact, conflict, accommodation and assimilation, as Wright lingers on the city as a source of fascistic sentiment:

> Do not hold a light attitude toward the slums of Chicago's South Side. Remember Hitler came out of such a slum. Remember that Chicago could be the Vienna of American Fascism! (1945: xx)

This was a worry that fed into Wright's creative writing. In the essay 'How Bigger was born', Wright recalls:

> I've even heard Negroes say that maybe Hitler and Mussolini are all right; that maybe Stalin is right. They did not say this out of any intellectual comprehension

10 See McCall (1988) who argues that racial misery was a form of indecent exposure.

of the forces at work in the world, but because they felt that these men 'did things', a phrase that is charged with more meaning than the mere words imply. (1987: 16)

Wright's words are reminiscent of Adorno and Horkheimer's (1986) *Dialectics of Enlightenment* in which they argue that liberalism had set up for 'the masses' an 'encrypted longing' for a freedom that they had not yet received, and that fascistic sentiments were born out of this sense of unfulfilment in modern industrialised societies. Yet Wright's purpose is to stress that, just as fascism in the form of Hitler's crimes was based upon an exploitation of the hunger and the longing that was in the hearts of Europe's masses, so the USA's urban slums were places where hope and humiliation were long-time bedfellows. Black people came to live in these conditions because, he contends, they responded to the cultural hopes of their times, leaving the South and coming 'to the cold industrial North' with the same impulse as had white men when they risked leaving 'the slumberous feudal world' (Wright, 1945: xxv). It is to the extent that the hope of succeeding within the terms of capitalist free enterprise is tenuous and unlikely to be realised, however, that there is an appeal in forms of ideological rejection, be they communism or fascism. This potential for ideological movements – for revolution – in the urban slums was one that was a result of the conditions in which these people were obliged to live. Wright shared and wished to add his agreement to the Chicago School sociologists' position that there was nothing peculiar about the people of the urban metropolis, but that the conditions of the metropolis could be studied through its impact upon them. Wright noted:

In *Black Metropolis*, the authors have presented much more than the anatomy of Negro frustration; they have shown how *any* human beings can become mangled, how *any* personalities can become distorted when men caught in the psychological trap of being emotionally committed to the living of a life of freedom which is denied them. (1945: xxvi)

Thus Wright maintained that there is a danger associated with the inequalities found in the industrial cities of the United States, one that was tied to 'race' and the history of enslavement, but was as much to do with the class structures formed by capitalist industrialisation. The danger was a result of the way in which urban life had 'evolved', the way the metropolis was responding to the movement of the culture within which it grew; and the conditions of urban living for black people were such that white America relied upon their hope and optimism. In the preface Wright is explicitly wondering about the psychological consequences that acceptance of these unacceptable conditions had on the urban black American:

[W]hat peculiar personality formations result when millions of people are forced to live lives of outward submissiveness while trying to keep intact in their hearts a sense of the worth of their humanity? What are the personality mechanisms that sublimate racial resentments which, if expressed openly, would carry penalties varying from mild censure to death? (1945: xxx)

Thus we return to the question that was also de Beauvoir's; how was it possible to live a submissive life, to manage to live as an objectified subject? In Wright's preface this condition has been raised as a question of political outlook. But the reaction of those who suffer the conditions described in *Black Metropolis* was not to be predicted. The relationship between suffering and politics resists easy formulations. Certainly it is clear that Wright was interested in moments of law-breaking, moments of fascism and moments of communist or workers' revolutions, as possibilities arising from similar sets of circumstances. However, as with the case of music mentioned earlier, he frequently reasserted that creativity, as often as fearful hatred, can arise from comparable, harsh situations. In a similar way, for de Beauvoir, as we have seen, the reaction to the situation of being 'the wrong side of the line' is not predictable: it could be one of mimicry and play-acting, an inauthenticity that was, nevertheless, comprehensible, or else it could be a reaction of revolt, an authentic reaction to structural disadvantage. Women were encouraged to the former, she argued, to a life lived in bad faith.

Wright is concerned to argue that anyone placed in the urban deprivation that both he and the sociologists documented would be affected by it. The racialised lines, the history of racist oppression that had brought black people to these conditions, were not to be denied or sublimated, but nor were they to be reified. Both Wright and de Beauvoir, I would want to argue, are suggesting in their different ways that there cannot be an ownership of oppression, that the similarities that both suggest across different forms of subjectivisation can be read as opening a space for a more radical critique than one based on ressentiment. De Beauvoir's few attempts in *The Second Sex* (1993, first published 1949) to relate the issues at stake to those of racism, and also to anti-Semitism, are moments at which she enables a reading that sees moments of connectivity, that reaches out to patterns of discrimination that are similar to, and reflect upon, gender discrimination. For example, *apropos* the frustration that women are obliged to cope with in not being able to register feelings and frustrations, not even through recourse to violence, de Beauvoir expands her vision away from the figure of the woman. As we have already seen, de Beauvoir seems to hold that women regard the order of things as fixed, and lack of physical power combines with this to produce her resignation to docility (1993: 348–9, first published 1949). The 'condemned passivity', the 'accursed alterity' has the effect of turning the objectified person inward, and, in that submission, there is a search for a way of conducting oneself in such a world. But this moment is another one at which de Beauvoir makes a comparison with the effects of racism in the United States, where, she suggests,

> it is quite impossible for a Negro, in the South, to use violence against the whites; this rule is the key to the mysterious 'black soul'; the way the Negro feels in the white world, the behaviour by which he adjusts himself to it, the compensations he seeks, his whole way of feeling and acting are to be explained on the basis of the passivity to which he is condemned. (1993: 348, first published 1949)

Her use of Richard Wright, if it is heuristic and rhetorical, is also an explicit attempt to acknowledge concrete, sociological similarities. Moreover, she expands her comments on race in the United States to comment, briefly, on the racial politics facing African immigrants to France:

> In *Black Boy* Richard Wright has shown how the ambitions of a young American Negro are blocked from the start and what a struggle he had merely in raising himself to the level where problems begin for the whites. Negroes coming to France from Africa also find difficulties – with themselves as well as those around them – similar to those confronting women. (1993: 732, first published 1949)

I have indicated above the problematic nature of these comparisons, both in terms of the way in which they make certain subject positions impossible, and the dubious model of power that they propose. They come too close to an attempt to spread the umbrella of oppression along the lines of a ressentiment politics. Nevertheless, I mean to conclude more positively, suggesting that however fumbled her effort, de Beauvoir's attempt is to make a case for the position of womanhood as a subjectivity that can be connected with other subjectivities, both internally and externally, and that the recognition of this might proffer women the possibility of an acknowledgement, a recognition and thereby an *existence* in the world. In this vein, she makes a further comparison toward the end of *The Second Sex* thus:

> The old Europe formerly poured out its contempt upon the American barbarians who boasted neither artists nor writers. 'Let us come into existence before being asked to justify our existence,' replied Jefferson, in effect. The Negroes make the same reply to the racists who reproach them for never having produced a Whitman or a Melville. No more can the French proletariat offer any name to compare with those of Racine or Mallarme.
> The free woman is just being born: when she has won possession of herself perhaps Rimbaud's prophecy will be fulfilled: 'There shall be poets! When woman's unmeasured bondage shall be broken, when she shall live for and through herself, man – hitherto detestable – having let her go, she, too, will be poet!' (1993: 750, first published 1949)[11]

Such a reading bases much, too much perhaps, on de Beauvoir's racialised metaphors and parallel arguments, those moments when her text enables us to 'see' connections that, in turn, enable one to argue that she surrenders a particularised gendered suffering. Nevertheless, these moments are there, suggestions of a different path, one that highlights the sense in which de Beauvoir's work is in line with an existentialist notion of 'situation', which in our contemporary vocabulary makes her argument clearly an 'anti-essentialist' one; the quotation above continues: 'it is through attaining *the same situation* as [men's] that she will find emancipation' (1993: 750, emphasis added, first published 1949).

---

11 De Beauvoir is quoting Rimbaud's letter to Pierre Demeny, 1871. Of course, it is highly debatable whether this line of argument is accurate or helpful. Several historians and writers work to illustrate that there have always been 'poets' and creativity amongst 'the oppressed'.

Similarly, in Wright's work, there are implicit and explicit suggestions that the way to challenge racism need not – indeed, would be inaccurate if it were to – model itself on the exclusivity of black people's sufferings. Both his relationship with the Chicago School of sociology and his Marxism would warn against such a characterisation of Wright's politics. Moreover, despite the charges of misogyny that have been levied at him, there are moments when his portrayals of women are nuanced and signal the further complexity of gendered positionalities. In the short story 'Long black song' (1978b), take, for example, the character of Sarah, who, significantly for this argument, has a sexual encounter with a white travelling salesman. There is not space to do justice to this short story here, but with the risk of being too cursory in my commentary, suffice it to remark at the complexity of Sarah's response as she tries to make sense of the white man's sexual advance, finding herself initially shocked, resisting and protesting, and then, turning 'inward' as the battle becomes one conducted with herself as she tries not to surrender to her body's response. As he touches her she repeats to herself 'But he's a *white* man! A *white* man!' (1978b: 268), and tries to hold her breath for fear of the feeling that surges through her:

> She could not see the stars now; her eyes were full of the feeling that surged over her body each time she caught her breath. He held her close, breathing into her ear; she straightened, rigidly, feeling that she had to straighten or die. And then her lips met his and she held her breath and dreaded ever to breathe again for fear of the feeling that would sweep over her limbs. (1978b: 269)

The story ends in a tragedy of masculine pride in a racist community, as Sarah's devastated husband, Silas, unconsoled by her remorse, attacks the salesman and another white man who come to the house in the morning, killing one of them. He knows he has lost everything he had worked for through this action, and remains in his house as the violent nature of white racism is mobilised against this black farmworker. As they set Sarah and Silas' home alight, the white men shout – 'Yuh think yohre white now, nigger?' (1978b: 285) – and Sarah watches from the fields in vain for her husband to run out. My point, however, is to suggest that in this story, Wright risked making sexual desire the site for another moment of connectivity across racial lines, one that is posited against the history that would read, with good reason, such an encounter as rape.[12] Despite the tragic outcome, and the 'punishment' that Sarah suffers – through, with and by Silas' own suffering – there is in Wright's story a sense that sexual desire can be such a place of connection, not without, but in spite of, racism. Such is perhaps too romantic a picture, where sexual desire is triumphant over racial disharmony, but it was certainly the case that Wright's own life involved a struggle with the attempt to live in the face of

---

12 This history of the rape of black women by white men is one that de Beauvoir herself comments on in *The Second Sex* (1993: 394, first published 1949).

prejudice against 'mixed race' relationships, to give them a status which would be free from the imagery of past histories, however true, real and important the remembrance of those histories was. And perhaps Levinas' notion that sexual desire has a specific, grasping relationship to the future is appropriate here, with this crucial different twist to it, for it is under the name of the caress that Levinas describes the erotic relationship as essentially and especially incomprehensible in the terms of power or knowledge; its peculiarity is unamenable to analyses that would speak of battling freedoms, each endeavouring to dominate or transcend the other. The erotic relationship is where Levinas defends his notion that to understand relationships as about the meeting of freedoms is to insist in advance upon an outcome which is the submission and enslavement of one and the triumph of the other (1987: 87). Without overdoing this thought, one might suggest that an attempt to recast de Beauvoir and Wright's futural visions might well draw strength from any image or impression where modes of connection are creative and open rather than fixed images that stem from models of power which attempt to reduce those connections.

By way of conclusion, therefore, I would argue that it is possible to read de Beauvoir with Richard Wright in such a way that refuses to characterise their politics as involving a spirit of ressentiment. For even at those moments when womanhood and the characterisation of Bigger Thomas are brought into proximity, where the vengeful and covetous are presented as the impulses to revolution or political argument, there is the possibility of reading differently. The notion of connectivity does not refer to a mundane sense of connections between people, but it is about the modes, the different ways – not just in terms of experiencing suffering, powerlessness or economic hardship, but also those possible through music, or through sex – that people's lives extend beyond the clarity often imposed by sociological models of power and subjectivity. Drawing on other routes of intertextuality, therefore, enables one to see models of politics that refuse the easy presentation of a bounded group of 'the oppressed' who, according to some very stark and reified division, demand to have the attributes and influences of the oppressor, as if their hope were to be remade in the very image of the oppressor.

4

APPEARANCE: THINKING DIFFERENCE IN THE POLITICAL REALM WITH HANNAH ARENDT

[T]he only polity that truly advances the freedom and plurality human beings are capable of experiencing, not to mention the conditions of existence they value and defend, is the polity that exhibits widespread participation in the public realm . . . politics unfolds as the communicative interaction of diverse equals acting together as citizens. (Arendt, quoted in Dietz, 1994: 247–8)

Hannah Arendt's relationship to feminist theory is one that has recently received much belated attention, focussing mainly on her declared non-allegiance to a politics which displayed facets of the forms of collective demand that she rallied against from her often controversial perspectives. One of her objections concerned the place of 'the body' and 'identity' in the political realm, since so-called 'life' issues, Arendt insisted, had no place in the realm of proper political debate; feminism constituted just the sort of assertion of a collective identity that signalled both a lack of engagement in political issues and an abuse of the possibility of true political debate. However, as Honig (1995) has commented, the feminism of the late twentieth century is one that is markedly different from that which Arendt dismissed so vehemently, and is one that concerns itself more with the issues to which Arendt herself devoted much thought. In this chapter, however, the intention is less to find the utility of Arendt's thought for feminism, but more to consider the constellation of issues that Arendt addressed in her explorations of the notion of 'the political'.

I want to use Arendt to explore further the notion of the political imagination because her work, whatever we may feel about its logic and conclusions, had a scope which was exactly about the *limits* of the political; that is, what was to be included within politics, what was outside, and what was 'at the edge' of politics. Not just for historical and geographical reasons were these questions configured by Arendt in ways that brought centre stage the concerns of identity, the place of certain personages within 'the political', 'proper' forms of political argument and the dangers of totalitarianism. In Arendt's work these issues move into one another and relate back and forth to one another, conceptually entangled in ways that are denied by contemporary reflections that seek to 'relate' them together as if their entanglement were never the case.

Arendt's work addresses several themes that occupy contemporary feminist reflection: in particular, I want to focus on what I am terming 'embodied participation'. To get to this idea, however, I will focus on the concept of *appearance* as a concept which informs Arendt's work and which links it with contemporary work on the notion of the 'public sphere'. These themes are famously addressed in Arendt's work to a large extent through the dual notions of the parvenu and the pariah. I will discuss them, however, through a lesser known article of Arendt's – 'Reflections on Little Rock' (1959a) – because, in this controversial piece, Arendt is taken explicitly into a discussion of identity and 'race' in relation to the nature and boundaries of 'the political'. Maintaining a focus on the concept of appearance allows one to stress this set of connections; it also allows one to emphasise the philosophical trajectories at play. The concern with appearance, for Arendt, was one with a profound philosophical impulse; it is one which is deeply implicated in her vision of democratic politics.

Approaching Arendt's work as a way to move back from and to rethink current feminist concerns, one is struck that feminist thought has in some senses been attracted in recent years to think issues of identity and appearance with Foucault in his most Nietzschean cast. But another important intellectual influence on Foucault was Heidegger, and the concept of appearance is one point at which we can read the influence of Heidegger's thought upon Arendt, giving us a counterpoint by which to think through the concept of appearance as it relates to present debates. Arendt took the concept of appearance from the same intellectual trajectory as both Foucault and Butler – especially from Nietzsche and Heidegger – and incorporated it into her political theory in a way that is markedly different. Here, I want to explore Arendt's troubling invention around 'Little Rock', and the way in which it treats the relationship between democracy and difference, in order both to provide a commentary on her vision of the political, and to provide a way of recasting certain questions that occupy feminist theory at the end of the twentieth century.

'Little Rock'

In 1959 one of Arendt's articles appeared in the journal *Dissent*, having been held back for a year because the critique she levies within it was thought too controversial to publish immediately. It concerned the Supreme Court's decision (*Brown*, 1954) to make the racial segregation of schools illegal, and the resulting events in Little Rock, Arkansas, one of only two southern states to comply with the ruling that year. The school board proposed a gradual, phased plan of integration. The decision to integrate schools, however, led to a vehement display of white segregationist fear and hatred in a state that had until that point seemed, in contrast to many southern states, relatively racially integrated and harmonious. Desegregation was delayed until 1957, and the number of black children who were accepted into the high school chosen for integration was pared down to a minimum – nine children who became known as the 'Little Rock Nine'. Amidst political wranglings between the governor, who had grown nervous about the lack of white support for desegregation plans and tried to halt the process, and the courts, who asked Governor Faubus to go ahead with the school board's plans, the first black high school students attempted to attend the school, Central High, in September 1957. Arkansas National Guardsmen were placed at the school's entrance; allegedly there to maintain order, they prevented the black students from entering. A white crowd had gathered to intimidate the black students, jeering and hurling abuse at them. One of the students, Elizabeth Eckford, was alone, and was surrounded by the crowd, who threatened her with lynching and caused her to flee; the others, as a group, were similarly not granted access, and were forced to turn back through the hostile white crowd. The situation became a struggle between federal and state government, and Faubus was eventually ordered to remove the guards who were still blocking the black students' enrolment. When the students finally did gain entrance, some three weeks later, the crowd again swelled outside the school, attacking journalists, and shouting at the school buildings. Eventually, for their safety, the children were removed from the school. Reluctantly, President Eisenhower sent troops to Little Rock, and mobilised the Arkansas National Guard, this time with orders to protect the black students; paratroopers lined the streets around the school, and the children were escorted there in convoy. With helicopters overhead, and surrounded by soldiers with bayonets drawn, the Little Rock Nine were eventually able to begin their attendance at Central High. The troops remained, and their presence became a source of political dispute surrounding the position and power of the governor, who maintained that he was opposed to forced desegregation. Faubus was re-elected in July 1958, and allowed schools to close for a year, until the Supreme Court ruled the closures as unlawful attempts to evade integration, and the schools were opened again (in August 1959) and integrated as the federal government required (Williams, 1988).

Arendt's position in 'Reflections on Little Rock', written in 1957, is fuelled by her notion of the political as a realm which is separate from the social and the private, and her argument brings with it, as we shall see, all the troubling questions that surround these distinctions as she presented them in her wider works. More than this, however, I want to suggest that the position developed in relation to education and desegregation has to be understood against the backdrop that also informs her development of those distinctions; that is, her personally and historically formed concern that the conditions of freedom be preserved and that the conditions that allow totalitarian rule be challenged. Her impulse is thoroughly and sincerely democratic. The curious and worrying feature of Arendt's polemic essay becomes, therefore, how the author of *The Origins of Totalitarianism* (1973), a writer who, she herself says in the added preamble to the finally published piece, 'as a Jew, takes her concern for all oppressed peoples for granted', could use her distinctive voice and judgement to speak out, like 'a poor joke', as one commentator at the time put it, *against* the decision to integrate schools in the South.

Arendt suggests that her thoughts were crystallised by seeing a photograph of a young black girl[1] accompanied by a white friend of her father's walking away from school followed by a 'jeering and grimacing mob of [white] youngsters' (1959a: 50). Arendt argued that the photograph was indicative of what progressive education asked of children: the black girl to be a hero, the white youngsters – or at least those who grow out of 'this brutality' – to attempt to live down this image that 'exposes so mercilessly their juvenile delinquency' (1959a: 50). What the desegregation policy meant was an abdication of responsibility by adults of the world into which they had borne these children: 'how have we come to the point where it is the children who are being asked to change or improve the world? And do we intend to have our political battles fought out in the school yards?' (1959a: 50). Arendt's argument suggests that she saw this burden on children as too easy a solution to entrenched political problems.

Arendt's position in 'Reflections on Little Rock' mobilises her belief in the idea of 'the social' or 'society' as a realm separate from both the private and the political realms. In the political realm, or the public domain generally, discrimination is unacceptable, as here the principle of equality reigns. But *only* in the political realm can we be equals, she argues, and 'what equality is to the body politic – its innermost principle – discrimination is to society' (1959a: 51). Within American society, people group together, argues Arendt, and 'therefore discriminate against each other, along lines of profession, income and ethnic origin' (1959a: 51).[2] Discrimination, she suggests, makes society possible; the freedom to associate and to form groups with whomever one wishes means that discrimination becomes for Arendt a right: 'discrimination is as indispensable a social right as equality is a political right' (1959a: 51). The task, therefore, is one of guarding the limits of these realms, since discrimination is destructive within the political and the personal spheres, but legitimate when confined within the social sphere (1959a: 51). The role of the legislator, therefore, is to avoid following social discrimination – there society would have become tyrannical (1959a: 53) – indeed, government is duty bound to ensure that discriminatory practices are not legally enforced (1959a: 53).[3]

Free association, Arendt continues to explain, is that which she might herself exercise were she to decide to holiday exclusively in the company of Jews; she sees, moreover, 'no reason why other resorts should not cater to

1 Presumably Elizabeth Eckford.

2 Arendt believes that in Europe the groups tend rather to be along lines of 'class origin, education and manners' (1959a: 51).

3 Religious institutions are the only public force that can fight social discrimination, Arendt suggests, and they can do so only in terms of the uniqueness of each person – churches are the only communal and public spaces in which appearances do not count, and discrimination within the churches would make them social rather than religious institutions (1959a: 53).

a clientele that wishes not to see Jews while on holiday' (1959a: 52). Discrimination has, she says, her language softening slightly here, 'greater validity than the principle of equality' (1959a: 52) in the social realm. The formation of social groups was, she thought, an aspect of social *preferences* that was not to be legislated against, and is even a *desirable* aspect of social life, insofar as it promotes plurality rather than a sameness that would quash the ability for new thought and directions that would be positive for 'the common world'.

The private realm, Arendt believed, is ruled by neither the political principle of equality nor by discrimination, but is based upon exclusiveness and the uniqueness of individuals to each other. Social discrimination lacks validity for the conduct of private life, and has no place there. Moreover, the notions of uniqueness and exclusiveness that provide the private realm with its special atmosphere are the ones that are fitting to the needs of children, who should be shielded from 'the demands of the social and the responsibilities of the political realm' (Arendt, 1959a: 55). The school is not an institution that fits easily into the distinctions that Arendt sets up. She argues her way around this by suggesting that although compulsory education is an intrusion into the rights of the parents to bring up their family as 'they see fit' (1959a: 55), it is one that comes about because of 'the right of the body politic to prepare children for adult citizenship' (1959a: 55). The school is therefore the first environment through which the child gains contact with the social world, and this is what makes it a preparation for (political) participation, in the sense, it seems Arendt means, that it provides children with the tools by which to participate to the best of their abilities, in democracy. But while the state's right to educate future citizens extends to the content of their education, it should not, according to Arendt, have any say in the social life and associations that the child develops through schooling.

The enforced desegregation of schools in the South, Arendt argued, meant depriving parents 'of rights which clearly belong to them in all free societies – the private right over their children and the social right to free association' (1959a: 55). The children are placed, moreover, in a situation of conflict between home and school, private and social life, to which they *as children* should not be exposed. When parents and teachers fail children as guides in and to the adult world, children tend toward conformity, Arendt believed, which can result in the sort of 'mob and gang rule' that, for her, the photograph of the white students presented. Children, she argues, have neither the 'ability nor the right' to develop public opinions of their own; it was exactly that demand that was being made of them in Little Rock, where the conflict between families and school demands effectively meant the abdication by both parents and teachers of their authority in, and their responsibility for, the world (1959a: 56).

I want to argue that Arendt's position in the 'Little Rock' article is one that can be understood through the concept of appearance as a philosophical concept to which Arendt gives a political twist. For argument's sake I will divide my discussion into two levels of appearance, although as we shall see they are strongly and hierarchically related to each other. First is the concept of appearance in the sense of 'appearing' in the political realm; second is the concept of appearing in the world; that is, birth, or what Arendt terms – for reasons that enable her to utilise the concept in her particular sense – 'natality'.

Appearing in the political realm

Arendt's concept of appearance has a route traceable back to Nietzsche and Heidegger, an inheritance recast within her theory of the different spheres. In this section I want to sketch this inheritance in order to understand how rich the concept of appearance is within Arendt's thought, but more than this to understand better how the essentially democratic impulse of her 'Little Rock' argument flounders on the tension between a concept of appearance and that of visibility. There is a complicated series of questions that follow such a moment, and I wish to pursue Arendt as they arise in her work because she reaches them with such a peculiar mixture of clarity and clumsiness.

The Nietzschean inheritance manifests itself in her argument that the public realm is fundamentally a space of appearance, and that, furthermore, democracy should allow thinking persons to appear, an argument fuelled by a disdain for the mediocracy in which, Nietzsche thought, liberalism can result. Arendt's argument that children should be offered the conditions to explore their individuality and develop their own thoughts and opinions is guided by the desire to base a democracy on a sphere in which an individual's brilliance will be allowed to shine and inspire. Arendt's distaste for the perspective that politics should target education and the young was due, in part, to the value she placed on allowing the young to develop their own, new and individual, thought. In 'The crisis in education' she wrote that 'to prepare a new generation for a new world can only mean that one wishes to strike from the newcomers' hands their own chance at the new' (1963a: 177), a sentiment resonant of Nietzsche's emphasis on individual heroic action that reaches beyond the herd mentality (see, e.g., Ansell-Pearson, 1994).

It is, however, possibly more pertinent to trace Arendt's Heideggerian inheritance on this point. For Heidegger, the 'forgetting' of Being has left man in a state of absorption with what is readily available. Heidegger's point is not that we are concerned with appearance while elsewhere there are more profound or pure truths; rather, his point is that our existence no longer astonishes us as it did the Greeks. The fact that there are beings may give us the suspicion of Being; but Being is not located elsewhere, for appearance and being are the same. Beings stand out – such that 'to let beings be as the beings which they are' (Heidegger, 1993a: 125) means 'to engage oneself with the open region and its openness into which every

being comes to stand, bringing that openness, as it were, along with itself'
(1993a: 125). The notion of openness, the 'unconcealed', is an appearance
that simultaneously involves a concealment: 'Letting-be is intrinsically at
the same time a concealing. In the ek-sistent freedom of Da-sein a concealing of being as a whole propriates. Here there *is* concealment' (1993a:
130). This concealment, however, is not to be thought of as in opposition
to unconcealment; indeed, Heidegger's point is that concealment 'preserves
what is most proper to *aletheia* (unconcealment) as its own' (1993a: 130).

When humanity is turned away from the mystery and turned only toward
beings, only toward the readily available, 'onward from one current thing to
the next, passing the mystery by', then 'this is *erring*' (Heidegger, 1993a:
133). Humanity's ek-sistence proceeds in errancy, a leading astray from
questioning, from the mystery that is forgotten; which is to say that
humanity is subjected to the turning to and fro between the 'rule of mystery
and the oppression of errancy' (1993: 134). It is only when we turn toward
that which is both nearest at hand and farthest from us – Being – with a
'resolute openness toward the mystery' (1993a: 134) that we ask the question
more originally. It is 'the glimpse into the mystery out of errancy' which is
itself a question 'in the sense of that unique question of what being as such is
as a whole. This questioning thinks the Being of beings' (1993a: 135).

As Dana Villa (1996a) has pointed out, Arendt is influenced by
Heidegger's framing of disclosure in terms of concealment/unconcealment,
and appropriates it for her 'disclosive theory' of action (Villa, 1996a: 147).
Moreover, in describing the profound interdependence between the public
and the private, Arendt writes in *The Human Condition* that 'the most
elementary meaning of the two realms indicates that there are things that
need to be hidden and others that need to be displayed publicly if they are
to exist at all' (1959b: 65). In the 'Reflections' piece, Arendt's concern with
the maintenance of the proper realm of appearance – the political – carries
the Heideggerian notion of a clearing, a disclosure, into a discussion of the
boundaries of the political. Arendt's realm of appearance relies upon
the more mysterious and unarticulated realms of the private and the social
in ways that mimic Heidegger's concealment/unconcealment. The argument
is complicated in the article on Little Rock, however, because Arendt is
mobilising these concepts within a discussion of 'race' and segregation in
the southern states, and this leads her to an attempt to disassociate the
notion of appearance from that which she terms 'visibility'.

Arendt begins her article in a way that sets up a tension between the
'equality' of all citizens as a principle of modern constitutional government
and the *visibility* of difference:

> [T]he Negroes stand out because of their 'visibility'. They are not the only 'visible
> minority' but they are the most visible one . . . while audibility is a temporary
> phenomenon, rarely persisting beyond one generation, the Negroes' visibility is
> unalterable and permanent. This is no trivial matter. In the public realm, where
> nothing counts that cannot make itself seen and heard, visibility and audibility
> are of prime importance. To argue that they are merely exterior appearances is to

beg the question. For it is precisely appearances that 'appear' in public, and inner qualities, gifts of heart or mind, are political only to the extent that their owner wishes to expose them in public, to place them in the limelight of the market place. (1959b: 47)

The problem of skin colour, Arendt seems to be suggesting, is that it has an unalterable visibility, that 'appears' as it were without the intention of the person, thereby marking a difference that disrupts a political realm that should properly be one of debate and deliberation, where one's distinctiveness is marked *only* through that debate. Alongside the distinction between the political and what lies 'outside' it, therefore, Arendt suggests a distinction that links, on the one hand, personality with action and *appearance*, and, on the other, the body and its attributes with non-action or mere *visibility*. Physical appearance 'appears', but it only appears in a weak sense:

> In acting and speaking, men show who they are, reveal actively their unique personal identities and thus make their appearance in the human world, while their physical identities appear without any activity of their own in the unique shape of the body and the sound of the voice. (Arendt, 1959b: 159)

In *The Human Condition* Arendt's argument suggests that the distinction between visibility and appearance that she makes in 'Reflections on Little Rock' is indeed one that is prompted by a notion of the greater profundity of appearance as rising from a darker place, whereas simply being always in view is another matter:

> [A] life spent entirely in public, in the presence of others, becomes, as we would say, shallow. While it retains its visibility, it loses the quality of rising into sight from some darker ground that must remain hidden if it is not to lose its depth in a very real, non-subjective sense. (Quoted in Villa, 1996a: 147)

Arendt's argument posits physical differences as visible but shallow, as provocative and even likely to increase social antagonism. The conception of racial difference as physically marked is one that regards the visibility of skin colour as unproblematic, as given. In 'Reflections on Little Rock' Arendt suggests that the principle of equality 'cannot equalize natural, physical characteristics', and a danger point arises when educational and social inequalities have been addressed, because it is then that such 'differences' will be resented and 'the more conspicuous will those become who are visibly and by nature unlike the others' (1959a: 48). This argument is one that had been prefigured in her discussion in *The Origins of Totalitarianism* in relation to anti-Semitism. There, she argued that

> Equality of condition, though it is certainly a basic requirement for justice, is nevertheless among the greatest and most uncertain ventures of modern mankind. The more equal conditions are, the less explanation there is for the differences that actually exist between people; and thus all the more unequal do people become. (1973: 54)

Arendt's argument is not that steps to achieve such equality should not be taken but that 'government intervention be guided by caution and moderation rather than impatience and ill-advised measures' (1959a: 48). Arendt suggests that while the legal enforcement of segregation obviously should have been removed from southern states, political equality does not *make* social equality; that equality, as she suggests in *The Origins of Totalitarianism*, should not be thought of as a social concept, because it is a political one.

Arendt struggles to keep her distinction between the social and the political intact in this discussion of racial desegregation, but despite her attempts she fails to convince, presenting a theory of the social as based upon spontaneous free association, underscored with a dubious psychology of 'like attracts like'. By contrast the political realm demands abstract or 'artificial' equality. In Little Rock, she suggests that the political was unfortunately disrupted by social – read, in this context, *bodily* – distinctions that have been introduced into the political realm, where such 'life' issues do not have a place.

We know that Arendt's position was, in part, fuelled by an attempt to understand and avoid ever again the totalitarianism that Europe had witnessed. Her view of the political is that of a realm in which not ourselves, as individuals or as embodied, but 'the world' is at stake; the public realm 'can nurture our worldliness . . . preserve the meaning and memory of action only insofar as it outlasts the life span of the individual' (*The Human Condition*, quoted in Villa, 1996a: 151). Arendt's plea in the 'Reflections' article could be construed as merely an argument about the *pace* of change, that racial discrimination will not be removed in one swift move of government legislation; social integration will not be forced. Hope for the future of the world will be encouraged through the removal of barriers to the progress of integration, certainly, but she is arguing that it not be hurried through a pressure to integrate where the welcome is not there. It is for this reason that Arendt contends, in the same piece, that the miscegenation laws should be a priority, for they represented a shameful denial of an elementary human right to marry whomever one wishes.

However one attempts to understand the impulses that motivate Arendt's distinction between visibility and appearance, there is a need to critique the sense of 'permanent visibility' that she uses in the 'Reflections' piece. Arendt privileges speech against physical action and associates what Frantz Fanon will term in the next decade the 'fact of blackness' with an intrusive, bodily, physical appearance in the realm of debate – the political – where action and courage appear through deeds and words. Thus in *The Human Condition* she writes:

> Speechless action would no longer be action because there would no longer be an actor, and an actor, the doer of deeds, is possible only if he is at the same time the speaker of words . . . though his deed can be perceived in its brute appearance without verbal accompaniment, it becomes relevant only through the spoken word in which he identifies himself as an actor, announcing what he does, has done, and intends to do. (1959b: 158–9)

Skin colour is too readily associated by Arendt with this form of 'brute appearance'. The tension that I highlighted at the beginning of this section – between visibility and equality – is far too crudely drawn by Arendt, ignoring as she does the role of racialised discourse in training the way in which bodies are seen (see Bell, 1996). Or, differently argued, she ignores the role of 'historicity' about which Fanon will write (and I will discuss in Chapter 6), suggesting a debt to Jaspers at that point, and to which Arendt herself alludes in *Between Past and Future* where she argues that 'automatic processes' are historically constituted:

> Our political life, moreover, despite its being the realm of action, also takes place in the midst of processes which we call historical and which tend to become as automatic as natural or cosmic processes, although they were started by men. (1963b: 168)

It seems that this champion of democratic processes was arguing that in a racist society black people cannot 'appear' or 'act' in the political realm because of their 'visibility'. On most sympathetic reading, one might argue that Arendt is only *describing* a racist response that has been historically constituted in the South, this place that she herself avoided:

> I have never lived in the South and have even avoided occasional trips to Southern States because they would have brought me into a situation that I personally would find unbearable. Like most people of European origin I have difficulty in understanding, let alone sharing, the common prejudices of Americans in this area. (1959a: 46)

Arendt's argument, while it purports to be an analytical argument of political description, relies upon the racist responses of white people in the South, historically and geographically constituted. The argument presented in 'Reflections on Little Rock' brings into sharp focus Arendt's inheritance of the ideal of disembodied political action, a line of argument that challenges the depiction of the realm of the political as a realm of appearance, of rising, since an attempt to take on board different skin colours forces her to make a distinction between appearance and visibility that is highly questionable.

I shall return to this conception of the 'space of appearances', the political realm, as one that involves, indeed requires, the appearance of abstracted or artificial equality as a condition of democratic participation. Before I do so, however, there is another sense in which Arendt's argument is 'about' appearance, which is the stronger sense of appearance 'in the world' or *natality*.

Appearance and natality

Throughout her work Arendt argues that the existence of natality prompts action and is thereby a source of freedom and hope. In 'What is freedom?', for example, drawing on Augustine, she argued 'because he *is* a beginning, man can begin; to be human and to be free are one and the same. God created man in order to introduce into the world the faculty of beginning: freedom' (1963b: 167). In 'The crisis of education', she wrote that it seems 'natural' to 'start a new world with those who are by birth and nature new' (1963a: 176), and for politics to focus on the education of children. However, this is a misconception, Arendt argues, because politics should involve the effort of persuasion and run the risk of failure; to base politics on 'the absolute superiority of the adult', to 'attempt to produce the new as a *fait accompli*' is a 'dictatorial intervention' (1963a: 176). In 'Reflections on Little Rock' Arendt argues that it was wrong to ask children to work out a problem which 'adults for generations have confessed themselves unable to solve' (1959a: 50).

In *The Origins of Totalitarianism* Arendt had suggested that totalitarianism has to deal with the 'the fact that men are being born and that therefore each of them *is* a new beginning, begins, in a sense, the world anew' (1973: 466). All forms of political government have to deal with this fact, of course, but for totalitarianism, because it attempts to 'still' action through terror in order to pursue the suprahuman law of Nature or History, birth is an 'annoying interference with higher forces' (1973: 466). In the last chapter of *The Origins of Totalitarianism* Arendt argues that totalitarianism differs from tyrannical lawless government because 'far from being lawless', it claims to go 'right to the sources of authority from which positive laws received their ultimate legitimation, that far from being arbitrary it is more obedient to these *suprahuman* forces' (1973: 461, emphasis added) such that 'far from wielding its power in the interests of one man, it is quite prepared to sacrifice everybody's vital interests to the execution of what it assumes to be the law of History or the law of Nature' (1973: 461–2). Totalitarian politics took from the recipes of nineteenth-century thought, argues Arendt, which saw a reconception of law as *motion* – Darwinian and Marxist accounts shared a sense of history as movement – and totalitarian politics adopts this idea in order to pursue the law of movement. Spontaneous human action cannot be allowed to interfere with the force of nature or of history that totalitarianism obeys; thus terror, the 'essence of totalitarian domination' (1973: 464), is employed to 'stabilize' men, to disallow any free action, and to 'liberate the forces of nature or history' (1973: 465). Terror is the execution, then, of a 'law of movement whose ultimate goal is not the welfare of man or the interest of one man but the fabrication of mankind' so that it 'eliminates individuals for the sake of the species, sacrifices the "parts" for the sake of the "whole"' (1973: 465).

Natality is a source of freedom and an interference to totalitarian regimes in the sense that it is necessary to quell that potential for new beginnings by bringing each generation under the control of the regime. The source of freedom that comes from the possibility of new beginnings, from natality, is at the heart of Arendt's theorisation of action.

In *The Human Condition* Arendt argues that the sense in which humans distinguish themselves – as opposed to being merely distinct – through speech and action recalls natality: 'with word and deed we insert ourselves into the human world, and this insertion is like a second birth, in which we confirm and take upon ourselves the naked fact of our original physical appearance' (1959b: 157). The impulse to act is an impulse that is a response to the beginning that was our birth: 'Because they are *initium*, newcomers and beginners by virtue of birth, men take initiative, are prompted into action' (1959b: 156). The fact of natality, then, is the source of the possibility of beginning, and as such, Arendt argues in 'What is freedom?', is not only a disruption to totalitarianism but is why we can say humans are free:

> Man does not possess freedom so much as he, or better his coming into the world, is equated with the appearance of freedom in the universe; man is free because he is a beginning and was so created after the universe had already come into existence. (1963b: 167)

The value that Arendt places on uniqueness, and the extension of that into a concern that childhood be spent predominantly in the atmosphere (ideally) provided by the private realm, where human uniqueness is a guiding principle, is a concern that she expresses in *The Human Condition* as follows:

> The fact that man is capable of action means that the unexpected can be expected from him, that he is able to perform what is infinitely improbable. And this again is possible only because each man is unique, so that with each birth something uniquely new comes into the world. (1959b: 158)

As Jean Elshtain has argued, Arendt's argument that children should not appear or be made to appear in the public realm, that their place was the private realm, was fuelled by a strong sense that this politicisation betrayed the newness of childhood. Elshtain points out that Arendt's memories of Hitler youth, and her notion of the parvenu who assaults her own dignity in order to go where she is unwanted, underlie her attitude in the 'Reflections' piece (1995: 269). Pushing children into a situation where they were unwanted, she argued, was humiliating and psychologically disturbing, and 'psychologically, the situation of being unwanted (a typically social predicament) is more difficult to bear than outright persecution (a political predicament) because personal pride is involved' (quoted in Young-Bruehl, 1982: 312).

Such concerns find an echo where feminist critic bell hooks has written of her experience of desegregation, since she remembers the events as a sudden loss of the innocence that had existed previously. Illustrating exactly the core of the issue here, hooks writes that, prior to desegregation, there was enjoyment in being segregated – 'we loved going to school then, from the moment we rushed out of the door in the morning to the lingering strolls home. In that world, black children were allowed innocence' (1991: 33) – but it was enjoyment in the context of an innocent ignorance of the situation of apartheid: 'We did not really understand the meaning of segregation, the brutal racism that had created the apartheid in this society, and no one explained it' (1991: 33). As a schoolgirl, hooks remembers a time of bewilderment at the actions of the 'grown black folks':

> It hurt to leave behind memories, schools that were 'ours', places we loved and cherished . . . I sat in classes where there was mostly contempt for us, a long tradition of hatred, and I wept. . . . I wept and longed for what we had lost and wondered why the grown black folks had acted as though they did not know we would be surrendering so much for so little, that we would be leaving behind a history. (1991: 34)

It is on these questions of pride and sacrifice that Ralph Ellison differs from Arendt. In an interview with Ralph Warren, collected in *Who Speaks for the Negro?*, Ellison argues that 'one of the important clues to the meaning of [American Negro] experience lies in the idea, the *ideal* of sacrifice' (Warren, 1966: 343). Arendt had failed to grasp this in the 'Reflections' article, he argued, positioning her in much the same standing as hooks describes herself – the bewildered schoolgirl in the desegregated school, not comprehending the actions of the grown up black folks. Ellison insisted:

> [S]he [Arendt] has absolutely no conception of what goes on in the minds of Negro parents when they send their kids through those lines of hostile people . . . they are aware of overtones of a rite of initiation which such events actually constitute for the child, a confrontation of the terrors of social life with all the mysteries stripped away. And in the outlook of many of those parents (who wish that the problem didn't exist), the child is expected to face the terror and contain his fear and anger *precisely* because he is a Negro American. Thus he's required to master the inner tensions created by his racial situation, and if he gets hurt – then his is one more sacrifice. It is a harsh requirement, but if he fails this basic test, his life will be even harsher. (Warren, 1966: 344)

According to her biographer, Elisabeth Young-Bruehl, Arendt felt that the parents of the children entering the hostile environment were forcing the child to treat education as a means for social advancement, denying the child the 'absolute protection of dignity' that her own mother had given her, instructing her to leave social situations where she was unwanted (1982: 311). Arendt wrote to Ellison, agreeing that she had not understood this ideal of sacrifice, that she had been unappreciative of the 'element of elementary, bodily fear in the situation' as an initation into the realities of a racist society (Young-Bruehl, 1982: 316).

Despite this acknowledgement to Ellison, Arendt's position was, and remained, concerned with the preservation of distinctions between the different realms. In terms of dignity, it was the dignity of the realm of politics that was uppermost in her mind. It is this that makes her position rather different from that of Zora Neale Hurston, who also objected to desegregation, but whose argument was directed against what she considered to be the pathologising 'tragedy of colour' school of thought that suggested that black people lived in deprivation, that it was a tragedy to be black, and that 'black students would only learn if they sat next to whites'; her position, directed against the NAACP's involvement in the *Brown* decision, was that one should instead direct efforts into the recognition and celebration of black people as dignified creators and of black traditions and institutions that had a long and proud history (see Hemenway, 1986:

329–37).[4] Arendt's concern with dignity was less for pride in Hurston's folkloric sense, and more in the preservation of the political realm, about the achievement of which there should be a collective pride. It has been argued that Arendt felt a gratitude for the citizenship granted her as an immigrant Jew escaping persecution in Europe to come to America (Benhabib, 1996: 154–5), such that her motivating impulse in 'Reflections on Little Rock', stronger than any sense of empathy with African Americans, was to preserve the merits, actual and potential, of the form of democracy she found there, a form in which the public realm was, Arendt believed, to be thought of as a 'space of appearances'.

Difference and/in the public realm

This discussion of appearance in relation to 'Reflections on Little Rock' has suggested the notion that appearance has philosophical bases in Arendt's thought concerning both the sense of 'rising' as the profundity of appearance in the public realm and that of appearance as the creative force of freedom cast as natality and the capacity of *beginning*. What emerges from the discussion is that Arendt's wish to preserve a public space of appearances led to some rather disturbing conclusions in her comment on the Little Rock events. Principally, I have wanted to show how the notion of disembodied participation cannot be sustained. While one may find the arguments presented in the 'Reflections' article thought-provoking and, in places, highly persuasive, there is a slippage in Arendt's argument which collapses appearance into visibility where she attempts to address the question of skin colour. It is as if the possibility of appearance in Arendt's thinking requires a disembodied participation; in part, this is as a result of Arendt's privileging of speech as the modality of appearance whereby an actor 'identifies himself' (1959b: 158, see earlier quotation). Bodily difference is positioned as an obstruction to participation as equal citizens in the public realm. As I have argued above, this might be an accurate description of the political situation in the South (and elsewhere), but Arendt seems to

4 Hemenway argues that Zora Neale Hurston's politics were formed out of an individualism that sometimes bordered on egoism, a suspicion of the Communist Party and indeed any collectivist government, combined with a suspicion of social science's emphasis on 'cultural deprivation'. Her celebration of folk heritage should be seen in this light, as should her dislike of the writings of Richard Wright, whose involvement in communist politics and literary use thereof abhored her, and the National Association for the Advancement of Colored People (NAACP), whom she felt pathologised black life. Her objection to desegregation (published in a letter to the *Orlando Sentinel*, August 11, 1955) delighted segregationists who used it to argue that black people themselves did not want this; the letter was reprinted and she received a card from a white supremacist group praising her stand. Her own background had been in the proud, self-governing all-black village of Eatonville, and while her views might seem by turns rather romantic or rather reactionary when applied as a general principle, they were based in that experience, and this enabled her to refute a pathologising of black life in social science that few were questioning 'from within' and to develop her notion of a black aesthetic.

elevate the argument away from description and on to a level of analyses which is highly problematic.

Arendt's theories posit a world in which social discrimination takes place, allowing a social plurality that somehow benefits the political realm, but her argument is that such discrimination cannot be allowed to *structure* that realm. Forms of free association, however, frequently have a relationship to forms of exclusion and political discrimination; the idea that spontaneous social discrimination has an innocence that is unrelated to forms of political discrimination is a utopian aspiration in Arendt's vision of an ideal political world. She writes as though this ideal situation were already the case, such that – and here I agree with the arguments put forward by James Bohman (1996) – she denies the way in which there is unequal access to the 'space of appearance' within which political decisions are taken. Moreover, the ability to challenge those decisions, or avoid their implications, means that Arendt assumes the concept of political equality rather than critiquing its failure.

Even as an ideal, however, there remain problems with Arendt's vision of the political realm. With the benefit of our contemporary perspective, and in relation to more recent theorising around the idea of public spheres, we are able to provide a critique of the way in which Arendt sees social plurality in relation to the political realm. There is an honouring of a form of authenticity in Arendt that also informs her arguments around the pariah and the parvenu. Seyla Benhabib notes how Arendt, borrowing her terms from the French journalist Bernard Lazare, utilised these terms as a way of understanding different strategies by which individuals maintained or denied their difference. Here her thought was, once again, informed more by reflection on European totalitarian regimes than by racial politics of the United States. Benhabib puts it succinctly:

> [W]hile the pariah is the one who is cast aside, marginalised and treated with contempt by society because of his or her otherness, the parvenu denies her otherness so as to become accepted by the dominant society. As the twentieth century progressed, the sociocultural paradoxes of maintaining particularistic identities gave way to a politics of annihilation of otherness through the racial policies of extermination in the hands of National Socialism. (1996: xxvi)

The same ideal of authenticity, however, sits uneasily when placed in the different context that has been the focus of this chapter. The figure of the parvenu is one that Arendt implies was being sought by those African Americans seeking access to previously all-white schools; yet, on the other hand, she denies African Americans the possibility of appearing in the political realm without being reduced to their group identification literally 'on sight'.

Both the question of authenticity – in the sense of a refusal of the position of the parvenu – and the question of how social discrimination feeds into the political realm are approached somewhat differently by those theorists of public spheres who have recently suggested that social diversity has produced what are in effect several, multiple, public spheres or 'counter public spheres' (Felski, 1990; Fraser, 1991; Gilroy, 1994). Arguing in terms of feminist or of 'black' counterpublic spheres, these arguments acknowledge the sense in which, in Arendtian terms, social discrimination *creates* political arenas that are public spaces of appearance. Rita Felski has promoted a notion of a feminist counterpublic sphere as a model for theorising 'the features and institutional locations of the feminist discursive community in late capitalism' (1990: 44). She suggests that the emergence of a feminist counterpublic sphere reflects women's greater, if still unequal, access to networks of communication and interpretation; in these discursive spaces dominant definitions of femininity are contested and redefined, so that whilst questions of the nature of female identity will not necessarily be resolved, they are addressed as 'a problem' (1990: 46). In a somewhat similar vein, Nancy Fraser (1991, 1997) has argued that the Habermassian concept of the public sphere is a useful one because it separates out the state and state apparatuses from what she describes as 'a theatre in modern societies in which political participation is enacted through the medium of talk . . . an institutionalised arena of discursive interaction . . . for debating and deliberating' (1991, 1997: 70). Such a theatre of talk, however, has to be conceived within a context of inequality. Fraser suggests that certain theorists have developed and utilised a concept of the public sphere in which social inequalities are bracketed. Because the public sphere exists within a social context of inequalities, however, to depict the public sphere thus is to engage in a conceit in which interlocutors are depicted *as if* they were social peers in this arena (Fraser, 1997: 79). Fraser's worry is therefore parallel to the concern expressed earlier in relation to Hannah Arendt, and her suggestion is that we might think and seek to protect a democratic society in which there are multiple publics, in which there are what she terms 'subaltern counterpublics' (1997: 81). The fact that these counterpublic spheres are *publicist*, Fraser argues, means that they are by definition 'not enclaves' (1997: 82), although they might have tendencies toward enclaving themselves from within as well as the threat of being enclaved from without. It is the dialectic between their dual functions of regrouping and withdrawal, on the one hand, and as bases and training for agitational activities toward the wider publics, on the other, that for Fraser gives these counterpublics their emancipatory potential (1997: 82).

Arendt's position, exemplified in the comments in 'Reflections on Little Rock', attempted to preserve the political realm separately from the social in an elevation of political principles above both the discriminatory practices of the social realm and the 'interior' concerns of the private realm. Bodily differences were assigned by her, as we have seen, to the later grouping. Arendt's attitude toward the feminist movements of her time arose from this conviction that the political realm be shielded from 'social' issues and 'life' questions. I have argued earlier that her attempt to maintain this distinction in relation to the Little Rock events floundered at exactly the point when Arendt made the decision to posit as 'social', and therefore as non-political, issues of visibility (in this case, skin colour) or, put in more general terms, of embodiment. Recent work on counterpublic spheres enables a challenge to Arendt's distinction between the social and the political insofar as it illustrates the routes by which social identities and social occasions can be both generative of political concerns and the vehicles for voicing those concerns. For feminism, specifically, this work enables one to expose the masculine nature of 'the political', both in terms of the ideal that Arendt describes (Cornell, 1997) and in terms of the inequities of realistic access. Moreover, it escapes the grandiose overtones by which Arendt links the realm of the political to the 'world at stake' through the quiet indication that there are several public realms and, in a certain sense, several different 'worlds' at stake. However, it is not altogether clear that one can use this work to refute all that Arendt says nor to resolve all the issues that the above discussion has raised. Before I conclude, I want to raise some of the questions that remain in thinking difference and/in relation to 'the political'.

The question that I have highlighted earlier concerning the relationship between appearance and visibility is one that needs some more excavation. For however poorly Arendt draws the distinction in relation to the events in Little Rock, there remains the question that her terms 'appearance' and 'visibility' were attempting to capture. That is, there is a tension between public spheres and publicity that remains in the work on counterpublic spheres and that turns on Arendt's point that profound participation is distinct from the shallowness of 'being seen'. The profundity of appearance seems a crucial facet of her argument, one that she trips over in relation to the 'Little Rock' article, but which remains, nevertheless, an intriguing and important conceptualisation of the political.

Arendt's arguments seem to suggest that merely making a group visible through the creation of communicative networks or through embodied display, whatever forms they might take, is not necessarily profound, dignified, political *participation*. Moreover, since Arendt's comments, history has illustrated how mere visibility, even as an initial strategy, can have a complicity with a visually dominated consumer capitalism (see Hennessey, 1995; M. Fraser, 1999) that undercuts the profundity of what is being said on a political level. Of course, the use of visibility *can* be and has been a political strategy. The occupancy of public space through demonstrations and marches, for example, has been a mode of making social discriminations visible through physical participation in the public realm (for example, one might point to the cases of the suffragettes, American civil rights movements or Gay Pride marches). The challenge to Arendt's theory here is that the visibility of a grouping – even a grouping around a 'shared identity' – need not be dismissed as merely social, an 'association' comparable to those of 'free association'. The counterpublic sphere might be seen, rather, as an acting in concert – a beginning, even – that brings it closer to an exercise in freedom in Arendt's sense. Furthermore, other forms of embodied participation might be seen in less overtly politicised public spaces, such as those created, for example, through musical communication or dance (Gilroy, 1994). However, such embodied participation cannot speak for itself. Its political message, in other words, has to be abstracted from the multiple bodies and the multiple ways in which that visibility might be understood. Another way of posing this debate, to borrow from Arendt's vocabulary, is to say that the issue at stake is how to maintain a profundity of appearance alongside or even *through* visibility.

There is not space to discuss here the various modes and languages by which theorists are entering this debate, for several positions and concerns crystallise at this point. It is necessary, however, to say that communication between 'counterpublic spheres', on the one hand, and other spheres or a wider political sphere, on the other (the difference is one of conceptualisation), can take many forms, but without some form, some sense of a communication 'out' – what Fraser (1997) considers to be a dialectic relationship between the tendency to become enclaves and the tendency to agitate beyond the counter public sphere's own bounds – the *political* impact is lost. This is the tricky step, for, with this step, counterpublic spheres have to engage in a 'wider' language, and take the risk of communication which may not necessarily be heard or heard in the way the speaker would wish (Bickford, 1995). Whilst the emphasis on 'the political' in Arendt and the public sphere in Habermas, as well as in work such as Fraser's (1997), may seem to abstract away from embodiment and consequently elevate speech and rational debate above the actual existence of the speakers themselves, there is a sense in which such a manoeuvre – to the question of communication – is unavoidable. In Arendt's work, as Bohman (1996) argues, the step to wider audience involves an implicit principle of compromise, and in these notions of counterpublic spheres, similarly, there seems to be a required model of democratic fora and compromise, lest the counterpublic spheres become hermetically sealed discussions that have no impact on any other except their own. The question then becomes how to make the movement 'out' to a wider public sphere in a way that does not involve a denial of that difference that each counterpublic sphere was designed, or formed, to support.

But this is surely a welcome challenge, and one that returns us to the notion of profundity. Several feminist theorists have worried – in a way that Arendt seems to have done – about the presentation of womanhood as a homogeneous group. The notion of a feminist counterpublic sphere runs such a risk in that, as in a crude model of multiculturalism, it can work to seal each 'counter' group into itself, imposing a homogeneity that may not exist. The status of the sphere as political as opposed to merely publicist, then, is guaranteed only to the extent that the profundity of the issues raised is challenged and debated. Have these issues 'merely' been raised into the realm of the visible or have they 'arisen' in the stronger senses that Arendt wrote about?

Such a role, one of challenge and debate, would be one fitting for the public realm of appearances as Arendt conceived it. In much of Arendt's work she writes in awe of the political realm as the realm of dignity and action; the world of appearances is the world in which profound thought will appear, and, indeed, should appear, for if it remains within the individualised intimate realm of the private, it constitutes a negation of the possibilities offered to humankind. The public realm, therefore, would indeed be the place where it is decided, in this new casting of Arendt's position, whether the concerns expressed or displayed in counterpublic spheres were merely publicist (simply made visible) or profound; this would also be the moment that any portrayal of 'interests' would be challenged (in terms of an assumed homogeneity, for example). As with Arendt's distinctions, these are ideal spaces and processes rather than descriptions of the presently existing contexts; but they are not removed from the realities of the present.

Conclusion

To conclude this chapter, I want to emphasise how Arendt's oeuvre maintained a relationship to the horizon that political limits form in the way that I suggested in Chapter 2, feminist politics implicitly does, and, indeed, should. There I argued that the debates that have ensued around the perceived threat of 'post-structuralist' theory for feminism and feminist thought might be approached not via the route of seeking to justify claims on either side, but by unpacking what this idea of 'danger' implies. For although much of these debates is based upon miscalls and misunderstandings, what they offer up is the opportunity to discuss feminism's 'political imagination' and *its* genealogy. The fear of 'post-structuralist thought', I suggested, felt most acutely in terms of the perceived lack of normative criteria and the relativising of Truth, is that in pursuing modes of thought that are intriguing or challenging, feminists might be seduced into a position of defenselessness when faced with the most extreme forms of right-wing politics. The 'threat' of post-structuralism, therefore, becomes transmuted into the threat of extremism.

For Arendt, the political limit that was the Nazi Germany that she fled is ever present in her work.[5] Her position in the 'Reflections' piece resonates with a concern to maintain democracy, even as she is led to the peculiar position that makes her echo the position of Governor Faubus, calling for a slower response that would await social change before political ideals are 'imposed' on children, and before children are able to 'begin' themselves. Arendt's articulated fear was that thought would be quashed were all moral

5 Even as her Judaism was a more complex and contentious issue (see Benhabib, 1995, 1996; Kaplan, 1995). Bat-Ami Bar On (1996) argues that although it is true that Arendt decentred gender in her analyses, this has to be understood in relation to her ethico-political commitment to her Jewishness. The decentring of gender, she argues, was a *traumatised* decentring that resulted from the way in which other issues – such as totalitarian regimes – were made central in her life.

considerations imposed from above. In *Eichmann in Jerusalem* (1977, first published in 1963), Arendt's controversial book that was composed of her newspaper reports on the trial of the Nazi war criminal Adolf Eichmann in Jerusalem in 1961, Arendt wrote that the banality of his character was signalled in his evident inability to *think*. 'The longer one listened to him', she wrote, 'the more obvious it became that his inability to speak was closely connected with an inability to think, namely, to think from the standpoint of somebody else' (1977: 49). He was not a 'monster', certainly, 'but it was difficult indeed not to suspect that he was a clown' (1977: 54); content with the elation that his clichés gave him, he consoled himself without any apparent awareness of his own glaring inconsistencies (1977: 55). Arendt suggested that, in relation to Eichmann, the ability to think for oneself, to have independent critical thought, was necessary, if not sufficient, for the exercise of political judgement and perhaps even for recognising justice (see Bradshaw, 1989: 67). Thinking, one might say, therefore, is a prerequisite for *profundity* in political judgement, and a guard against totalitarian regimes' ideological impositions. The increasingly automatic nature of judgement in mass society, where most are not involved in judging but form opinions without independent thought, was for Arendt a signal of increasing and worrying thoughtlessness (as Villa, 1996b, argues). One might see Arendt's response to desegregation in Little Rock as a fear that the judgement was too 'automatic'; and one might see, moreover, her response to Ellison as a consequence of thought on her part, a reflection (if not a retraction) on her own 'Reflections' article. As Villa writes, Arendt's 'Thinking and moral considerations' (1984) sought out Socrates as exemplary of a man who forced his conversational partners to think. In that article, she admires Socrates not for his teaching, but for infecting others with his own perplexity (1984: 22); her attachment to thinking is due to the sense in which a consideration from a 'distance' awakens conscience because thinking involves a relationship to oneself whereby one bears witness to oneself and judges oneself (1984: 35).

It is arguably because Arendt had the political limit of totalitarian regimes firmly 'in view' that her later work took this turn toward the value of thinking as profound withdrawal, diminishing her previous elevation of public debate above individualised 'interior' activities and reversing her previous argument that regarded truth as coercive where politics is persuasive (Bradshaw, 1989: 68). Arendt's disdain of solitary withdrawal in *The Human Condition* (1959b) is lessened then, as she considered Eichmann as thoughtless, as not having that 'twoness'. His inability to think meant he would not mind contradicting himself, and would not be perturbed by his inability to account for his actions except through clichés; it was not an inherent wickedness that Arendt saw in Eichmann but an inability to think that made him 'capable of infinite evil' (1984: 36). Further, as she considered the life of Martin Heidegger, her previous mentor and lover, whose support for Nazism she attempted to understand in relation to the occupation of the philosopher, she presents her arguments for an understanding of thinking as an activity that requires some withdrawal from the world of appearances where one 'is never alone and always much too busy to think'. Arendt's (1978b) 'apology' for Heidegger, an essay written for his eightieth birthday, was one that depicted him as erring in his attempt to move into the public world of human affairs.[6] Heidegger's retreat to the seclusion of his thinking was an entirely appropriate response to his 'collision' with the public world, for thinking requires 'essential seclusion from the world' (Arendt, 1978b: 299). Arendt's position seems to be that, unlike Eichmann, Heidegger recognised his error and restored his capacity for judgement by retreating and thinking in the 'place of stillness' appropriate for thought (Bradshaw, 1989: 70), concording with Heidegger's own position in his 'Letter on humanism' that thinking must not be inscribed in a 'technical horizon' – as a means toward acting or making – but may be regarded as the pursuit of thinking Being, that which is 'farther than all beings and yet nearer to man than every being' (Heidegger, 1993: 234). For the Arendt of 'Thinking and moral considerations' (1984), and of *The Life of the Mind* (1978a), thinking can prevent immoral action in the world, and therefore it has to become 'ascribed to everybody; it cannot be a privilege of the few' (quoted in Bradshaw, 1989: 73). In *The Life of the Mind* (1978a) Arendt suggests that everyone has conscience and that everyone acts, and that the conflict which can arise between these two makes the experience of the 'two-in-one' of thought a common experience. This 'two-in-one' of thinking connects thought to the performance of deeds, and action in the world. In 'Thinking and moral considerations' Arendt concluded that judging is the by-product of thinking, and judging makes thinking 'manifest in the world of appearances' (1984: 37), especially important in those times in history when 'things fall apart', when the majority are swept away unthinkingly. At these times, 'those who think are drawn out of hiding' and then thinking, while never the same as judgement, facilitates judgement, the 'most political of man's mental abilities' (Arendt, 1984: 36).[7]

Thus, despite the fact that Arendt's turn to thought, withdrawal, solitude and truth in her later work seems to contradict some of her earlier

6 See Ettinger (1995) on the relationship between Arendt and Heidegger; Dana Villa's (1996a) book is excellent on the philosophical connections.

7 Arendt is explicit that she has Kant in mind when she introduces judgement as dealing with things close at hand (as opposed to thinking, which deals with invisibles). Her arguments around thought and around political debate are infused with this Kantian concern with judgement. Ronald Beiner explains that it is 'the faculty of judgement that fits us into this world of phenomena and appearances, and makes it possible for us to find our proper place within it. It is precisely because the political world is defined by Arendt as a realm of phenomenal disclosure [the realm of appearances] that the faculty of judgement assumes such importance for her' (1983: 14, see also pp. 15–19, and pp. 119–25 where Beiner discusses the Eichmann case in relation to those who criticised Arendt's cool analyses as betraying a 'lack of love for the Jewish people'). For feminist uses and critiques of Kant, see Flax (1993), Schott (1997) and Hutchings (1996), the latter of whom also places Arendt in relation to Kantian notions of judgement, explaining that Arendt was anxious to avoid the idea of judgement as law governed.

propositions, in the light of this chapter I would argue that it can be seen as an attempt to give a route to profundity. That is, as we have seen, Arendt's concern is that appearance in the public realm should not be merely a case of deeds and actors being 'seen', but that deeds and actions should have 'arisen'; they should have some profundity about them. While great thinkers are a rarity, thought is a human capacity which should be developed in all. Her concern was to counteract the tendencies of a world of automatic thought that relied upon the 'bannisters' provided for it, by arguing that thinking, whilst necessarily a solitary and still activity, is required by a public realm of appearances that, in its absence, would be merely publicity and dangerously without *gravitas*.

For contemporary feminist thought, this discussion indicates the complexity of imagining the political realm. Participation in the public realm might be generally considered positively, but this chapter has illustrated the sense in which imagining 'the political' involves one in considerations of philosophical visions and divisions.

As Honig has argued, although Arendt dismissed feminism, regarding 'the woman question' as one that it was inappropriate to pose politically (Honig, 1995: 135), feminism is very different now from the feminism that surrounded Arendt, and many of the concerns of current feminist theory resonate with Arendt's work insofar as she was a theorist of an 'agonistic and performative politics' (Honig, 1995: 136). Honig argues that because Arendt poses 'an agonistic action in concert that postulates difference and plurality, not identity, as its base' (1995: 160), she can be useful in thinking through the question of how feminism might motivate future action without postulating identity – or any other foundationalism – as its ground. In this chapter I have focussed on one aspect of Arendt – her use of the concept of appearance in the public realm – to illustrate the provocations and the problems in thinking 'the political' with Arendt. I would also wish to suggest that, as well as making an excellent counterpoint to current attempts to theorise the public sphere, Arendt makes for a thoroughly intriguing figure for the project of thinking through feminist political imagination on a more general level. Reading Arendt makes one think about what feminism *is*.[8]

Thinking about what feminism is, as I have suggested in preceding chapters, involves considerations of temporo-spatial nature – Where is the 'target' of the intervention? Where is the audience? Which forum will the intervention occupy? Where are the boundaries of its constitution? When and how are we to measure success? – as well as considerations of enunciative positions that revolve around issues such as: Who is speaking? For

---

8 Young-Bruehl in May and Kohn (1996) argued that she did not consider Arendt's thinking as very helpful in current feminist projects that are attempting to integrate perspectives and find analytical categories to articulate the 'resistance of multiple victims' (*sic*). However, she argues that what she has done is to make feminists usefully think about feminism.

whom are they speaking? How will they be heard?[9] Here I have argued that Arendt's thoughts on the demarcations between different realms – political, social, private – provocative as they may be, are too rigid for contemporary feminism; but, more subtly, I have wanted to suggest through the discussions in this chapter that her notion of appearance, along with the concepts I have herein appended to it – notably, those of visibility and profundity – gathers around it a set of concerns that are central to thinking about feminist political imagination. Thus, while other writers have often explored Arendt and feminism with reference to the way in which she deals with 'our' question of identity – particularly in relation to the question of using or denying difference (which is the issue behind the parvenu/pariah distinction) – I have explored Arendt in order to show how even as her own interventions were flawed or, as I would argue in the case of the 'Little Rock' article, deeply misguided, her work was centrally about how the political realm is imagined. There was an explicit quality to the horizons and limits in Arendt's life and work; and it is partly because of the fear of one positive evil – the repetition of totalitarianism – that it seems Arendt added a peculiar voice to another discriminatory practice – the continued racial segregation of schools. For the purposes of this book, she is a thoroughly intriguing figure, a theorist who illustrates the connections between the philosophical and the political, between the embodied and the abstract, and between fear and the power of imagination. She illustrates the arguments that how we philosophise affects the way we articulate and target our politics, how we abstract 'the political' affects the way we consider and experience embodiment, and, perhaps most graphically, how we fear affects the shape and force of our imaginations.

9 Dietz's discussion of Arendt and feminism takes a different form from mine, but she similarly asks questions that concern the politics of speaking for and as women, of maintaining, respecting, and challenging difference in the public realm: 'What constitutes an ethic of communicative interaction among citizens? How can the diversity of speech and speakers be maintained and allowed to flourish? Do women bring a different voice of female consciousness to the public realm? How has it manifested itself?' (Dietz, 1994: 249).

5

MIMESIS AS CULTURAL SURVIVAL: JUDITH BUTLER AND ANTI-SEMITISM

> Wittig understands gender as the workings of 'sex', where 'sex' is an obligatory injunction for the body to become a cultural sign, to materialise itself in obedience to a historically delimited possibility, and to do this, not once or twice, but as a sustained and repeated corporeal project. The notion of a 'project', however, suggests the originating force of a radical will, and because gender is a project that has cultural survival as its end, the term strategy better suggests the situation of duress under which gender performance always and variously occurs.
> (Judith Butler, 1990: 139)

Why is it that, as we exit the twentieth century, we 'feminist scholars' are engaged in projects that emphasise performativity, and debating ways of understanding what a commitment to anti-essentialism leaves us with? If an emphasis on performativity aids us in comprehending our gendered subjectivities, does it also reveal something about our historical positionality? In this chapter I want to begin from the observation that this 'century of women' has also been the century whose political visions have been sadly and brutally challenged by the need to understand the reproduction and tenacity of essentialist forms of belonging. In addressing the genealogy of a particular concept – mimesis – that has become popular within feminist theorising of identity, I mean to imply that the popularity of 'the mimetic' within contemporary feminist thought has much to do with the way in which the conception of identity as the 'stylised repetition of acts' (Butler, 1993a) offers the opportunity to conceive identity 'beyond essentialism' and thus to be a part of the demand that this century close with its intellectuals engaged in an optimism that responsibly remembers.

I want to illustrate here the sense in which 'mimesis' has an intellectual heritage, or what I would term a 'specific genealogy', that was moulded by the events of the twentieth century, a social–theoretical history that has centrally involved grappling with racism and, of particular concern here, with anti-Semitism. I focus on Judith Butler's highly influential work on gender (1990, 1993a, 1997a, 1997b) in order to suggest that it reveals a certain feminist inheritance of an emphasis on mimesis and imitation that resonates with the ways in which theoreticians responded to the calamitous events of essentialist politics and versions of belonging that were central to the political vision of Hitler's National Socialism and to the events of the Second World War. In her writings, Butler offers a certain trajectory of her work, and explicitly calls upon her intellectual heritage, one that is headed in name by Nietzsche and in attitude by genealogy, but that also includes significant psychoanalytic, deconstructionist and existentialist inheritances. Rather than rehearse that trajectory, my intention is to point to this other trajectory, to the ways in which her attempts to think gender non-essentially have a specific relation to attempts to theorise anti-Semitism. This is to give Butler's work a genealogy that traces the notion of mimesis back into work which employed the concept within sociotheoretical responses to anti-Semitism.

I am treading a specific path through this ambitious argument, one that illuminates certain important thinkers at the expense of others. I begin by introducing Butler's arguments through her indebtedness to de Beauvoir, before emphasising the role that the concept of mimesis takes in Butler's work. In the next section I take a cue from the work of Jonathan Boyarin, who highlights the underplayed notion of cultural survival in Butler's work, in order to shift focus on to the history of mimesis in sociotheoretical thinking about anti-Semitism. That section therefore addresses the influential text of Adorno and Horkheimer, *Dialectic of Enlightenment* (1986), where the concept of mimesis was employed, rather differently, in their attempts to comprehend anti-Semitic fascism in the context of the unfolding of capitalist 'civilisation', as well as in the important, if highly criticised, work of Jean-Paul Sartre, *Anti-Semite and Jew* (1965). This tracing is presented not in order to replace that which is more visible in Butler's work, but in order to supplement it with a particular concern in mind. Nor is the chapter intended as a critique of Butler's position; indeed, it applauds Butler's position, and is intended as a certain form of defence, by seeking to give it a specific genealogy in this way. My concern is to answer the critiques which regard the attention to performativity and mimesis as ahistorical and apolitical, as 'obsessive' about 'the subject', by illustrating and to some extent reorientating the debate. Within that reorientation the idea of 'cultural survival' will be crucial, since it ties Butler's work on gender explicitly with this work on ethnicity and racism and forces attention on to the specific historical and political context within which mimetic behaviour and identity performance takes place.

Butler, mimesis and imitation: carrying on gender

In Butler's *Gender Trouble* Simone de Beauvoir is the source of a series of questions for Butler, centring on the notion of 'becoming a woman':

> The phrase is odd, even nonsensical, for how can one become a woman if one wasn't a woman all along? And who is this 'one' who does the becoming? Is there some human who becomes its gender at some point in time? Is it fair to assume that this human was not its gender before it became its gender? . . . And, perhaps most pertinently, when does this mechanism arrive on the cultural scene to transform the human subject into a gendered subject? (Butler, 1990: 111)

Butler pushes de Beauvoir's thesis to its extreme position, suggesting that de Beauvoir invites further questioning on the relationship between sex and gender, ones that the latter herself did not pursue. First, if one is not born, but 'becomes' a woman, the distinction between sex and gender allows one to interrogate further the cultural construction of sexes and genders: 'it does not follow that to be a given sex is to become a given gender; in other words, "woman" need not be the cultural construction of the female body, and "man" need not interpret male bodies' (Butler, 1990: 112). For de Beauvoir there *is* an anatomical factor in the causality of 'becoming', since she argues that there is a psychic interpretation of the anatomy, whereby the boy has the ability to assume an 'attitude of subjectivity' because he has – through the psychic interpretation of the penis – an 'alter ego', a point by which to compare himself with his companions. The girl, by contrast, cannot 'incarnate herself in any part of herself', such that she has a diffuse and inward-looking attitude, and this is, de Beauvoir contends, the function of the doll, with which the girl identifies, enabling her to act towards 'herself' (1993: 292–3, first published 1949). Thus masculinity, for de Beauvoir, is indeed tied to the male body, and feminine behaviour to the female, albeit in a negative sense in the latter case. Taking a cue from Foucault's *History of Sexuality Volume One*, Butler refuses to make the sexed body the anchor for a discussion of gender *tout court*, for, as Foucault suggested:

[I]t is precisely this idea of sex in itself that we cannot accept without examination. Is 'sex' really the anchorage point that supports the manifestations of sexuality, or is it not rather a complex idea that was formed inside the deployment of sexuality? In any case, one could show how this idea of sex took form in the different strategies of power and the definite role it played therein. (1981: 152)

In emphasising this point, Butler pursues a line of questioning that leads from de Beauvoir on towards her own thesis. Perhaps, Butler posits, *contra* de Beauvoir, there are 'genders, ways of culturally interpreting the sexed body, that are in no way restricted to the apparent duality of sex' (1990: 112). The apparent duality of sex may be the effect, she argues, of the deployment of compulsory heterosexuality. Moreover, de Beauvoir's use of the term 'becoming' leads Butler to wonder further:

[I]f gender is something that one becomes – but can never be – then gender is itself a kind of becoming or activity, and that gender ought not to be conceived as a noun or a substantial thing or a static cultural marker, but rather as an incessant and repeated action of some sort. (1990: 112)

Butler employs de Beauvoir as part of the build-up to her own position, which is one that continually questions the cultural conflation of gender and sex, and their production within compulsory heterosexuality, emphasising instead the performative aspects of gender. In a Foucauldian (and Nietzschean) manoeuvre, Butler questions the way in which the performance of gender produces the *effect* of an organising principle – an identity –

that appears to *cause* the behaviour. Gender is 'performative', constituted by the various acts of gender, a 'construction that conceals its own genesis', such that 'the tacit collective agreement to perform, produce and sustain discrete and polar genders as cultural fictions is obscured by the credibility of those productions' (1990: 140). There is thus a 'trope of interiority' whenever the body (or the sexed body) is regarded as *causing* gender. Although gender is generally understood to be interior, stable and causative, it is better interrogated, Butler is suggesting, as a cultural fiction, as a way of producing the effect of 'identity', and, therefore, as the exterior, contingent resultant of repeated 'acts, gestures, enactments' which are

> performative in the sense that the essence or identity that they otherwise purport to express are *fabrications* manufactured and sustained through corporeal signs and other discursive means. That the gendered body is performative suggests that it has no ontological status apart from the various acts which constitute its reality. This also suggests that if that reality is fabricated as an interior essence, that very interiority is *an effect and function of a decidedly public and social discourse*, the public regulation of fantasy through the surface politics of the body, the gender border control that differentiates inner from outer and so institutes the 'integrity' of the subject. (1990: 136, emphasis added)

I want to focus on the argument that gender is a 'truth effect' of a public and social discourse, for Butler's argument here is that gender is *imitative*. What does Butler mean when she argues that gender is imitative? In her reply to other contributors in the volume *Feminist Contentions* (1995), Butler states that femininity is 'an impossible ideal, on which compels *a daily mime* that can, by definition, never succeed in its effort to approximate that ideal' (Butler, 1995: 142, emphasis added). Here, she gives her position a trajectory that is somewhat different from that gleaned from *Gender Trouble* in that she highlights the role of linguistics in the development of her thesis.[1] She emphasises that, from linguistics, one learns that the performative act is one that brings into being or enacts what it names; and that, further, any sense of a prior agency is the effect of the utterance. The subject, although seemingly the source of the utterance – the 'doer behind the deed' – is in this way performatively constituted. From this, Butler argues that one can also think of gender as involving an ensemble of performative acts which draw upon conventions that the acts 'cite' and by which they are understood (Butler, 1995: 134). The 'public and social discourse' of the above quotation can be thought of, as Butler refines it in *Excitable Speech* (1997a), as historically sedimented linguistic conventions that have a 'sedimented iterability'. Gender is, as it were, an embodied citing of sedimented ideals. Gender is an embodied performativity that attempts to mime the impossible ideals of the public and social discourse,

---

1 Butler mentions therefore J.L. Austin's *How to do Things with Words* (1962), Derrida's 'Signature, Event, Context' in *Limited, Inc.* (1988) and Paul de Man's readings of Nietzsche in *Allegories of Reading* (1986).

the historically sedimented conventions that demand one displays a gendered subjectivity.

Where lesbian sexuality is derided as a fake or bad copy (of heterosexual relations), Butler's position redirects attention on to the assumptions that result in the privileging of heterosexuality as the original which homosexuality is then said to copy (Butler, 1991: 17). Heterosexuality, too, her argument runs, involves a process of mimicry, where the ideals that are mimed are the publicly and socially reiterated norms. The use of the notion of imitation in Butler, then, is one that attacks the thinking that would imply that lesbianism is a kind of miming, and argues that 'all gendering is a kind of impersonation and approximation' (1991: 21). The imitation that is gender is one that produces the notion of the original as its effect: 'the naturalistic effects of heterosexualised genders are produced through imitative strategies; what they imitate is a phantasmatic ideal of heterosexual identity, one that is produced by the imitation as its effect' (1991: 21). The project of heterosexual identity is an endless repetition of itself, a compulsive production or mimicry of its impossible ideals.

In contrast to other understandings of mimesis, there is no judgement of mimesis in Butler's work, and no judgement of one who participates in mimetic behaviour since all individuals are involved in imitation. There is, similarly, no attempt to place mimesis on either side of the dichotomies good/bad, natural/unnatural. Hegemonic heterosexuality involves all in mimesis, and yet the ideals that are being mimed are *impossible* to mime completely. They are impossible to occupy in terms of their own logic, for hegemonic ideals are never truly separate from that which they would exclude. The ideals remain discursively tied to one another, and those who live amidst them are necessarily engaged in performances which, once interrogated, reveal the sense in which the purported identity and the excluded identity are also profoundly tied to one another at the level of the psyche.

Butler argues that the maintenance of ideals of masculinity and femininity involves the performance or repetition of a heterosexual matrix which is inherently unstable. Heterosexuality offers subject positions (ideals) which can only be 'taken up' (mimed) by the subject through a process of repression or renunciation. Butler states: 'no "subject" comes into existence as a speaking being except through the repression of certain possibilities of speech (this is the significance of psychosis as impossible speech)' (1991: 139). For the order of heterosexuality to reign, and, in turn, its related gendered positions to be comprehended, there is a repression of forbidden impulses or desires, such that particular ways of naming the self become unviable. 'Oppression works', she writes, 'not merely through acts of overt prohibition, but covertly, through the constitution of viable subjects and through the corollary constitution of a domain of unviable (un)subjects – *abjects* we might call them – who are neither named nor prohibited within the economy of the law' (1991: 20). As Butler argues in *Gender Trouble*, there is, with respect to gendered heterosexuality, a psychic process which can be likened to melancholia, whereby the lost (the forbidden) loved object is carried within the ego, forming part of it. Heterosexual ideals demand that the very possibility of homosexuality be refused by the subject: it is the forbidden path. The possibility that is repressed and refused is to be *continually* refused, and the homosexual becomes thereby 'encrypted' within the heterosexual:

> There are structures of psychic homosexuality within heterosexual relations, and structures of psychic heterosexuality within gay and lesbian sexuality and relationships . . . the ideal of a coherent heterosexuality that Wittig describes as the norm and standard of the heterosexual contract is an impossible ideal, a 'fetish' . . . (1990: 121–2)

This encrypting is melancholic in that it carries the lost or 'forbidden' object with it in a way which elsewhere Butler likens to the way that Melanie Klein saw guilt operating 'as a way of preserving the object of love from one's own obliterating violence' (in Butler, 1997b: 25). It is exactly this psychic carrying *with* that makes heterosexuality an anxious project – heterosexuality is 'consistently haunted by that domain of sexual possibility that must be excluded for heterosexualized gender to reproduce itself' (Butler, 1993a: 125). The fear of difference that this focus on mimesis reveals is not that which it is common for campaigners for gay rights to point to – that between heterosexuals and homosexuals – but that between the performance, the ideal and the necessary excluded (see Girard, 1978, on this point). When the 'gaps' are illuminated, and made seeable, the exposure of gender as performative threatens the very idea of identity in the sense of a fit between mind and body. This is exactly why Butler returns to the example of drag, which reflects the imitative structure of hegemonic gender, disputing the claim that bodies and genders 'fit', and that heterosexuality is natural and original:

> To claim that all gender is like drag, or is drag, is to suggest that 'imitation' is at the heart of the *heterosexual* project and its gender binarisms, that drag is not a secondary imitation that presupposes a prior and original gender, but that hegemonic heterosexuality is itself a constant and repeated effort to imitate its own idealisations. (1993a: 125, original emphasis)

It is at this point that Butler comes closest to Irigaray's argument that mimesis might become a strategy. For Irigaray, mimesis is a strategy that has the potential to reveal the construction of Woman by illuminating through 'playful repetition' what is supposed to remain invisible. She writes,

> To play with mimesis is thus, for a woman, to try to recover the place of her exploitation by discourse, without allowing herself to be simply reduced to it. It means to resubmit herself – in as much as she is on the side of the 'perceptible', of 'matter' – to 'ideas', in particular to ideas about herself, that are elaborated in/ by a masculine logic, but so as to make 'visible' by an effect of playful repetition, what was supposed to remain invisible: the cover up of a possible operation of the feminine in language. (Irigaray, 1985: 76)

Irigaray's focus is different from Butler's insofar as Irigaray believes there is something one can term 'the feminine' in language which masculine logic has attempted to exclude. Mimesis is used differently by the two writers because, for Irigaray, mimesis is on the level of strategy – one that reveals through its repetition of ideas about women – and not of constitution, as it is for Butler.[2] However, Butler also sees in the mimetic nature of gender, as she understands it, the possibility of disruption, and comes close to Irigaray if only in the sense that Butler often uses a language of revealing the unseen relation between discursive and hegemonic ideals, on the one hand, and the constitution of the subject, on the other.[3]

Butler implies that heterosexuality remains hegemonic because it produces the idea of homosexuality whilst simultaneously disallowing its articulation as an identity, as owned in the same way that heterosexuality is 'owned'. But because of its reliance upon a simultaneous renunciation, Butler suggests – and this is the window of hope – there is a 'promising ambivalence of the norm' (1997a: 91) in the sense that there is the possibility of exposing the alterity within the norm, and the failure therefore of 'the norm to effect the universal reach for which it stands' (1997a: 91). What in *Excitable Speech* Butler terms the authorised and the 'deauthorised', elsewhere the viable and the (allegedly) abject, are sites of enunciation or 'identities' that are created at the very same moment.

It seems that Butler's refusal to judge mimesis *per se* is coupled with a sense in which the possibility of miming differently is held out as an *illuminating* possibility, due to the instability of heterosexuality and its attendant genders, and the possibility of showing that the alterity within the norm is regarded as *'promising'*. This might imply, and some have indeed taken it to imply, that the refusal to mimic hegemonic ideals is the implied 'solution' to the division of gender and sexuality, and the inequities that rely upon these divisions. And yet there is also a sense in which Butler implies that mimicry as a strategy of resistance or subversion – either in Irigaray's sense, or in the sense of attempting to mime the 'wrong' ideals, to flout the hegemonic relations between bodies, identities and performance – might frequently be one that would simply entail too many *risks*. Hence the importance of the term *hegemony* to Butler. That heterosexual matrices and gender ideals are hegemonic implies not simply that they are held up as normal, but also that the boundaries are *policed* so that the traversing of these boundaries entails various judgements, even punishments. Butler refuses to go so far as to actually *advocate* the crossing of boundaries – even if she speaks of performativity as open to 're-signification' (in Benhabib, 1995: 135) – remaining instead 'merely' the astute analyst of situations where the illumination of 'the gaps' occurs. Just as those who transgress are not elevated into heroines, so those who perform and thus maintain

2 See Schor, 1989.
3 For Butler's own response to Irigaray, see the discussion in *Bodies that Matter* (1993a: 36–55).

hegemonic ideals and norms are not to be automatically judged negatively. It is to these *risks* and the *policing* of gender that I now turn, in order to focus on the importance of placing mimesis in the context, and especially in terms of the power relations, in which it takes place.

Cultural survival

Towards the end of *Gender Trouble* Butler argues that 'gender is a project that has cultural survival as its end' (1990: 139). The notion of cultural survival, to which Boyarin (1995: 1322) has drawn attention, makes Butler's work sound much more ominous than the playful way it is often presented. What Butler talks about in terms of 're-signification' (or in her earlier terms of 'parody' and 'subversion') is rendered dangerous in this phrase, which implies that compliance with the 'sedimented norms' must be seen within the context of the risk involved in behaving otherwise. She continues the point: '[so that] the term strategy better suggests the situation of duress under which gender performance always and variously occurs' (1990: 139).

The category of mimicry as Butler employs it in her work is one that I would argue carries with it a sense of sadness, both of forfeiting (possibilities of being otherwise) and of resignation to 'carrying on' under duress. There is no playful repetition here. Gender performance is regarded as a strategy of *survival*, formed within a heterosexual matrix which, while not compulsory, is hegemonic, such that the psychic structures it deploys are analogous to melancholia, in which the lost object is incorporated into psychic life as part of the ego, object of ambivalence; that is, both loved and hated. Moreover, wherever a performance is situated on the 'outside', in a non-hegemonic position, it is frequently named by the terms which reincorporate it to the 'inside'. There may be times when such enunciations illuminate the 'gap' between ideals and performances, but there is no necessary connection there. Most of the time, gender is performed, and (presumably) 'read' or seen, because there is an issue of *survival* at stake.

Jonathan Boyarin (1995) makes an intriguing intervention into the debate around Butler's work within which he begins a rumination on the place of Jewish communities in relation to the arguments in *Gender Trouble*, and how her arguments would translate into a Jewish context. One of the themes of his article is that of cultural survival, in terms of how persistently *non-hegemonic* identities are figured by Butler. Non-hegemonic identities, he explains, would be those that persistently resist the hegemonic epistemic regime that Butler is exploring in relation to gender; these might 'not only be Jews in a Christian or post-Christian society, but "religious" Jews in a secular Jewish society' (Boyarin, 1995: 1318). Boyarin's purpose is to bring the performativity of identity into an account of cultural genealogy, to expose a sense in which a Jewish political subject can be thought as founded upon 'generational connection and its attendant anamnestic responsibilities and pleasures' (Boyarin and Boyarin, 1993: 701) making possible a maintenance of cultural identity thought through notions of generation and diaspora in such a way that highlights the Jewish embrace of the idea that there is no pure originality, that all subjective action takes place through at least a moment of imitation (Boyarin and Boyarin, 1995: 29). In the tradition of rabbinic Judaism, Boyarin and Boyarin write, 'discovering that something has already been said by someone greater is no diminution, but an enhancement, and there is an explicit value attached to citation' (1995: 29). Thus Boyarin and Boyarin suggest a reading of mimicry – that is, of citation and embodied performativity – as a project of survival that can be both a *healthy* sustenance of a culturally given and temporally sustained identity, as well as the site of a politics of interruption.

In this manner, the work of Jonathan and Daniel Boyarin offers a way of reading Butler's emphasis on the mimicry of ideals as a way of producing the effect of identity through a Jewish tradition, so as to connect her thesis of mimesis to a notion of *generational* mimicry and non-hegemonic identities as projects or strategies of survival. In what follows I also wish to move the context within which Butler is read, and to suggest that there is a tradition of thinking mimicry within a history of thought around anti-Semitism.[4] Before elaborating the implications of placing cultural survival more strongly to the fore, I wish to draw out the relationship of Butler's mode of theorising to some key figures in the theorisation of anti-Semitism. I do so in order to argue that it is not simply a case of regarding Butler's mode as requiring translation into a different context; in tracing this specific genealogy of the concept of mimesis, I mean to suggest a stronger argument which is that Butler's work already has, in its intellectual heritage, a connection with these attempts to comprehend anti-Semitism and anti-Semitic fascism. The connections will then allow a further set of questions to be asked about the relationship of Butler's feminist theory to differing usages of the concept of mimesis.

Judaism, anti-Semitism and mimesis

The classic text of Adorno and Horkheimer, *Dialectic of Enlightenment* (1986), is an important forerunner to the work of Boyarin and Boyarin. In response to the events of the Second World War, Adorno and Horkheimer felt obliged to surrender the 'innocence of philosophy' as they attempted to understand the 'indefatigable self-destructiveness of enlightenment' (1986: xi, first published 1944). Read as setting the context for later social–theoretical responses to anti-Semitism, this work offers a place from which to embark upon the specific route for thinking about more recent debates concerning identity and mimesis.

---

4 As there is a history of thinking racism in relation to the concept of mimesis, and which is the backdrop for much of the recent work on mimicry in relation to passing. See, for example, Fanon (1986) or Bhabha (1994).

Dialectic of Enlightenment gave a crucial role to the concept of mimesis, but one which was very different from that which both Butler and Boyarin and Boyarin would later present. The idea of mimesis was utilised by Adorno and Horkheimer, within their historical context and with their specific theoretical inflections, in order to make an argument about anti-Semitism and fascism.[5] Their concept of mimesis is not easily assimilable to the post-Derridean understanding, for it is employed to name a natural process. Although natural, however, it is also susceptible to control. In their writings they mean to illuminate the historical and socio-economic contexts in which mimetic processes took place, and, in particular, to understand the fascistic attempts to denigrate and repress mimetic behaviour. They wrote:

> [A]nti-Semitism is based upon a false projection. It is the counterpart of true mimesis, and fundamentally related to the repressed form; in fact, it is probably the morbid expression of repressed mimesis. Mimesis imitates the environment, but false projection makes the environment like itself. For mimesis the outside world is a model which the inner world must try to conform to: the alien must become familiar; but false projection confuses the inner and outer world and defines the most intimate experiences as hostile. (1986: 187, first published 1944)

In contrast to the way in which Butler uses the notion of mimicry as copy (of a hegemonic norm) mimesis was described by Adorno and Horkheimer as a mode of adaptation, part of a healthy assimilation and accommodation of the environment within which one moves. Such a conception is indebted to psychoanalytic ideas of identification, by which Adorno and Horkheimer were profoundly influenced. Its fundamental assumption, which is not necessarily in itself a psychoanalytic one, is that the infant naturally imitates the environment around it, responding to the gestures of first contact. However, civilisation has attempted to control human physical adaptation to nature, replacing

> organic adaptation to others and mimetic behaviour proper, by organised control of mimesis, in the magical phase; and finally, by rational practice, by work, in the historical phase. Uncontrolled mimesis is outlawed. (1986: 180, first published 1944)

Thus Adorno and Horkheimer argue that the reflection of nature that mimesis involves has been suppressed, and is suppressed in each generation, in order for humans to fit into the capitalist schema which holds up

---

5 Adorno and Horkheimer also give a complex place to women in relation to mimesis, suggesting that gender has a differential relationship to the historical changes they chart in relation to mimesis. On the complexities of women, representation and the representation of women in their schema, see Hewitt (1994). I am aware that I am avoiding a discussion of these complexities because I wish to stress the use of their concept of mimesis in relation to anti-Semitism by way of drawing a continuity and a contrast with Butler's use of mimesis in relation to gender.

other modes of being as necessary for its particular order of things. Where mimesis appears *qua* mimesis, including the forms of magical and religious rituals, it is suspect and disallowed. Only activity – rational practice – is allowed.

Mimesis is described by Adorno and Horkheimer as both a positive natural response to adaptation, and as an activity that social interests – here, capitalist ones – are involved in attempting to control. Yet, like all suppressed inclinations, mimetic behaviour is never completely destroyed, and it reappears. Even though capitalistic civilisations would wish to be rid of mimesis – to individuate and make humans merely 'human', as it were – this is an impossible desire. Those 'blinded by civilisation', Adorno and Horkheimer argue, experience 'their own tabooed mimetic features' in the behaviours and gestures of others, and they respond to them as old-fashioned, embarrassing and fearful remnants that survive in the rational environment of civilisation (1986: 181–2, first published 1944). Any expressiveness is experienced as an exaggeration in a civilisation where only an 'unmoving and unmoved countenance' is acceptable. For the anti-Semite, it is the Jews who are seen to engage in expressive mimetic behaviour, responding to natural impulses and ignoring the requirements of civilisation in which a 'fit' between individuals and the socio-economic system has been elevated above that between individuals and human nature. This would be a point at which Boyarin and Boyarin would be curiously in accord with Adorno and Horkheimer, insofar as they argue that rabbanic traditions allow, even encourage, a mimesis. The difference, of course, would be that for the former, this mimesis is a mode of continuance of tradition in the name of cultural and generational reproduction – the project of survival – whereas Adorno and Horkheimer suggest that in the minds of the anti-Semites the mimesis is not of cultural traditions, but of natural, emotional inclinations, inclinations which should, according to their repressive (and repressed) logic, be controlled in the name of civilisation.

In anti-Semitic fascism, however, a certain form of mimesis was allowed, Adorno and Horkheimer argue, that can be thought as a second level of mimesis. Anti-Semites both blame the Jew for engaging in forbidden mimetic behaviour – of flouting the demands of civilisation that one should avoid giving in to suppressed emotive expressivity – and at the same time, engage *themselves* in a form of mimicry of 'the Jew'; that is, the image which anti-Semitism presents of the Jew. Anti-Semites imitate their image of the Jew, in a false version of natural response to others, and are thereby themselves able to enjoy an activity forbidden by civilisation:

> There is no anti-Semite who does not basically want to imitate his mental image of a Jew, which is composed of mimetic cyphers: the argumentative movement of a hand, the musical voice painting a vivid picture of things and feelings irrespective of the real content of what is said, and the nose – the physiognomic *principium individuationis*, . . . Anti-Semites gather together to celebrate the moment when authority permits what is usually forbidden, and become collective

only in that common purpose. Their rantings are organised laughter. (1986: 184, first published 1944)

This is the mimesis of mimesis, then, in which it matters little whether Jews really do have the mimetic features that the anti-Semite sees there, because anti-Semitism is based on a *projection*, whereby 'impulses which the subject will not admit as his own even though they are most assuredly so, are attributed to the object – the prospective victim' (1986: 187, first published 1944). The mimesis of mimesis is a process in which the subject mimes because (s)he longs for the other, desires in some way what (s)he imagines the other to be. This sense of mimesis is also that which Sartre describes in *Anti-Semite and Jew*, where the anti-Semite gives himself[6] the pleasure of ranting, reporting and voicing evils which he attributes to the Jews:

> He [the anti-Semite] can thus glut himself to the point of obsession with the recital of and criminal actions which excite and satisfy his perverse leanings; but since at the same time he attributes them to those infamous Jews on whom he heaps his scorn, he satisfies himself without being compromised. (1965: 46, first published 1946)

The recitation that is taking place here, therefore, is one which gives the speaker pleasure, and is a mimicry that is 'a basic sadism' (1965: 46, first published 1946). For Sartre, this mimesis is based on fear, not of the Jews, but of the anti-Semite's own situation, a fear of 'himself, of his own consciousness, of his liberty, of his instincts, of his responsibilities, of solitariness, of change, of society, and of the world' (1965: 53, first published 1946). The ambivalence towards liberty is similarly important in the argument of Adorno and Horkheimer, for whom anti-Semitic fascism has to be viewed in the context of a frustration that is the gap that yawns between the potential that civilisation's discourse of liberty holds up for people, and its actuality.

The psychic processes involved in repressed mimesis are to be understood, Adorno and Horkheimer argued, in the context of the mockery that the masses had suffered insofar as they had had repeatedly to suppress the longing for happiness which liberalism and capitalism had promised them. The hatred felt by the anti-Semites was directed at an image of that happiness, which they perceived the Jews as having achieved despite the fact that the latter did not have any real access to power (1986: 172, first published 1944). Through this argument, Adorno and Horkheimer dovetail their analysis of anti-Semitism with a critique of capitalism, arguing that instead of pointing to the real villains of the new mercantile industrial age, the anti-Semite points to the scapegoat, the population who had seemingly created their own happiness, wealth and community within, but despite, the capitalist structures with which they, the masses, had been obliged to live. Fascism is the crystallisation of a general condition in which it becomes superfluous for man to plan his own happiness because in a world

---

6 Sartre writes with the masculine pronoun.

where repression and a capitalist mentality reign, all responsibility is to the apparatus, and reflective thought is anathema. Thus 'the dialectic of Enlightenment is transformed objectively into delusion' (1986: 204, first published 1944).

Sartre's work had a different route of philosophical indebtedness from Adorno and Horkheimer's, one that speaks less of capitalism and its inequities in its attempt to comprehend anti-Semitism, and more of inter-subjective economies. There is for Sartre an investment in anti-Semitism as an attachment to a tradition and a community: 'The phrase, "I hate the Jews" is one that is uttered in chorus; in pronouncing it, one attaches himself to a tradition and to a community – the tradition and community of the mediocre' (1965: 22, first published 1946). The citation of what would be termed 'hate speech' in contemporary America was thus for Sartre, as it is for Butler, a citation that keeps alive a discourse which, at the same time as it excludes, creates a community of same-thinking speakers. The community network of anti-Semites, Sartre argued, binds in anger those whom other hierarchies would disaggregate (1965: 30, first published 1946). It is in this bonding quality of anti-Semitism that Sartre sees the anti-Semite attaching himself to a tradition formed in relation to the pretext of the Jew. Although there were particular reasons why it was the Jews who were chosen as objects of revulsion, elsewhere it might be 'the Negro or the man of yellow skin' (1965: 54, first published 1946). The Jew would be invented by the anti-Semite did he not exist, writes Sartre (1965: 13, first published 1946), since, one surmises, the Jew fulfils a necessary function for the anti-Semite, to 'stifle his anxieties at their inception by persuading himself that his place in the world has been marked out in advance' (1965: 54, first published 1946).

Insofar as Sartre's work posed anti-Semitism as an imagined remembrance through repetition, and despite its functionalist structure, it is an argument that prefigures Boyarin and Boyarin's position on the maintenance of Jewish traditions themselves, with the important difference, of course, that there is a disparity between the two cases in terms of the nature of the subject's reflection on their embodied reminiscence of tradition. That is, there is a difference between the way that Sartre implies that the anti-Semite 'remembers' and the way that Judaism is remembered according to Boyarin and Boyarin. This concerns the nature of reflection.

Sartre's argument was that the anti-Semite was unreflective, a man who had chosen 'to live entirely outside himself, never to look within' (1965: 21, first published 1946). As such, Sartre echoes the argument of Adorno and Horkheimer, who, trying to understand the psychological state of the anti-Semite within a Europe which had attached itself to a narrative of liberalism and enlightenment, asserted that anti-Semitism was a projection that was not a problem because it was projection as such – since for them projection is present in all perception – but because of 'the absence from it of reflection' (1986: 189, first published 1944). Anti-Semitism involves a process which projects onto the world without taking in what is given back to the subject, such that projection makes the world a void; just as with the paranoiac, so with the anti-Semite, there is no limit to the ego's projections, no information that causes the ego to reflect upon itself (1986: 189–90, first published 1944).

For Sartre, the Jews in an anti-Semitic society, in contrast to the anti-Semite, are forced to be overly self-reflective – there is 'the necessity imposed upon the Jew of subjecting himself to endless self examination' so that he assumes a 'phantom personality' (1965: 78–9, first published 1946). The existential situation overdetermines the Jew, Sartre argues, for there is nothing determinate about the synthesis of characteristics (psychical and physical, anatomical, social, religious) that make up 'the Jew'. The bond between Jews is the shared experience of being placed as a Jew:

> It is neither their past, their religion, nor their soil that unites the sons of Israel. If they have a bond, if all of them deserve the name of Jew, it is because they have in common the situation of a Jew, that is, they live in a community which takes them for Jews. (1965: 67, first published 1946)

The mimicry that the Jew is obliged to participate in is one that Sartre bases in the concepts of authenticity and inauthenticity. The authentic path is to live within the situation, to be conscious of it, and to assume its responsibilities and risks (1965: 89, first published 1946). But authenticity requires one to live in a situation which 'is quite simply that of a martyr' (1965: 91, first published 1946). The inauthentic situation must be more tempting, reasons Sartre. But it is exactly the inauthentic Jew whom the anti-Semite focusses upon; that is, the one who attempts to 'pass'. The avenues of flight that characterise the route of the inauthentic Jew are collected into the 'monstrous portrait' that is made to stand for the 'Jew in general' (1965: 94, first published 1946). While Sartre argues that inauthenticity implies no moral blame, he does suggest that the assimilating Jew is acting in bad faith (1965: 99, first published 1946) and that he has 'allowed himself to be persuaded by the anti-Semites' (1965: 94, first published 1946), even that he makes himself anti-Semitic wherever he sees the traits that he denies in himself in other Jews (1965: 106, first published 1946). Furthermore, Sartre implies that there is a felt moral responsibility to the extent that the Jew sees authenticity as continuing a tradition and keeping open the possibility of being Jewish:

> To be a Jew is to be thrown into – to be *abandoned to* – the situation of a Jew; and at the same time it is to be responsible in and through one's own person for the destiny and the very nature of the Jewish people. For, whatever the Jew says or does, and whether he have a clear or vague conception of his responsibilities, it is as if all his acts were subject to a Kantian imperative, as if he had to ask himself before each act: 'If all Jews acted as I am going to do, what would happen to Jewish life?' (1965: 89–90, first published 1946)

Thus the theme of cultural survival has a place in Sartre's arguments too, in the form of an obligation to continuance, a theme which is also present in Levinas' later reflections on National Socialism and anti-Semitism, in which he argued that after Auschwitz there is a 'commandment to faithfulness', an obligation to live and remain Jews. For Levinas, however, this becomes also a commandment to defend the state of Israel:

> To renounce after Auschwitz this God absent from Auschwitz – no longer to assure the continuation of Israel – would amount to finishing the criminal enterprise of National Socialism, which aimed at the annihilation of Israel and the forgetting of the ethical message of the Bible, which Judaism bears, and whose multi-millennial history is concretely prolonged by Israel's existence as a people . . . The Jew, after Auschwitz, is pledged to his faithfulness to Judaism and to the material and even political conditions of its existence. (1988: 162–3)

The situation of 'remaining Jewish', however, is not a straightforward one in Sartre's argument, for the Jew, even and especially the authentic Jew, attempting to live the situation in which he is taken for a Jew, is in danger of denying the possibility of Jewish existence. Forced to observe himself through the eyes of others, he becomes simultaneously a witness and an object, such that, for Jews, wishing to know the Jew through introspection is also to deny him ('the Jew') (1965: 97, first published 1946). In making himself subject, he makes himself object.

Boyarin and Boyarin would dispute Sartre's position, finding the language of authenticity and inauthenticity objectionable and restricting, so that even as they would share, I believe, the broad political impulse behind the work, they would differ on the manoeuvres that Sartre's philosophical position obliges him to take. For although Boyarin and Boyarin also would wish to rethink the bonds that make up a 'Jewish community', they would argue that being 'taken for a Jew' does not *constitute* that community, such that the focus is less on the perception of Jews from without, and more on the continuance of various practices that internally, as it were, constitute Jewish traditions. They would maintain that there is a place for a non-essentialist but genealogical, non-biological *performative* sense of continuity, where questions of authenticity are inappropriate. Sartre's existentialism places him in a position where there is a privileging only of the present, only of the *situation* within which human actors meet, and of judging their behaviour at that moment. Tradition in Sartre is demoted to the status of a self-pitying lie: 'If it is true, as Hegel says, that a community is historical to the degree that it remembers its history, then the Jewish community is the least historical of all, for it keeps a memory of nothing but a long martyrdom, that is, of a long passivity' (1965: 66–7, first published 1946). The questions of continuing remembered traditions arc more active and crucial than this for Boyarin and Boyarin, but not as an impulse to Zionism. Levinas entwined a pledge to faithfulness to Judaism with the question of land; that is, the continuation of the state of Israel. Boyarin and Boyarin refuse the presumptive link between tradition and land as a dangerous one, and distance themselves from it. I will now focus upon the arguments of Boyarin and Boyarin as a route to thinking mimesis in a way that brings Butler's thesis back into this discussion.

As I have mentioned earlier, Jonathan Boyarin considers how Butler's work would position Judaism, and would translate into a Jewish context (1995), a line of questioning that focusses on a notion of cultural survival. Via an emphasis on cultural survival, the Boyarins' purpose is to link the notion of performativity with an account of cultural genealogy, to expose a sense in which a Jewish political subject can be thought as founded upon generational connection and embodied practices (1993: 701). If one accepts that Judaism values imitation *qua* citation, there is a way of reading Butler's emphasis on the mimicry of ideals as producing the effect of identity in a way that connects her thesis to a notion of *generational* mimicry and non-hegemonic identities as projects or strategies of survival. As both a sustenance of a culturally given and temporally sustained identity, as well as the site of a politics of interruption, mimicry can be understood as an alternative theoretical framework for considering embodied performativity, one that avoids the negative associations of genealogical ways of thinking about ethnicity that have often been associated with racism. The embodied citational practices of Judaism in a diasporic context, may have, Boyarin and Boyarin suggest, a particular contribution to make to this politico-theoretical manoeuvre.

In an influential article published in 1993 – 'Diaspora: generation and the ground of identity' – Boyarin and Boyarin argue that scholars of identity have inherited a tendency to refute genealogical ways of thinking about group identity from the attack that was launched at the very beginnings of Christendom in the Letters of Paul, where coming together in spirit was elevated above any genealogical bodily connection between people. But, they point out, there has been a sustained Jewish counter-discourse to this position. They wish to propose a notion of critically grounded identity as a way to confront those forms of 'pure theory' (1993: 694) that, in line with Pauline tradition, make 'things of the body . . . less important than things of the spirit', and in which the physical connection of common descent from Abraham and the embodied practices with which that genealogy is marked off as difference are rejected in favour of a connection between people based on 'individual re-creation and entry de novo into a community of common belief' (1993: 695).

Thus in Paul was made a move toward wholeness and unity that, despite itself, unintentionally devalued what could be seen as the mimetic nature of Jewish practice so that: 'to stand for anything other than what the apostle stands for is to articulate for oneself a place of difference, which has already implicitly been associated with discord and disorder' (Boyarin and Boyarin, 1993: 696). The drive to sameness in Pauline discourse can also, Boyarin and Boyarin argue, be seen in the politics of group relations. As Paul became the source of Christianity *tout court*, the 'coercive move toward sameness' became directed to the Jews: 'the place of difference increasingly became the Jewish place and the Jew the sign of discord and disorder in the Christian polity' (1993: 697). This is despite the fact that Paul intended to include the Jews, and, in an important sense, saw his position as the fulfilment of Judaism.

Boyarin and Boyarin argue that the right to remain different has to be kept at the level of practice and descent, for otherwise the Jew risks becoming an ideal which works to deprive Jews of their difference. Their position is one that attempts to avoid the idealisation of difference, and rejects, for the same reasons, those well-intentioned theoretical positions that regard as always and necessarily pernicious those communities that uphold their specialness (1993: 698).[7] Their purpose, then, is to articulate a modern, but non-Zionist, Jewish subject:

> We suggest that a Jewish subject position founded on generational connection and its attendant anamnestic responsibilities and pleasures affords the possibility of a flexible and nonhermetic critical Jewish identity. (1993: 701)

No doubt Sartre's *Anti-Semite and Jew* (1965) would be cast from such a position as one of the attempts to idealise Jewishness, not in the sense of valorising Jews, but in the sense of diluting difference through an attempt to avoid adopting a position which feels too close to that of the racist or anti-Semite. Sartre's repeated attempt to employ existentialist concepts in such a way that continually denies grounds of difference is a means to avoid anti-Semitism, but comes perilously close to the Pauline form of idealisation. Thus his work would be situated in what Boyarin and Boyarin would see as a Platonic mode of claiming (spiritual) equivalence between human subjects: 'the valorisation of any kind of elective and affective connection between people over against the claims of physical kinship is deeply embedded in the Platonic value system Europe has largely inherited from Paul' (1993: 702). But genealogical ways of thinking about identity, the Boyarins are suggesting, need not be immediately saddled with the baggage of racist discourse. Indeed,

> The insistence on the value of bodily connection and embodied practice that is emblematic of Judaism since Paul thus has significant critical power vis a vis the isolating and disembodying direction of Western idealist philosophies. (1993: 705–6)

For Boyarin and Boyarin, therefore, one needs to think about the generational forms of mimicry that take place within all the complexities and contingencies of the diaspora. Their position shares an affinity with Butler's emphasis on performativity and the mimicry of ideals, but the contextualisation is different. This is due, in part, I believe, to the differences

---

7 Thus they criticise, for example, the work of Jean-Luc Nancy – especially *The Inoperative Community* (1991) – because he seems to suggest that since violence that has been done in the name of communities and solidarity, any already existing community is relegated beyond consideration by virtue of its existence to a world we have lost or never existed.

between thinking about gender and sexuality as performed identities, and the thinking about religious and ethnic identities. It seems that feminist theory is entering a stage in which the difficult work of thinking about the relationship and differences *between* different modes of difference – class, 'race', sexuality, ethnicity – demands to be thought of as a central issue, so that the list does not substitute for the complexities of engagement. The recent debate between Butler and Nancy Fraser in the journal *New Left Review* (N. Fraser, 1998), is, in part, about the possibility of thinking through the construction and relationships between differences (here, between class and sexuality), and, indeed, the debate between Rita Felski and other feminist scholars in the journal *Signs* (Felski, 1997) on the topic of difference, similarly suggests that this is a new agenda for feminist thought. In the next section I will pursue these questions in relation to my specific genealogy of Butler's use of mimesis.

Mimesis in a new agenda

How does this discussion of mimesis in relation to the thinking of anti-Semitism and Judaism give a context in which to return to Butler's work? Reversing the manoeuvre of the Boyarins we are now in a position to ask, what does this revisiting tell us about gender and mimesis? The notion of cultural survival is highlighted, I think rightly, by these discussions. For both Adorno and Horkheimer, and for Sartre, this was also a very real issue at stake, as they pondered how recovery from the atrocities of the Second World War was to take place. The way in which Butler thinks of cultural survival is less overt, but, nevertheless, it is a place from which to think about the role of several key turns and distinctions in her work. In pursuing this term, however, I think it is important to give some consideration to the different domains that have been brought together in my earlier discussion. How similar is the use of the term mimesis in the work of various authors? Can the term 'cultural survival' smooth over any differences in the ways these writers are using the term?

There are several ways in which Butler's use of the term mimicry parts company with that of Adorno and Horkheimer. Not least because of the naturalisation of mimesis in the latter's work. For Adorno and Horkheimer, mimesis is posited as a foundational and natural process. For them, mimetic behaviour is positioned as almost equivalent to a notion of accommodation such as one finds in Piagetian developmental psychology, a *natural* mode of human adaptation to being in the world. In the context of capitalism, however, and this is their contribution, this natural developmental process is suppressed, and where it erupts it takes on a distorted form with potentially fascistic qualities. But whereas, in Adorno and Horkheimer, repressed mimesis is the eruption of a natural process suppressed by the socio-economic order, in Butler there is nothing 'natural' about the process of mimicking either 'the norms' or 'the other'.

A second reason why one would expect a different twist in the concept of mimesis in Adorno and Horkheimer from its usage in Butler is because of the different theoretical inheritances of each, and in particular the different understandings of power that these entail. Adorno and Horkheimer write within their Frankfurt School context, premised on beliefs and utilising terms that would be anathema to Butler's Foucauldian persuasion. In Butler, economic contexts are downplayed, if not altogether absent,[8] but it is certainly the case that although the socio-economic context does not suppress a *natural* behaviour, certain modes of mimicry either uphold or deviate from the contexts in which they are performed. In this sense, Butler is interested in processes of domination, just as Adorno and Horkheimer were. Moreover, the notion of cultural survival points to the importance of hegemony in Butler's thesis, and this in itself is instructive. Butler speaks of hegemonic norms which are mimed in the process of subjectification and identification, and implies that the mimesis of these norms is difficult – if not impossible – to avoid. The leftist framework is betrayed both by the term hegemony, and by Butler's usage of Althusserian notion of interpellation. More than merely indicative of a sense of the power relations within which mimesis occurs, these terms, taken together with the argument that gender is oftentimes a matter of cultural survival within a 'situation of duress', imply that mimesis is a strategic mode of 'going on' with a specific socio-cultural context, in which other corporeal styles are abjected, foreclosed or simply too risky.[9] Within the hegemonic heterosexual project, subjects are produced that are engaged in a repeated endeavour to imitate the idealisations of that project (Butler, 1993a: 125); those whose desires take them outside that project are obliged to monitor the safety of the spaces they inhabit before corporeal styles and gender performances transgress or stretch the hegemonic regulatory norms.

The embodied repetition of hegemonic norms needs to be understood within the context of these power relations and their various modes of policing, because it needs to remain clear that Butler's account attends to the differing modes of survival for which mimetic behaviour occurs. Several factors can influence the degree to which heterosexualised genders are performed; these can concern perceptions of personal safety, for example, but they may also concern one's subjective need or desire to mark oneself as gendered. The embodied repetition of the non-hegemonic (in all countries bar Israel, and perhaps even there) identity – 'Jew' – of which Boyarin and Boyarin speak, resonates strongly with Butler's arguments,

8 In the *New Left Review* debate, mentioned earlier, Butler herself has turned attention to this question (1998) where she argues that the regulation of sexuality is central to the functioning of political economy. See also the reply by Nancy Fraser in the same volume.

9 These alternatives have different psychoanalytic implications. In the last the decision can be conscious risk assessment; foreclosure implies something more than repression, a situation where the alternatives could not be brought to consciousness because they do not reside in the psyche; with abjection, there may be the possibility of recovery of the alternative possibility from the unconscious.

as they recognise, and in terms of religious ritualised bodily movements and markings this is especially the case. Jonathan Boyarin has illustrated how his own partaking in Jewish communal activities has had just this quality; that is, an embodied marking out, the performance of which can be more or less strongly marked according to one's response to changing situations and one's changing sense of requiring community bonds. Mimicry across a generational boundary is attractive, comforting even, but also, to differing degrees, and particularly as one reaches adulthood, a matter of felt need within contexts, a fact that becomes particularly apparent when one travels and reconnects to the 'community' in different locales (see Boyarin, 1996).

In this, there is a similarity between the work of Boyarin and Boyarin and that of Butler. There is, however, a sense in which the mimicry of which Boyarin and Boyarin speak approaches a functionalist sociological notion of cultural reproduction, and is related, in turn, to a notion of respect for one's ancestry, especially in terms of their sufferings, that manifests in an embodied remembrance of one's genealogically given positionality. The 'double mark of the male Jew', as they term it, involves embodied remembrance, both by altering the body (of one's sons), but also by displaying embodied difference (oneself); even if the marking practice of circumcision unites Jews in terms of numbers, they point out that it is the wearing of the yarmulke, the (relatively removable) headcovering, that marks the body of the Jew Jewish for spectators (Boyarin and Boyarin, 1995). In Butler, by contrast, gender performance is regarded less as a means of being faithful to gendered cultural inheritances, an obedience to traditions out of generational respect, and more in terms of the disciplinary mechanisms that surround divergence from those norms of performance: 'acting out of line with heterosexual norms brings with it ostracism, punishment and violence' (1991: 24). Cultural survival is therefore not that which it is for the Boyarins – a form of remembering and reproduction borne out of a genealogically given selfhood, and a desire to remain faithful – but is presented in Butler as a more regulated mode of conformity that is less conscious of its positivity and its need for reproduction and more conscious of the shaming and punishments (and less often, but sometimes, of the pleasures[10]) of deviating from those norms. It is a training, in the Foucauldian sense, that is disciplinary. In considering the ways in which cultural ideals of womanhood operate to discipline women's movement through space, the presentation of her body, and her use of facial expressions, Sandra Lee Bartky (1988) has argued the sense in which femininity is not an insignificant matter of sexual difference, but a matter of disciplinary power, in Foucault's sense that women become self-regulating subjected subjects, but also in the sense that performing differently carries

10 The quotation referring to punishments for transgressing heterosexual norms continues 'not to mention the transgressive pleasures produced by those very prohibitions' (Butler, 1991: 24).

regulative punishments, especially, in Bartky's examples, punishments relating to sexual availability and reputation.[11]

Although it might be attractive and even fruitful to think of gender as a mode of belonging in which each socially designated female conforms out of generationally given respect for her maternal line (is it our mothers we would disappoint if we were able to 'give up' gender?), gender feels, from the point of view of this discussion, and paradoxically perhaps, much less 'in the family' than religious or ethnic affiliation. Moreover, whilst Judaism of course entails rules and regulations, as well as means for the casting out, disciplining and disowning, of those who do not conform, Boyarin and Boyarin are focussing upon the sense in which the maintenance of Jewish ways of life is a matter of the positive survival of Judaism within a diasporised context. In order for Jews to survive *qua* Jews, such repetition must occur. In Butler, by contrast, the survival is less that of a culture within another culture, and more the survival of the self within a (gender-regulated) culture. Taking up the abject position 'beyond' gender is at the linguistic level a complex manoeuvre, she suggests, (hence the reference to psychotic speech, earlier[12]), whereas in our multi-faith world, one might imagine, altering one's religious affiliation, or moving in and out of an intensity of affect around it, is a *communicable* – if by no means trivial – matter.

It feels somewhat misguided to allow the discussion to move in such a direction, as if it were possible to compare either 'religious' or ethnic affiliation with gender allegiance. These authors are aware that the performance of ethnic or religious affiliation can be the site for gender performance (and vice versa) so that, for example, the Boyarins write: 'the marks we ground our selfhood in are only imposed on and available to *male* Jews – although in nonorthodox communities women are increasingly adopting the yarmulke – and hence they are inescapably inscriptions of hierarchising and reifying difference' (1995: 17, emphasis added). Moreover, there are evidently dangers and costs involved in the altering of ethnic and religious affiliation, as there are gender. The point is not to criticise the authors' awareness of such complexities, but to suggest that the similarity that the

---

11 There would be another line of discussion to pursue here that would take this feminist work on Foucault's concept of disciplinary power back into conversation with Adorno and Horkheimer's *Dialectic of Enlightenment* in order to pursue the argument there that women are included in the thesis presented there by virtue of their exclusion from philosophical discourse. As argued by Andrew Hewitt, 'women are instrumentalised as the representatives of the possibility of exclusion understood as an escape from the all inclusive system of power . . . the initial – and damning – exclusion of women from the philosophical project is reworked as a potential exemption from the totality both of power as ontologised domination and of reason as a system of closure' (1994: 147). Hewitt's excellent article explores the contradictions and potentials of attempting to think about the place of women in relation to the argument of *Dialectic of Enlightenment*.

12 And despite the fact that gay communities do attempt to subvert these, using 'inappropriately' gendered pronouns, etc.

Boyarins draw between their position and that of Butler's may be a little rushed. The mimicry of the norms of one's (persecuted) cultural allegiance is a matter of enabling the survival of one's genealogy throughout, at least, one's own generation. The 'citation' of gender(ing) norms, however, is not posited by Butler as a means of maintaining that which our maternal line has bequeathed us, for gender is not in itself *a* culture, but is, rather, a mode of distinction that is culturally constituted. This divergence in argumentation, subtle as it may be, becomes important as it highlights the need to avoid reproducing the tendency to think ethnicity and gender as parallel and comparable processes. Such a tendency falters because it refuses to think through the modes by which 'culture', including ethnic or religious cultures, 'transport' gender within themselves, and, conversely, modes of gendering can 'transport' ethnicity.

There is a further worry that leads me via another route to argue that gender mimicry and generational ethnic mimicry need to be kept analytically separate, such that their simultaneity be better traced. This concerns the processes that Butler captures with her notion of encrypting. This relates to the use that Butler makes of Freud's writings on melancholia – in particular the way she employs a notion of encrypting the possibility of being otherwise as analogous with a melancholic encrypting of the other – which implies that in embarking upon a route of gender survival one cannot avoid encumbering a certain specific kind of psychic baggage. The performance of (either) heterosexualised gender 'carries' the abjected possibility of being the other (gender and sexuality) with it.

Interestingly, the encrypting of homosexuality within the psychic structures of heterosexuality is a process the effects of which might be likened to the role of repressed mimesis in Adorno and Horkheimer in a specific sense. It is perhaps taking liberties with the texts to suggest this connection, for there are several principles – particularly about subjectification and, relatedly, about how psyches operate within a socio-economic context – that I pass over to make this leap. Nevertheless, it would seem that one could liken the phenomena of drag as presented in Butler to the repressed mimesis of the anti-Semitic fascist in Adorno and Horkheimer. For just as in repressed mimesis the anti-Semite mimics the other in order to engage in forbidden mimetic behaviour that (s)he mistakenly or otherwise projects onto 'the Jew', in drag men impersonate the qualities they impute to feminine performance in such a way that it matters little, as Sartre also said of the relation between the anti-Semite and the Jew, whether women do truly have those qualities. Where Butler points to drag she does so, as I have explained, in order to provide an analysis of what is illuminated there; that is, crucially, the distance between sex, gender identity and gender performance. There is no *need* implied in Butler – that is, the men who impersonate women have no psychic need to engage in mimesis. Nevertheless, the notion of encrypting suggests there is a form of release – even if that release is a non-subjectively felt illumination of the heterosexual matrix. Although it is without the element of naturalised psychic need, therefore, there is an echo of repressed mimesis in drag, and, as with the rantings of the anti-Semite that mime mimesis, of the correlative sense of ambivalence toward the loved/hated object mimed.

That said, and to whatever extent one concedes this peculiar connection, my understanding is that the encrypting of the 'unviable' subject identity is fundamental to gender identity within the heterosexual matrix, principally because there is, currently, no available third sex (despite Monique Wittig's attempts to make 'lesbian' do this work). The structure of melancholia is such that the encrypting of what is 'given up' in order to mime the subject position of one's gender/sexuality requires a 'knowledge' of that forbidden other as an integral part of the process of performing the 'chosen' identity (see Benjamin, 1997), even if that knowledge is a distorted form of knowledge such as arguably one finds in those instances of drag that refuse the heterogeneity of women by miming the exaggerated 'ideal', with all the ambivalence that that implies.

In the case of ethnicity, it is more difficult to assert that there is *an* encrypted other, a comparable 'knowledge', accurate or distorted, faithful or unfaithful, that is *required* for the identification to take place. If this is the case, it would be a reason why one has to be careful about moving too quickly from the analysis of gender to that of 'race' or ethnicity. For with Butler's stress on this encrypting, there is a sense in which, in the case of gender, mimicry is a process in which the 'other', the non-mimed, is nevertheless also 'known' and carried with the mime, encrypted as, if not its opposite exactly, as its limit. The performance of gender always involves the process of abjection, renunciation, or differentiation; heterosexual femininity requires, by definition, a relation to masculinity (the desired) and homosexuality (the abjected), *as formational*. As Butler describes it, the constitution of gender is melancholic, impossible because it carries its alleged 'opposite' with it. However, in the Boyarins' notion of mimicry across generations, there is no *necessary* knowledge of 'the other' implied. Even in a multi-religious community one can be a practising Catholic, say, without the 'knowledge' of how, by which embodied citations, one would be a practising Jew. The mimicry of one's generationally given knowledge and practices requires knowledge of the prior generation and its practices, but the ethnic self does not seem to rely for its very *constitution* upon knowledge of 'other' ethnicities or religions, even if these religions themselves historically and discursively defined themselves through the boundaries and connections they form with each other. The melancholias that may accompany the ethnic mimesis of which the Boyarins write, are therefore, *psychically* speaking, of a different order from those that concern gender, based as they are on generational reproduction of a faith and sense of *lineage* (be that more or less embodied) rather than on the reproduction or 'citation' of a *line of differentiation* (masculine/feminine), each side of which is defined by even as it rejects its opposite.

There is an important point that flows from these questions and which concerns the relationship between citation and self-constitution. The various writers brought together here do not lead one to regard every instance of mimesis as self-constitutional. Is it the case, for example, that the rantings that link the anti-Semite to a tradition of anti-Semitism, as Sartre describes, are as self-constitutive as the mimicry of gender citation? And how are these instances of mimesis to be understood in relation to the mimesis of one's own ethnic or religious genealogy?

Butler has a notion of citation that links her thesis explicitly with the maintenance of tradition, and that uses the philosophical perspective developed in relation to subjectification and gender to speak about racist speech. In an argument reminiscent of Sartre she writes in reference to racist speech:

> [N]either the law nor hate speech are uttered exclusively by a single subject. The racial slur is always cited from elsewhere, and in the speaking of it, one chimes in with a chorus of racists, producing at that moment the linguistic occasion for an imagined relation to an historically transmitted community of racists. (1997a: 80)

This form of citation, therefore, is one that provides a self-identity that is not singular but, due to its citational nature, a placing of the self within a racist community and tradition. In doing so, one positions others in order to construct and bolster one's own sense of superiority as a racialised subject: both those who have previously agreed, and those of whom one speaks. Adorno and Horkheimer suggest something to this effect when they speak of the anti-Semite engaging in a mimesis of those whom he judges as anachronistically mimetic; that is, when the anti-Semite gives in to a suppressed desire to engage in mimesis himself. The anti-Semite produces an image of the Other that enables a self-constitution as not-Other, even at the very moment that he proceeds to enact that Other: 'they are so awful', he says, 'they are just like this, just as I am being now'. In Butler, however, racist citation is not given the self-constitutional role that is the citation of gender norms. The imagined relation to a tradition of racists may be a situating of the self, an aesthetics of existence, but its power emanates from the imagined community that gives one an imagined place amongst others, rather than, as is the scenario with gender, where the subject is engaged in a performative constitution of oneself as a 'one'. It is, indeed, a source of political hope that this is the case; moving beyond racist speech is not about moving beyond linguistic resources that make one 'culturally intelligible'.[13] Although the hope for absolute non-repetition of racism, the dream of censorship, is not viable, for repetition will occur, Butler suggests, the question is how that repetition can be different, or interrupted. The interruption of gender norms is similarly posited by Butler as a possibility; indeed, her whole thesis is to stress the temporal, repeated and therefore interruptable nature of gender performativity (the question of 'agency' is for her about the possibility of resignification). However,

---

13 Except perhaps in the most racist of societies where – it is an empirical question – the possibility of 'moving beyond' is so tightly constricted that one is rendered unintelligible.

even if such an interruption is 'visible' in certain cultural phenomena, such as drag, is not comparable to the way in which Butler speaks of interrupting racist hate speech. This is because the citation of the racist slur is not self-constitutional in the way that gender (currently) is, in the sense that the discursive possibilities for moving 'beyond' gender are not as readily available as are those of moving beyond a racist enunciative mode.[14] This relates to the notion that becoming gendered is about being 'culturally intelligible'; that 'sex' is not what one has or is, but 'how "one" becomes viable at all' (see Butler, 1993a: 2). The difference turns on the possibility of surviving outside that subject position. Again, the notion of 'cultural survival', together with the intentions and visions of the speaker, become all important. In each instance, therefore, it seems pertinent to enquire whether citations are self-constitutional, or whether they are 'merely' citations, for it is exactly the connection between subjectivities, embodiment and modes of affiliation through citation that these writers help illuminate.

It may be that I have set up these questions falsely here. Is it ever possible to think about gender outside the question of ethnicity? Hegemonic ideals must surely be simultaneously both 'about' gender and 'about' ethnicity, since the mimesis of hegemonic ideals, the 'style of the flesh' they involve, varies both within and between cultures. 'Masculinity' and 'femininity' do not exist 'without' or 'outside' or 'before' ethnicity. And yet it feels politically important for an anti-racist position to attempt to distinguish between self-constitutive mimesis and mimesis that is not related to subject-constitution. The political thrust of this work is to reach a point where one is able to contemplate how subjects are constituted in relation to notions of themselves and others, but, more so, how these are mobile and changing relations. But does this make the projects of anti-racism and feminism the same? Isn't there something different, presently at least, about attempting to resignify ethnicities in an anti-racist manner, as opposed to attempting to resignify gender differentiations?

Indeed, the importance of reading Butler with Boyarin and Boyarin against earlier work on mimesis and anti-Semitism revolves around the issue of thinking about subjectivities in relation to realigning political commitment and cultural identities. The work of Boyarin and Boyarin is crucially about how one might be able to think ethnic difference without falling into racism. They do so by arguing that it is possible to rescue the notion of personal genealogy from its racist overtones. The Boyarins pose their argument against, *inter alia*, that of Jean-Luc Nancy, whose work, they suggest, has as its political impulse the refusal of modes of argumentation that have fascistic potentialities, but whose argument leads him to repeat a Pauline utopia that poses the coming together of political

14 Note that this sentence concerns moving beyond a racist position, not moving beyond ethnic affiliations. Moving beyond ethnicity may be as difficult as moving beyond gender, and the questions are surely entwined on the personal level.

groupings as a necessarily disembodied connection. In stressing the citational but embodied nature of identities, the Boyarins join Butler in positing a political hope that affiliations, genealogical or not, can be – and frequently, *are* – wrested from any associations of inscribed destiny.[15]

This sense of a joint purpose – between the feminism of Butler and the anti-racism of Boyarin and Boyarin – is undoubtedly important. Clearly, an attention to the constitution of identities and how they might be realigned or subverted links these authors' work. However, I am arguing that one might hesitate a little longer before endorsing the suggestion that the Boyarins make. That is, they argue that one might think of gender along the same lines as they speak of Jewish communities, as a sort of 'diasporised gender identity':

> We suggest that a diasporised gender identity is both possible and positive. Being a woman is a special kind of being, and there are aspects of life and practice that insist on and celebrate that speciality. (1993: 721)

The impulse to make this connection is made clear; that is, the notion of diaspora in relation to gender emphasises the unfixed nature of identity and bodies, and avoids dualisms, such that 'we can substitute partially Jewish, partially Greek, bodies that are sometimes gendered and sometimes not' (Boyarin and Boyarin, 1993: 721). However, for the reasons discussed previously, I would wish to resist this manoeuvre: the similarities in thinking about embodied performances do not suffice. As the Boyarins themselves suggest, there is an issue of land or territory involved here. The notion of diaspora involves a notion of a remembered or promised land (Gilroy, 1993; Clifford, 1997), and frequently an imagined 'homing' sentiment (Brah, 1996). The special position that Jewish communities have as models of thinking more flexibly about the term 'diaspora' (see, e.g., Gilroy, 1996) is due to the way it can act as a model for prising open the 'deadly discourse' that couples 'race and space' (Boyarin and Boyarin, 1993: 714):

> Cultures, as well as identities, are constantly being re-made. While this is true of all cultures, diasporic Jewish culture lays it bare because of the impossibility of a natural association between this people and a particular land. (1993: 721)

While gender is indeed a marked or 'special' way of being, it does not have this association or even disassociation with a land. (For although the use of space is certainly gendered, there is not *a* place, or *a* land, that is mythically

15 For this reason the idea of 'tradition' that Boyarin and Boyarin use needs to be repeatedly problematised. When 'tradition' in Boyarin and Boyarin is likened to the position of hegemonic norms in Butler, as this discussion implies it must be, it becomes perhaps more clear that any notion of 'tradition' needs always to be related to the mode of remembrance, and the circumstances of its citation and performance, in order to avoid a conservative position that simply sees tradition as that which has been repeated and passed on, and to keep an emphasis on the contingency and complexities of both memory and performance. Very often it is through the lens of present circumstances and situations that the repetition of past traditions is deemed important.

or otherwise, 'home' to all women.) It is preferable, therefore, to connect ethnicity and religion and gender on the lines of embodied performativity, watching how modes of mimicry and citation occur in the forms of embodiment that produce effective subjects, but without rushing to assimilating them. It is for this reason perhaps that Butler has spoken of ways of thinking of race and gender non-sequentially, in terms of how one may operate as the 'unmarked background' of the other.

Conclusion

Although mimesis as a concept has a history of marking a division between the real and the copy, the work that I have discussed breaks with this sense in order to point to the norms that govern people's modes of subjectification and affiliation. In this chapter I have argued that there is a way of resituating Butler's work as a feminist inheritance of attempts to theorise anti-Semitism in the post-Second World War period. This is not a straightforward trajectory, since although Sartre's work was clearly important for Butler's intellectual development, these would not be connections that she herself would emphasise, nor maybe even accept as important. Nevertheless, through the concept of mimesis, I have suggested that it is possible and fruitful to rethink Butler's position alongside those who employed the term in ways that are related but that involve crucially different assumptions. What has arisen from such an exercise is the importance of the issue of cultural survival, which throws a certain light on Butler's sociopolitical vision. Cultural survival is a concept which relates to Butler's retention of a notion of hegemony, such that the interpellation of subjects of which she speaks is not a process that is either natural or foreclosed in any given culture, but is a process which takes on the appearance of being both, because it takes place in a disciplinary context.

The texts considered here illustrate the sense in which mimesis is a concept that has been employed in different ways, such that, although I have focussed upon the concern to think of non-essentialist identities in terms of embodied performativity – a concern that is shared by Butler and the recent work of Boyarin and Boyarin – I would also argue that the earlier text of Adorno and Horkheimer and that of Sartre indicate the importance of clarifying just how these contemporary uses of the concept are to be related to former issues of the natural and the artificial, to repression and freedom, to authenticity and inauthenticity, as well as to questions of socio-economic context and cultural traditions.

The question of mimesis in this new agenda is significant, therefore, in its reutilisation of the question of mimesis in a way that moves the focus away from assumptions of the repressed natural process that underpinned Adorno and Horkheimer's thesis, and towards the complex manoeuvres of continued performances and continued 'tradition', away from judgements of authenticity and towards the reasons why people maintain certain

embodied subjectivities. Such a perspective raises the questions of generational relations, of foreclosed possibilities and of affective attachments to
identity that reach beyond the Nietzschean sense of a wounded attachment.
A focus on the responsibilities and pressures of 'cultural survival' seems
fruitful as a guiding concept in this exploration of the connections between
identification, affiliation and the power contexts within which mimesis, as a
form of repetition or 'citation', occurs.

6

ESSENTIALISM AND EMBODIMENT:
THE POLITICS BEHIND THE PARANOIA

Assessing where we are now, it seems to me that feminism stands less in
danger of the totalizing tendencies of feminists than of an increasingly
paralyzing anxiety over falling (from what grace?) into ethnocentrism
or 'essentialism.' (The often-present implication that such a fall indicates deeply conservative and racist tendencies, of course, intensifies
such anxieties). (Susan Bordo, 1993: 225)

In this chapter I address certain questions that have hovered at the margins
of the previous chapters and that turn on the concept of difference in
relation to the question of embodiment. Several feminist theorists and
philosophers have been engaged of late in discussions about how to adequately theorise the body. From a range of disciplines, feminists meet at the
site of the body, concerned to understand the power constellations that are
constructed there, refusing to accept the body as 'merely' natural, or the
'given' on which power or domination does its work, and agreeing if only
upon a commitment to dispose with the mind/body dualism that Western
thought has inherited from Descartes' meditations some three centuries ago.
I wish to place that feminist concern with the theorisation of the body in the
light of the argument of this book. I do so by revisiting the notion of
essentialism, as a, if not the, primary target against which theoretical
feminist work on embodiment is set, in order to follow through Diana Fuss'
(1989) arguments that essentialism might be best understood as a term
descriptive of political strategy, and that, when it is so understood, the
feminist response to it may move beyond one which privileges the substi-
tution of the essentialising terms with a term such as 'social construction'. I
wish to argue that when essentialist arguments are regarded as *deployed* in
this way, as mobilised within various power/knowledge networks, one's
sense of them may be very different. Furthermore, I argue that embodiment
has remained a problematic for feminism, not only due to a continuing
legacy of Cartesian thinking, but also because, at the end of this century,
feminism's political imagination has become – properly and necessarily –
entwined with thinking not just sexual difference but a variety of modes of
difference in a way that is non-essentialising. That is, essentialism is not just
a concern for those critiquing the forms of knowledge that work to maintain
gender equality, but it is similarly a concern for all those wishing to
challenge modes of knowing that seek to fix and to categorise people hierarchically. Moreover, in making these connections one highlights the sense

in which being able to speak of embodiment in terms that acknowledge its import for subjectivity may have a political importance that is missed by those who fear talk of the body as essentialist and reject it on those grounds.

The chapter is structured in four sections. In the first I elaborate upon Diana Fuss' influential arguments, arguing that her path-breaking intervention implies a further set of questions that in some ways precede those that she investigated. The section argues that if we pursue the power of the term 'essentialism', its ability to rouse the argument and anxiety within feminist theoretical fora of which Susan Bordo writes in the quotation that heads this chapter, one suspects that the issues it subtends concern not only the Cartesian legacy in its various permutations, but also events that are much closer to the present and that are those of twentieth-century forms of politics. Indeed, the movements of Fuss' own book, and the way the debates have been posed in feminist work, suggest as much. I argue that the issue of essentialism in feminist thought has become, and for good reason, entangled with endeavours to think both 'race' and gender. Following this cue the chapter addresses the dangers of essentialism and the question of embodiment by considering work outside specifically feminist debates, in order to argue that feminist work shares a concern with other thinkers who have addressed these issues in their writings, and in ways that tie feminist questions to issues of 'race' in a particular way, one that is infused with the history of the twentieth century. I discuss, in turn, the work of Emmanuel Levinas and of Frantz Fanon, with specific foci in mind. In particular, these writers enable a consideration of the dangers of disavowing a sense of embodiment, of moving 'culture' or 'social' into the place of 'biology' or 'nature' as if that were a solution to the issues in hand. These second and third sections argue that much more rests on our articulation than this solution comprehends. That is, how to respond to the need to acknowledge felt embodiment as central to identity, while simultaneously placing that sense within a critique that refuses to replicate the divisions that feminist theory has managed so well to question. I want to argue that the juxta-position of feminist debates with these older texts adds weight to the feminist arguments, because feminist debates are currently exploring how one might be able to both *recognise the affect of embodiment while simul-taneously recognising the production of that affect*. I argue that these concerns can be placed within the terms of Levinas' notion of proximity and the 'mediation' of Fanon's historicity. Such considerations then enable me to return in the fourth section to feminist theory, and in particular to the work on the thinking of anti-essentialist models of embodiment and to see how noticing the shadow of these concerns might retrain one's sight on feminist theory's engagements with 'embodiment'.

Essentialism and paranoia

Diana Fuss' (1989) *Essentially Speaking: Feminism, Nature and Difference* made an important intervention into feminist debate, setting out her argument that the essentialist/constructionist debate within feminist theory had 'foreclosed more ambitious investigations of specificity and difference by fostering a certain *paranoia* around the perceived threat of essentialism' (1989: 1, emphasis added). It is this sense of paranoia that interests me, for it suggests a prior question to the direction Fuss takes: what is it about essentialism that has the ability to make feminist theorists feel paranoid? Before I pursue that thought, however, let me summarise Fuss' position.

The idea that constructionism offers a theoretical critique and alternative to esssentialist modes of thought may be, Fuss argues, an assumption that avoids tackling the conceptual difficulties within that very critique: the triumphant transcendence of essentialism may be illusory. For although constructionism attempts to dismiss essentialism through an emphasis on complex discursive strategies that produce essences as effects, the constructionist position itself depends upon being able to recognise and to avoid essentialism. Fuss' argument is that the possibilities for both recognition and avoidance are doubtful. First, she argues that 'there is no essence to essentialism' (1989: 4), and to treat the term as if there were is to engage in the construction of essence as irreducible. As with the paranoid, Fuss seems to suggest, constructionists in their various guises construct that of which they live in fear. Essentialism is not 'always already knowable' (1989: 21). It takes many forms; and the conservatism or radicalism of essentialist modes of thought 'depends to a significant degree, on who is utilizing it, how it is deployed, and where its effects are concentrated' (1989: 20). Moreover, I take Fuss to mean that the accusation of essentialism, as much as the essentialist modes of thinking themselves, should be regarded as a term deployed within strategies, the politics of which may have a full range.

Secondly, the possibility of avoiding essentialist modes of thought may be more problematic than many 'constructionist' arguments allow. The pluralising of terms – feminisms, women, histories, deconstructionisms – has been an attempt to signal anti-essentialism, as have been the various attempts to shift attention on to the social and linguistic and away from the ahistorical conceptions of the natural. However, these manoeuvres, Fuss argues, frequently amount to a deferral of the encounter with essentialism, rather than its avoidance altogether. In themselves, they do not necessarily avoid essentialism, for it is an assumption that 'nature and fixity go together (naturally) just as sociality and change go together (naturally). In other words, it may be time to ask whether essences can change and whether constructions can be normative' (1989: 6). Questioning the anti-essentialism purportedly found in Lacanian psychoanalysis and in Derridean deconstruction, Fuss wishes to disrupt the polarities within this debate: for, she believes, essentialism and constructionism are co-implicated with one other (1989: xii). The suggestion that has been made from some quarters, furthermore, that one might 'employ' essentialism politically – that essence may have to be 'risked' (Heath, 1978: 99) as a feminist strategy – implies that essentialism is a tool or method that one can utilise or avoid. However, to focus on one conceptual element 'within' a wider strategy, in this way, obscures the fact that it is always the strategy itself that is risky – its configurations, contexts and its timing – not any one aspect of its argumentation.

Agreeing with these points, I want to argue that there is an issue which precedes Fuss' discussion and which relates to her statement about 'paranoia'. My interest is in pursuing this term – essentialism – one that has been for feminism 'the prime idiom of intellectual terrorism and the privileged instrument of political orthodoxy . . . endowed . . . with the power to reduce to silence, to excommunicate, to consign to oblivion' (Schor, 1989: 40). If one accepts Fuss' argument that notions of essences can take many forms and can contribute to many different strategies, the politics of which one cannot know in advance, then the question becomes: why has essentialism been so feared? If its effects and intentions have the possibility of being innocuous, how is it that the term essentialism has bred such 'irrational fear', or, in Bordo's words, such 'paralyzing anxiety', around itself? I want to argue that essentialist modes of thought are feared in part because essences imply fixity and therefore the impossibility of change, such that the fate of feminism is frustration. That feminist argumentation itself may mimic essentialist modes of thought engenders the possibility that feminism itself prevents its own realisation: that feminism may unwittingly be a suicidal project. This issue animates the debates that seek to avoid essentialism or to 'use' – but not be taken in by – essentialism. But, more than this, I want to suggest that in contemporary feminist debates, essentialist modes of thought are also 'feared' because of an awareness of that which has historically been carried out in political complexes that have deployed essentialism as a mode of hierarchical classification. And it is for this reason, I would suggest, that it is particularly at the site of the body and around questions of 'race' and feminism that the essentialism debate takes place. For constructionists, as Fuss summarises, 'the body is never simply there, rather it is composed of a network of effects continually subject to sociopolitical determination. The body is "always already" culturally mapped; it never exists in a pure or uncoded state' (1989: 5–6). If the 'social' is always privileged over the 'natural' in constructionist accounts – even when the shape of argument may not be dramatically altered and may need, consequently, more thought – it is, I believe, in part because such a privileging enables a distance to be taken from those times when bodies were so dramatically essentialised, when people were reduced to an essence as part of an order that placed them within cruel and deadly hierarchies.

My argument, therefore, is that although there has been a tendency in feminist theory and philosophy to recount the essentialism debate as an abstract one that begins with Platonic and Aristotelian attitudes to women or as a legacy of Cartesian meditations and Enlightenment reifications, there are twentieth-century formulations and legacies to which feminist theory is also responding. Indeed, the direction of both Spelman's and Fuss's books suggests that the debate about essentialism is also a debate about the place of 'race' in feminist thought, as each of them moves her discussion to encompass, *inter alia*, the possibilities of thinking 'race' non-essentially. The fear of essentialism that feminist thought responds to is, *in part*, therefore, a response to the twentieth century and to the political contexts which have encompassed the deployment of essentialist racist ideas. The paranoia that one finds in feminism, that of which Fuss writes, is paranoia in the sense that it constructs its object of fear while at the same time believing itself to be merely responding to it, but, furthermore, it is paranoia because its fear is actually of something else, something wider, of which a certain way of speaking or mode of address is metonymic. That something else is, at least in part, I am suggesting, the twentieth century's experiences of hierarchical racisms. The fear is that feminist theory might be engaging itself in ways of theorising and arguing that themselves replicate or resonate with the essentialist ways of thinking that have wrought so much damage. Thus the debate on essentialism is tied up with the question of how feminism can embrace all women without unwittingly reinforcing dangerous hierarchies.[1]

For these reasons I wish to write about essentialism by pulling our attention 'backwards' – not as far back as Plato or even Descartes – but to a couple of key writers of this century who were engaged with thinking through and beyond essentialism. My position is one that takes seriously Fuss' argument that one should approach essentialism as a deployment, that consequently it is not a case of ever truly being able to denounce, let alone avoid, simply by 'crying "essentialism"' (1989: 21). Instead, it is crucial to monitor the way in which ideas about the body, categorisation and possibilties of change are made to function within particular configurations. These are highly political terms, and the way in which they are set to work may take many different forms.

I wish to engage in this debate in order to reach a point in the discussion that is able to address the question of embodiment as a current concern of feminism within a twentieth-century history of racism. The debate is infrequently related to the context in which I am placing it here – Fuss' own later work (e.g. 1994) is one exception – and doing so makes one think, I believe, rather differently about the debate's purpose and direction. Thus, even if my strong argument that feminism is responding indirectly to the deployment of essentialism within fascistic and racist political complexes is overplayed, there is a weaker and less controversial version, which is that something provocative might emerge from attempting the conversation.

My first provocation is to argue that feminism has too quickly associated any talk of the body as pertaining to nature, biologism and essentialism. There is a risk that feminist attempts to develop anti-essentialist modes of

---

1 Schor suggests that the critique of false universalism of essentialist thought has been in large part a feminist endeavour which has arisen from discourses of 'black, Chicana, lesbian, first and third world feminist activists' (1989: 42).

thought have subsumed 'the body' beneath a notion of 'the social' or 'culture' or 'discourse' or 'ideology' – the differences depend upon the theoretical proclivities of the writer – in such a way that the experience of embodiment is understood as, through and through, social, cultural, discursive or ideological. I am not the first to make such a point, but I want to argue, further, that there is a risk that this manoeuvre, the motivation for which is completely laudable, may have the opposite effect from its intention. By denouncing talk of the experience of embodiment as a basis of identity, by associating 'body-talk' with anti-social constructionism and as 'risking essentialism', the experience of embodiment is left open to any articulation. I mean this in the sense that there is an intended alienation that has long been part of the importance and power of feminist intervention, a punctuation which raises a question mark over how women (first, but theoretically everyone) experience their embodiment. (Along the lines of: *why* do you experience your body as too fat, or too thin? *Why* do you think beautiful requires the modifications you ritually, expensively, painfully pursue? And so on.) But in the attempted dissociation from hierarchical modes of classification, in the attempt to argue that one's experience of the body does not 'belong' to oneself, that there are ideological forces at work on our most intimate perceptions of our bodies, there remains a danger that the body becomes a site for alternative accounts. Alternative accounts, that is, that appeal to or explain embodied experience, including those that mobilise essentialism within politically reactionary strategies. In this chapter I want to follow an argument to this effect made by Emmanuel Levinas, in order to make the argument that contemporary feminism's task in this debate can be regarded as one that takes up the challenges of this century in the sense that fascism's appeal to bodies signals that the experience of embodiment, and a sense of descent, have been used in political deployments that take advantage of scenarios where embodiment has been unaddressed or denied. Seeking to avoid a situation whereby the removal of experienced embodiment *tout court* leaves feminist theory unable to respond to those who would appeal to the body as a certain Truth, therefore makes it – and has made it – encumbant upon feminist theorists to search for another mode of intervention.

My second provocation is that there are good reasons why it will not do to respond to the first provocation by simply reasserting the truth of embodiment over and above cultural mediation, to swing the pendulum back, as it were, to make acceptable again an unmediated embodied experience 'below' or beyond culture. For these reasons, I turn to the work of Frantz Fanon, who, within the context of colonial racism, so powerfully portrayed the sense in which to speak of the experience of embodiment is not to assert an independence or essence to the body, but to consider the interdependence of what he terms 'bodily schemas'. The feminist theoretical work on embodiment has taken on exactly this direction, as I argue in the final section of the chapter, where I want to make explicit the significance of recent theoretical work on embodiment in terms of the explorations that are the concerns of this chapter. In the next section, I introduce those concerns through an early piece by Emmanuel Levinas that addresses the question of embodiment in relation to Hitler's fascism.

Appealing to the body: re-reading Levinas on the body and Hitlerism

There have been some creative and exciting meetings between the thought of Emmanuel Levinas and feminism, ones that illustrate the problematic nature of his masculinism and heterosexism, as well as pursuing the possibilities of a feminist appropriation of Levinasian thought (see, e.g., Chanter, 1995; Irigaray, 1986, 1991). In this section, however, I am less concerned with the uses of Levinas' philosophy for feminist theory, and more concerned to use one small early piece of Levinas' – 'The politics of Hitlerism' – in order to consider feminist theory's take on embodment 'from afar'. The questions that are urgent for feminist theory today, I am suggesting, have a deep resonance with those that were urgent for Levinas then. The theorisation of embodiment is placed, in Levinas' prophetic piece, in a highly charged political context, where the careful articulation of felt embodiment is posited as a primary task for a philosophy that is otherwise rendered impotent in the face of appeals to the body.

Writing in 1933, Levinas contemplated the question of the body in relation to the politics of Hitlerism,[2] suggesting that in order to grasp the appeal of the Nazis' version of fascism, one needs to place the body in its European context, and, in particular, in relation to the Christian notion of the soul as detachable from the body, as able 'to free itself from what has been . . . so it can regain its first virginity' (1990: 66, first published 1933). Versions of this notion that the body can be separated out from the soul – that the soul, with its different temporal existence, is superior to the mere container of the body – are maintained, according to Levinas, in the models of liberalism that early writers on democracy proposed, and that linger in our present, insofar as they posit Reason in the place of the spirit, making all bodies (theoretically) irrelevant. Reason, disembodied and in the form of the general will, represents the individual wills of the social body. So too in Marxism, insofar as the latter envisaged a breaking free – a flight – from the social relations that attempt to place the body and consciousness in a particular formation. The body has thus been regarded, in religious, political and philosophical contexts, as an obstacle, breaking the free flight of spirit, and catching it within the body (Levinas, 1990: 67, first published 1933).

To 'answer' such a tradition of thought, it does not suffice to insist that the body is 'material', to simply negate the idea of spirit; rather, Levinas

2 In the text under discussion, Levinas refers to 'the Germanic ideal' and modern Germany rather than Hitlerism, but I use this term for clarity and because the article of 1990 is entitled 'The Politics of Hitlerism'.

suggests, attention needs to be directed to the question of body more specifically through the notion of identity. The body is the primary way in which we experience the world, not just because it is 'closer and more familiar to us than the rest of the world' (1990: 68, first published 1933), but because a sense of identity – a feeling of identity between our bodies and ourselves – can be rendered acute in certain circumstances. Here Levinas turns toward the experience of pain – 'is it not the case that the sick man experiences the indivisible simplicity of his being when he turns over in his bed of suffering to find a position that gives him peace?' (1990: 68, first published 1933) – a theme to which Levinas returns in later work (e.g. in *Time & the Other* (1987), in the interviews collected as *Ethics and Infinity* (1985) and in the piece 'Useless suffering' (1988)). In his analysis of pain, he argues that man is 'backed up against Being', where there is no retreat, and pain is unbearable – it will not be borne – and in that sense 'can not one say that analysis reveals in pain the spirit's opposition to this pain, a rebellion or refusal to remain with it and consequently an attempt to go beyond it?' (1990: 68, first published 1933). The attempt is desperate, as the spirit in this sense, 'remains inelutably locked within pain' (1990: 68, first published 1933).

The body cannot be dissociated from the self, and in this sense cannot be likened to a relationship with a merely material object in the world. Any attempt to refine, and redefine the relationship of self and body in terms of a dualism, is, Levinas argues, 'to betray the originality of the very feeling from which it is appropriate to begin' (1990: 69, first published 1933). Levinas implies here that a sense of identity involves the body, definitionally, such that there is an infelicity in any attempt to subordinate the body in the name of a 'higher' identification. The way in which people respond to the challenge that such a realisation poses for Western traditional modes of thought, however, is where Levinas sees the politics of Hitlerism dovetailing with the demise of such modes of thought. If democracy relied upon a sense of the future as open to the choices of the individual, as if liberalism had (as had Christianity) the ability to tame the past through the triumph of a disembodied spirit, then Hitlerism relies upon returning a sense of that history and embodiment.

It is as if Levinas is suggesting, in a way that prefigured Adorno and Horkheimer's similar argument, that the appeal of Hitlerism was in its ability to capitalise on the disappointment that political liberalism has resulted in; for the recognition of the impossibility of flight from the body sits antagonistically with political liberalism's denial of the feeling of embodiment. Hitlerism provided a new conceptualisation in which 'to be truly oneself does not mean taking flight once more above contingent events that always remain foreign to the Self's freedom; on the contrary, it means becoming aware of the ineluctable original chain that is unique to our bodies, and above all, accepting this chaining' (1990: 69, first published 1933).

The 'chaining' to which Levinas refers here is one that chains the self to the body, and the body to blood, to heredity and, therefore, to the past.

When the image of the openness of the future upon which liberalism relies no longer comforts, when the notion that there is the possibility of the assimilation of spirits (or of wills) no longer reigns, that is the time in which the appeal of a 'society based on consanguinity', one that concretises the spirit, becomes possible (Levinas, 1990: 69, first published 1933). Moreover, the danger in regarding the future as open to man's choices is that those who steadfastly abide by such a notion become unconvinced of their own convictions, since every decision may be altered in the open future, so much so that the very ideal of freedom is rendered insecure, and the threat of Hitlerism looms. The logic of Hitlerism appeals to a sense of chaining, to a sense that the future is not open, the spirit or will is not free of the body, but is always bound to its past, anchored in flesh and blood. The choice of the citizen, under this logic, is not one that is freed from the body, nor is it one that can be altered in the future. For the person accepting his or her chaining to his/her body and the past, truth is not for contemplation from afar: it is 'under the weight of his whole existence, which includes facts on which there is no going back, that man will say his yes or his no' (1990: 70, with Levinas' masculine pronoun, first published 1933).

A further corollary of this stance, Levinas argues, is that the idea of community, under such a formulation, can only come about by blood. Rational or mystical communion between spirits – indeed, any form of community that attempts to deny the body or recreate dualisms – is positioned as suspicious, untruthful. Furthermore, the truth that National Socialism upheld was not to be shared or 'taught' exactly, for that would be to engage in another form of equalisation, or, reading Levinas back on himself, to reimpose an idea of spirit by making a community through (rational, read spiritual) conviction. The universal truth of consanguinity is characterised not by propagation of an idea, but by force, by expansion. Those who submit are universalised by the propogation of war and conquest; even as they become forcibly 'included', they do not become equal.

Levinas' point, as he says in his 1990 preface to this early piece, is that philosophy has to protect itself from leaving open this appeal of racist movements. In the preface he writes: 'We must ask ourselves if liberalism is all we need to achieve an authentic dignity for the human subject?' (1990: 63). The philosopher's task is to find a way to speak and validate the experience of embodiment in a way that does not fall into either religious or racialised modes of genealogy. Much of Levinas' life's work was arguably a philosophical attempt to think through the relation of Self to the body in ethical and political contexts. In particular, his concern to think of embodiment in relation to the question of Being, read in the light of the early article I have been discussing here, can be regarded as an attempt to allow embodiment into philosophy, and thereby into the politico-ethical realm, without replicating dualisms that will not hold and that, upon their dissolution, enable pernicious political philosophies to gain credence.

This early piece demonstrates the power of Levinas' work. The reason I utilise it here is because it illustrates how the way in which understandings of embodiment are related to the political complex in which bodies are spoken about and acted towards, as Fuss has argued. The essentialist mode of argument that was contained within Nazi Germany's regime was one which was arguably able to gain credence because its racism fostered and allowed a sense of embodiment, a sense of genealogical belonging – one that it then tied to territorial expansionist claims – that appealed so powerfully that it made other forms of political identification appear weak and ineffectual.

More than this, Levinas' arguments illustrate the connections between essentialism, embodiment and history by suggesting that the fascism of Hitler was an attempt to replace the futural abstractions and promises of liberal discourse with the material embodiment of history. Hitlerism deployed a mode of essentialising discourse, therefore, that made the flow of the blood, the physical genealogy of the person, the foundation for political and territorial programmes. On such a basis, the work of categorisation and the making of hierarchies takes place.

In current feminist theory and philosophy there is a concern that links with these issues and this history, and the 'paranoia' that surrounds debates on 'feminist essentialism' is fuelled, at least in part, I believe, by the legacy they have left intellectual thought. So the questions of sexual and racist essentialism have become entwined. In her *Imaginary Bodies: Ethics, Power and Corporeality* (1996), feminist theorist Moira Gatens argues that the need to think of identity in an anti-essentialist fashion involves one in the politics of remembering and forgetting, a statement that takes her into a discussion of exactly these issues. Noting how feminism's commitment to anti-essentialism has led to various interrogations of the way in which 'woman' or 'women' has functioned as a discursive category throughout history, Gatens notes further how that form of enquiry is close to Nietzsche's concept of genealogy, and that this connection, as I argued in Chapter 2, leads one into debate around Nietzsche's complicity with fascistic forms of thought (1996: 76–7). It is as if Gatens hears the interlocutor's question as: have anti-essentialist approaches bequeathed feminism a rudderless anti-ethical epistemological basis (such as some have suggested[3] with Nietzsche)? Gatens' response to this is to argue that anti-essentialism is not rudderless, but is about how to remember those things which are important in order, as Foucault would put it, to 'understand and remember how we became what we are, not in order to live what we have become as our "truth" but rather as our conditions of possibility for that which we may become' (1996: 77). She thereby moves her discussion to the politics of remembering and in the same gesture motions toward the oppression of several categories of people:

> Jews, blacks, women have been (and often still are) treated very badly merely by virtue of their membership of the group or 'type' 'Jew', 'Black', 'Woman'. These

3 She refers explicitly to Alasdair MacIntyre's (1990) critique of Nietzsche.

groups have been subject to various pogroms: the Holocaust, mass lynchings and witch hunts. Remembering such things involves great pain which could be alleviated by acts of forgetting. Yet there are some things which cannot and should not be forgotten. (1996: 77)

Gatens' connections thus encourage a reading that pulls the question of essentialism onto the terrain of fascistic programmes and racist violence, and concludes the same paragraph with an indication that these are the reasons why one has to maintain an anti-essentialist stance. Remembering in order to pursue the question of what we may become, she argues, is an issue of thinking of identity as without essence. Quoting Rajchman (who is following Foucault), her suggestion is that one should adopt a philosophy that '"instead of attempting to determine what we should do on the basis of what we essentially are, attempts, by analysing what we have been constituted to be, to ask what we might become." This is precisely not to understand one's identity as a given, an a priori, in short *an essence*' (1996: 77, italics added).

Too often, anti-essentialism has been associated with a flight from the materiality of the body, from questions of felt embodiment. Even where this is an inaccuracy of interpretation, the debate is often structured in this way, as if to speak of the experience of embodiment as mediated culturally or discursively constituted is to deny embodiment. The power of Levinas' work is that he warns against thinking about the body in this way. He did not 'leave' the body as he took up his task of philosophy, for that would be to tread the fault lines of abstract liberalism and of Christian ideas of spirit. If he is correct – and this is admittedly a big 'if' – it would mean that wherever 'anti-essentialist' feminist theory flees 'the body', it might even work against its very commitments, creating a vulnerable discursive space where the appeal of essentialist political arguments may flourish. All this is contingent on the events and multiple contexts that surround such statements, it goes without saying, which is why I put the point tentatively here. But Levinas' piece acts as a warning to the debates about essentialism, in the sense that it forces us to address embodiment and to think, as Fuss has suggested, about essentialism as a mode of argument that can enter into several different strategies at different points in time. The abstraction away from the body, as well as the assertion of the materiality of the body, can both be rendered politically suspect. Presently, the terms of debate used in the feminist discussions indicate this sense of needing to make connections with dangerous essentialist moments in history, and portray an understanding that there is more to the discussion than the struggle against essentialist notions of the gendered body. Furthermore, there is an awareness that waving the banner of anti-essentialism, in and of itself, does not necessarily offer protection.

Before I return to feminist debates on embodiment, I want to pursue this aspect of the debates, adding to what I have said so far by turning to the work of Frantz Fanon, a figure who now enjoys a central place in cultural analyses of 'race' and racism, and who appears in the margins of feminist work (including in the work of Fuss herself (1994)), although not without some ambiguity, given his handling of sexuality and gender within his work, especially in *Black Skins, White Masks* (1986, first published 1952) (see, e.g., Bergner, 1995; Young, 1996), a point to which I will return below. Fanon serves the argument here well insofar as his work addresses the complexities of thinking about the relationship between a sense of embodiment, historically specific articulations of the body, and the temporal placement of the body. His work adds a further layer to the argument insofar as it speaks of these concerns within the context of colonial racism.

Emerging bodies, exploding bodies: the work of Frantz Fanon

At around the same time that de Beauvoir was writing about the complexities of 'becoming a woman', Frantz Fanon was writing his own treatises on the complexities of living the position of objectified subject in terms of 'blackness' and colonial regimes. When the two met, de Beauvoir found him to be 'an exceptional man. When one was with him, life seemed to be a tragic adventure, often horrible, but of infinite worth' (quoted in Moi, 1994: 205).[4] The two writers were not, however, engaged in each other's thought in their own texts,[5] although the two were linked much more explicitly through their relationships with Jean-Paul Sartre. Sartre championed Fanon's reception in Europe, imploring Europeans to read Fanon, for, as he wrote in his preface to *The Wretched of the Earth*, Fanon would enable them to 'get to know yourselves in the light of truth' (1969: 12, first published 1961), since his words were a diagnosis of the death of Europe:

> This doctor neither claims that she is a hopeless case – miracles have been known to exist – nor does he give her the means to cure herself. He certifies that she is dying, on external evidence, founded on symptoms that he can observe. As to curing her, no; he has other things to think about; he does not give a damn whether she lives or dies. (Fanon, 1969: 9, first published 1961)

But the challenges that Europe's colonial powers were experiencing, and especially in the case of France in relation to Fanon's adopted home, Algeria, were not to be regarded as evidence of a lack of humanity, even where actions were extremely violent. No, according to Sartre, read Fanon and discover that 'this irrepressible violence is neither sound nor fury, nor the resurrection of savage instincts, nor even the effect of resentment: it is man re-creating himself' (Fanon, 1969: 18, first published 1961).

The notion of 'recreation' here is a theme that runs through Fanon's work. Peoples in colonised countries had been placed within the colonial machine

---

4 As Moi points out, she is writing retrospectively of a political ally.

5 And remarkably little has been written about their relationship since, with Moi's (1994) comments making a notable exception.

that was 'violence in its natural state' (1969, first published 1961), he argued, and their intellectuals were caught up in praising and defending Western values. The 'recreation' of the colonised would be violent, would have to attack territorially and intellectually, and out of that state of emergency, as Homi Bhabha (1986: vi) writes, there would be a state of emergence. Similarly, Sartre wrote in his introduction to the poetry anthology *Black Orpheus* that the celebration of Negritude that the collection represented was a 'becoming':

> Strange and decisive divergence; the race has transmuted itself into historicity: the Present black explodes and temporalises himself; Negritude inserts itself with its Past and its Future in the universal history; it is no more than a state, neither even an existential attitude; it is a Becoming . . . a patient construction, a future. (1963: 57)

For Fanon, the notion of recreation, of becoming, is one that involves a violent, explosive moment. The embrace of historicity, taking up a place within the events that make up history, involves a movement, a transmutation, an insertion, that will shatter the regimes – of power, of thought, of space – that upheld colonialism. The dramatic language of the emergency/emergence indicates the rupturing with the position into which Western ideologies had placed the colonised. The point at which the 'natives' act upon the sentiments they feel is one at which they challenge the settlers' rule, certainly, but with that, they also challenge Western modes of thought, both modes of categorising people and ways of understanding History. Moreover, when the colonised act collectively, they are making the demand to be allowed to desire, and refusing the implications of racist discourse that left only the possibility 'to turn white or disappear' (Fanon, 1986: 100).

The moment of explosion, recreation and insertion is one that Fanon wishes to wrest from Hegelian dialectical views of history, in the sense that he wanted to refute the claim that this emergence was merely a moment in a historical movement – the 'antithesis' – that would fall away in time and become resolved through synthesis. In *Black Skin, White Masks* Fanon makes this point (1986: 132, first published 1952), *contra* Sartre, indicating that their alliance was not a trouble-free one (indeed, throughout Fanon's works one finds him both indebted and infuriated by the politics of Sartre's philosophy). Although Fanon also argues that Negritude is a creation of the black man – '[i]t is the white man who creates the Negro. But it is the Negro who creates Negritude' (1989: 47) – he argues that that reaction is not merely reactionary, but is creative, and is not automatically to resolve in synthesis, but is worth dwelling upon in its own right. To see history as always already tending toward synthesis is to know it in advance; that, Fanon would assert, is a comfort of which the world cannot afford to pretend.

The point that I wish to emphasise in this discussion of Fanon is that the moment of emergence is one that is not simply about land, although it is crucially about reoccupying space, nor about claiming a place in history, although it is about marking historical situations (Fanon, 1969: 40, first published 1961), but it is also, fundamentally, about the *body*:

> The violence which has ruled over the ordering of the colonial world, which has ceaselessly drummed the rhythm for the destruction of native social forms . . . that same violence will be claimed and taken over by the native at the moment when, deciding to *embody history in his own person*, he surges into forbidden quarters. (1969: 31, emphasis added, first published 1961)

The explosion that is the liberation movements of colonised peoples is a refusal of an imposed positionality. The coloniser – like the racist, more generally – attempts to fix the native, the black man; the moment at which their eyes meet is one which produces an effect in each. The coloniser feels threatened, correctly in Fanon's view, as 'he ascertains bitterly, always on the defensive "they want to take our place"' (1969: 30, first published 1961). The recreation that takes place happens with the body, producing a sense of historicity within the body, an embodiment which could be embraced, celebrated, as, in some profound way, carrying forward history in a way that colonialism had attempted to destroy.

Here is the connection with Levinas' piece on Hitlerism. For it is as if Fanon were arguing that the body which emerges is one that the liberation movements oppose to the dominance of a History that would not accommodate them, or that accommodated them in ways that did not allow them a sense of genealogy that they felt or thought was accurate. Liberation requires that the individual colonised's own sense of embodiment is redefined away from that which the colonial regime would allow. It is a movement from a position in which colonised bodies were allowed only material status, to a position of forcing recognition of a hitherto repressed, or unarticulated, social body. Moreover, it is an assertion of the individual's *personal* embodiment, an attempt to redefine the relation of self to body away from racist discourses and back to a sense of identity between self and the very vitality of the body. Thus Fanon is writing on the very cusp of the problem Levinas locates; that is, how to speak and live embodiment in such a way that does not abstract into dualisms, nor descend into fascisms.

This theme is also present and placed centrally in *Black Skin, White Masks* where Fanon again offers an image of explosion which is at once an intellectual explosion and one that is felt bodily, that crucially concerns the relation of the self to the body; that is, embodiment. Again, there is a meeting of eyes:

> I was satisfied with an intellectual understanding of these differences [between black, mulatto, white]. It was not really dramatic. And then . . . And then the occasion arose when I had to meet the white man's eyes. An unfamiliar weight burdened me. The real world challenged my claims. In the white world the man of colour encounters difficulties in the development of his bodily schema. Consciousness of the body is a solely negating activity. (1986: 110, first published 1952)

Fanon shows the sense in which colonial regimes and racist modes of categorisation mark the body such that the experience of embodiment emanates neither from 'inside' nor from without. Struggling with a sense of corporeality within a racist society is to struggle too with the impossibility of being other; there is struggle on the level of what Fanon terms 'the bodily schema'. Although Fanon's work requires feminist critique on several counts (see, e.g., Bergner, 1995; Young, 1996), this aspect of his thesis is reminiscent of the paradox that de Beauvoir commented upon when she argued that becoming feminine involves being object while retaining a sense of oneself as subject; the colonised battle with their sense of humanity in the face of a racist discourse that speaks of them as objects or animals. Fanon writes:

> The native . . . laughs to himself every time he spots an allusion to the animal world in the other's words. For he knows that he is not an animal; and it is precisely at the moment that he realises his humanity that he begins to sharpen the weapons with which he will secure its victory. (1969: 33, first published 1961)

The possibility of explosion, therefore, haunts the project of identity in an unequal society. The project of identity is interrupted because the attempt to maintain a sense of one's own body is shaken when that body is taken by others to signify otherwise. The thesis of *Black Skin, White Masks* is that in a colonial society black people were obliged to operate as if they were white, to adopt a mask, to mimic the role of the white person, in a situation that made them learn an imposed language, and take on a complex relation to their own bodies, one that opened out the space between subjectivity and the body. Whereas the subject develops a sense of corporeality, a 'bodily schema', through the movements of the body, racism imposes different ways of viewing the black body that disrupt and problematise that sense of embodiment, forcing the subject himself or herself, to question and redefine their prior sense. Thus, in the oft-quoted passage where Fanon describes an incident in which the narrator's black body is seen by a small white boy through what he terms the 'racial epidermal schema', the child interprets the black body in ways over which the narrator has no control:

> 'Look, a Negro!' The circle was drawing a bit tighter. I made no secret of my amusement.
> 'Mama, see the Negro! I'm frightened!' Frightened! Frightened! Now they were beginning to be afraid of me. I made up my mind to laugh myself to tears, but laughter had become impossible.
> I could no longer laugh, because I knew that there were legends, stories, history, and above all historicity, which I had learned about from Jaspers. Then, assailed at various points, the corporeal schema crumbled, its place taken by a racial epidermal schema. (1986: 112, first published 1952)

Fanon is describing here the sense in which visuality is not neutral but a 'racially saturated field' (Butler, 1993b: 17); the small white boy sees the colour of the man's skin, and sees it 'discursively' (Bell, 1996) so that the narrator – Fanon – becomes 'responsible at the same time for my body, for my race, for my ancestors' (1986: 112, first published 1952).

Contemplating his own body, Fanon recognises the connections that the boy had made. From the 'fact of blackness' Fanon's 'objective examination' makes his black body an object that conjures up a series of images that batter and dislocate him: 'tom-toms, cannibalism, intellectual deficiency, fetishism, racial defects, slave-ships, and above all else, above all: "Sho' good eatin"' (1986: 112). The sight of the black man is understood through 'a thousand details, anecdotes, stories' (1986: 111). While he rejects the 'thematisation' of his body in this way, wishing only to be 'a man among other men', he recognises that embodiment moves in a value-laden world, where seeing colour is seeing according to the categories of racist logic. Even when white people were welcoming, the issue of colour was mentioned: 'When people like me they tell me it is in spite of my colour. When they dislike me, they point out that it is not because of my colour' (1986: 116). His contemplation of this incident explodes the corporeal schema that had been formed by moving as a human being in the world – 'my body was given back to me sprawled out, distorted, recoloured, clad in mourning in that white winter day' (1986: 113).

The racial epidermal schema explodes the bodily schema that would have been formed through the experience of the body in its interior space and the relation of that space to the world in which it moves. This experience of embodiment for Fanon was one which he felt in these terms:

> I know that if I want to smoke, I shall have to reach out my right arm and take the pack of cigarettes lying at the other end of the table. The matches, however, are in the drawer on the left, and I shall have to lean back slightly . . . a slow composition of my self as a body in the middle of a spatial and temporal world – such seems to be the schema. (1986: 111)

Fanon is close to Freud here insofar as Freud suggested that the ego was, at least initially, a bodily ego. There is for Fanon a structuring of the self, a formation, within the world that is about the sense of becoming familiar with the co-ordinates of one's own living body within space. This more holistic spatiality is refused by the spatiality of discursively and historically constituted conditions as they are violently recast by the racist epidermal schema. In the midst of this description of corporeal explosion, Fanon makes reference to Sartre's *Anti-Semite and Jew* (1965), for there he saw a connection in terms of being caught between oneself and the idea of one that others held.[6] Sartre had written that the Jews in an anti-Semitic society 'had allowed themselves to be poisoned by the stereotype that others have of them, and they live in fear that their acts will correspond to this stereotype' (in Fanon, 1986: 115). Fanon treats the figure of the Jew as always white, and suggests that if this is the situation of overdetermination from 'within', as Sartre suggests it is, then 'Negroes' are overdetermined

---

6 The problem, in fact, that Arendt's issue of appearance threw up in Chapter 4, and the one that Susan Bickford (1995) takes up.

from 'without' (1986: 116).[7] It is this overdetermination that means that the skin marked by the colour black cannot mimic the white world around him, for the white masks that one might take up, including those of language or of education, will not gain one equality as long as the racial epidermal schema maintains its hold.

The relationship between discursive conditions and the body is necessarily one that involves historical, spatial, even architectural conditions. The sense in which colonialism places bodies not simply discursively, by overinvesting the bodily schema within colour-coded forms of racism, but also within spatialised parameters, was a theme to which Fanon returned often. Most explicitly perhaps, Fanon turned to this question in the essays collected in *The Wretched of the Earth* (1969, first published 1961) and *Studies in a Dying Colonialism* (1989, first published 1959). In the essay 'Concerning violence', quoted earlier, Fanon speaks of the spatial configuration of the colonised city, in which there is a Manichean divide between the zones occupied by the settlers and that occupied by the 'natives'. The motif of eyes meeting recurs once more:

> The town belonging to the colonised people or at least to the native town, the Negro village . . . the reservation, is a place of ill fame, peopled by men of ill repute. They are born there, it matters little where or how; they die there, it matters not where or how. It is a world without spaciousness; men live on top of each other, and their huts are built one on top of the other. The native town is a hungry town, starved of bread, of meat, of shoes, of coal, of light . . . The look that the native turns on the settler's town is a look of lust, a look of envy; it expresses his dreams of possession – all manner of possession: to sit at the settler's table, to sleep in the settler's bed, with his wife if possible. The colonised man is an envious man. And this the settler knows very well; when their glances meet he ascertains bitterly, always on the defensive 'they want to take our place'. It is true, for there is no native who does not dream at least once a day of setting himself up in the settler's place. (1969: 30)

The decision to embody history, therefore, is one which requires a removal of imposed spatiality – and the resultant control of movement(s) – on many levels. It is a decision to make history through a challenge to the violence of the colonialists both through revolutionary struggle – colonialism is violence in its natural state and 'will only yield when confronted with greater violence' (1969: 48) – as well as through an intellectual or discursive challenge that involves an assertion of the bodily schema.[8]

The themes of struggle concerning corporeal insertion into history and the attempted colonial control of bodies – where and how they move, where and how they are seen – emerges again in Fanon's 'Algeria unveiled'

7 On Fanon's use of the figure of 'the Jew', see Cheyette (1995).

8 Fanon's disappointment in the colonised intellectuals might be read in this light, for they had been too long convinced of certain eternal values, taught to them by the West, that they had implanted in their minds a 'vigilant sentinel' guarding the 'Graeco-Latin pedestal' (1969: 36), and were unwittingly engaged in a mimicry of the values of the West that worked to impede collective opposition.

piece, which returns us also to the notion of mimicry. At a certain stage in
the liberation struggle, Fanon tells us, Algerian women became involved in
a crucial role. The boundaries of the city of Algiers reflected the divisions
of a colonised city, with Europeans living separately from the Algerian
population. With the violence that marked the liberation struggle, however,
the French sealed off the Algerian city and had French soldiers patrol the
exits from the Algerian city into the European city that surrounded it. It
was because the colonisers had become aware that Algerian women were
carrying messages and weaponry to men who were engaged in attacks
within the European areas of Algiers that the tactics of the Algerians
changed. Women were now to pass through the patrolled boundaries disguised as European women, unsearched and unimpeded. Although Fanon
states that these women were not involved in imitation, in the sense that
they were not copying the image of espionage that had been known
imaginatively or from films and stories (1989: 50, first published 1959), they
were involved in a mimicry in the sense that they assumed the clothes,
attitudes and demeanour of French women. She crossed the patrolled
boundary with 'revolvers, grenades, hundreds of false identity cards or
bombs' (1989: 58, first published 1959) about her person, enabling the
attacks on the European city to continue.

The essay is important in this discussion because it draws attention to
the unreliability of the visual cues on which the authorities relied in order
to categorise and 'know' the individuals who moved before them. These
incidents expose sight as discursively and historically constituted, such that
the assumption of Algerian status is not based upon seeing the body as
much as it is about reading the body in its context. But more than this,
Fanon's essay is intriguing in this context for how he returns to the notion
of the corporeal schema, the interior sense of embodiment. Although the
disguised Algerian woman 'moves like a fish in the Western waters' (1989:
58, first published 1959), she is experiencing her embodiment anew because
of the very different positionality that she is obliged to adopt:

> [T]hat young girl, unveiled only yesterday, . . . walks with sure steps down the
> streets of the European city teeming with policemen, parachutists, militiamen.
> She no longer slinks along the walls as she tended to do before the Revolution . . .
>
> The shoulders of the unveiled Algerian woman are thrust back with easy
> freedom. She walks with a graceful, measured stride, neither too fast or too slow.
> Her legs are bare, not confined by the veil, given back to themselves, and her hips
> are free . . .
>
> Without the veil she has an impression of her body being cut up into bits, put
> adrift; the limbs seem to lengthen indefinitely. When the Algerian woman has to
> cross a street, for a long time she commits errors of judgement as to the exact
> distance to be negotiated. The unveiled body seems to escape, to dissolve. (1989:
> 58–9, first published 1959)

Passing for a European, the revolutionary Algerian woman is obliged to
re-establish a relationship with herself-as-embodied, as she relearns a sense

of embodiment in this new relationship to the world. It is not that the imitation taking place here is a form of altering one's relationship to one's identity (indeed, it is a form of imitation that does not involve identification, as Fuss (1994: 27) comments) but what is happening here is that the corporeal schema has to adapt to the conditions in which the body is moving, re-co-ordinating interior with exterior spatiality. In this way, Fanon's thoughts on the role of the revolutionary Algerian woman complement the way in which he describes the explosion of the corporeal schema in the face of the racial epidermal schema, illustrating the argument that her embodiment is actually experienced differently when the configuration of histories and expectations that surround that 'body' is altered.[9]

What does this reading of Fanon's work add to the feminist debates and conversations around embodiment? I have wanted to suggest that although Fanon's use of a notion of corporeal schema may appear at first to replicate an inner to which the racial epidermal schema is the outer and the more powerful, his work offers an apt opportunity to consider embodiment in the manner in which Levinas suggests. That is, as an exploration of the way in which inner and outer are unstable, mobile and entwined, Fanon's writings address the need to maintain a focus on the identity that a sense of the body can give, while at the same time emphasising the changing historical and political, discursively and non-discursively given conditions of that sense. His work enables one to illustrate the argument that while there is nothing essential, in the sense of fixed and unchanging, about one's sense of embodiment, one's identity is 'about' one's body in the context of its insertion into these conditions. Thus Fanon's work is crucially about the notion of embodying history and the effect of historically constituted discourses (including the discipline of History itself) on embodiment; it is also crucially about the political need to challenge the ways in which bodies are 'put into discourse'. His arguments therefore raise exactly the questions that are the concerns of this chapter. At its most succinct and most ambitious: how the sense of the individual body in motion relates to the movements of history. To return to the argument made above, one is engaged here in a risk that, politically speaking, one is impelled to take. Any

9 Marie-Aimee Helie-Lucas (1990) argues that any sense of women's part in the struggle being regarded as equal to men's should be aware that few women were allowed to register for veteran status, and that women's roles were frequently cast as merely 'helping' the men (even though the French authorities would acknowledge her actions by imprisoning, torturing and killing her). Women in Algeria have since had to tread carefully between political and feminist positions, as issues of contraception, wearing of the veil, and feminist agitation all become highly problematic when one is caught between notions of fidelity to one's people and identification with other oppressed women. Helie-Lucas calls for international perspective that collective organisation might challenge those moments when women are asked to suffer discrimination and inequalities in the name of defending or supporting 'the community'. On the question of the veil, see also essays by Elia, Goldberg and Souffrant in Gordon, Sharpley-Whiting and White (eds) (1996). For theoretical comment and contextualisation of the work of Helie-Lucas, see Spivak's (1993) Chapter 7.

attempts to know or to theorise this relationship run the risk of imposition. Who is ever in a position to articulate embodiment for another? Fanon makes the point very graphically that such articulations impose definitions that define lives through their powerful categorisations and associations; he also illustrates, and has been rightly criticised for it, how even a radical, such as he, can contribute to certain discursive associations around women, 'race' and sexuality. Indeed, Bergner has argued that Fanon's treatment of black women's desire in the second chapter of *Black Skin, White Masks*, 'The woman of colour and the black man', illustrates 'his own desire to circumscribe black women's sexuality and economic autonomy in order to ensure the patriarchal authority of black men' (1995: 81). Yet *not* to think this relationship – that between the motion of the body and the movements of history – may be a misguided abdication, for if people's identity is experienced through the body, and their relationship to the world, to others and to historical change is experienced with the body, then the contingent ways in which that experience is given significance are the pertinent and necessary sites of investigation and intervention.

Embodiment in feminist theory

This manoeuvre cannot be a reassertion of that which the flight from the body wished to avoid. The task, then, is to theorise the body in a way that captures the import of the proximity of the body, the debt of identity to the body, but, at the same time, that maintains a thoroughly anti-essentialist stance. What I mean to suggest here is that being 'anti-essentialist' need not be a reason not to consider the phenomena and import of embodiment; 'anti-essentialist', as a feminist slogan, is a rallying point directed, with good reason, against strategies that have sought to govern women's lives. However, I have enlisted the help of Levinas and Fanon in order to argue that the consideration of embodiment, and the historical, discursive and power-crossed nature of that embodiment, is not aided by rehearsing that slogan; and, indeed, the neglect of embodiment may work against the very intention of that anti-essentialist stance.

This is not to return to essences. As Gayatri Spivak has suggested, as with 'anti-essentialism', 'essentialism' is not a topic of investigation in and of itself. Although there may be a need to reckon with the 'fragments of essences' (Spivak, 1993: 21) in theoretical work, this is not equivalent to a return to essences, as if to attempt to produce 'a theory of essences' (1993: 15). But there may be a place for a return to the empirical, which is too often confused with an essentialist manoeuvre (1993: 16). The exploration of embodiment as an empirical investigation means a consideration of the ways in which bodies are 'value-coded', in Spivak's terms (1993: 20), in the context of politico-economic strategies, which are often explicitly and consciously strategic. To mistake these as *theories* which critics must counter with attempts to produce 'anti-essentialist theories' is to conflate strategy and theory.[10] Instead, critiquing these codes and contexts must involve the critic in a persistent self-critique in terms of the fetishised nature of 'the masterword' (such as 'woman' or 'the body'). Wherever there is a tendency toward centring (around these terms), deconstruction, as a re-reading, enables one to see how essentialism is both useful and dangerous. It does not lead to a new theory – an anti-essentialist theory – but leads rather to a counter-intuitive position which is to leave open the question as to whether there are or are not essences (1993: 10), and look instead, Spivak implies, to how bodies become *significant* in their relation to other bodies (1993: 20) in their various contexts and strategies.

Much feminist work is, I believe, presently engaged in an attempt to speak about embodiment which falls within this remit. There are grounds for reading contemporary feminist work as already beginning the difficult explorations of embodiment that my discussion implies, for there seems to be a reaching for the possibility of theorising 'beyond' the terms of previous debates, for the possibility of theorising embodiment without conservatism, with an awareness of the possibilities and dangers of 'essentialism'. The work of Elizabeth Grosz (1994), Moira Gatens (1996) and Iris Marion Young (1990), to name a few, have this, in their different ways, as (one of) their tasks. Some of the turns to the work of Bourdieu, similarly, search for possibilities of thinking about felt embodiment, by considering what he termed 'le sens practique', the dispositions and competencies of the body that embodiment displays, while keeping open the variability of the body across space and time. Bourdieu's notion of 'habitus' is one that feminists have considered since it enables one to speak about embodiment as embodied history 'internalised as second nature and so forgotten as history . . . the active presence of the whole past of which it is the product' (1991: 56); although how far feminism can use Bourdieu's thought is a matter of debate, centring predominantly around different conceptions of social reproduction, the efficacy of language in that process and the corporeal accommodation of dominant symbolic codes (MacNay, 1999; Butler, 1997a).

To take an exemplary case, Elizabeth Grosz has pursued her work in ways that can be regarded as complementary with the task such as it is emerging here. Grosz argues that she is motivated in part by an attempt to salvage the feminist debate from under the strain of an either/or choice between a feminism organised around a concept of 'women' that has been challenged as an essentialising and universalising categorisation, on the one hand, or a dissolution of feminism 'into localised, regional, specific struggles, representing the interest of particular women or groups of women' (Grosz,

10 Here Spivak is responding to the debates that have taken place around her suggestions that essentialism may need to be 'risked' in the sense that it is a strategy in a political world. In this interview Spivak implies an exasperated impatience with the attempts to outline an abstract position that expresses what might be meant by 'strategic essentialism' and the debates that have ensued around her earlier comments.

1990: 341–2), on the other. Her work draws upon several philosophies, but, in particular, on Deleuze and Guattari's (1984) provocative work *Anti-Oedipus* – a work which, intriguingly for this discussion, Michel Foucault wished to think of as an *Introduction to the Non-Fascist Life* (1984b: xiii) – to think about embodiment outside the 'mire of biologism in which it has been entrenched' (Grosz, 1994: 188). What her work also does, I would argue, is to point in a direction that may indeed salvage the question of embodiment away from the back and forth of the debate on essentialism. Grosz gives us the opportunity, following through the suggestions of this chapter, to consider the question of embodied experience as constituted by historically and culturally specific discourses but as also crucial in maintaining, intervening in or embodying historical (discursive, social and political) movements.

Grosz's model is one that she offers feminist enquiry in the hope that it moves beyond some of the traditional theorising of the body. In her words, the model

> acknowledges both the psychical or interior dimensions of subjectivity and the surface corporeal exposures of the subject to social inscription and training; a model which resists, as much as possible, both dualism and monism; a model which insists on (at least) two surfaces which cannot be collapsed into one and which do not always harmoniously blend with and support each other; a model where the join, the interaction of the two surfaces, is always a question of power; a model that may be represented by the geometrical form of the Möbius strip's two dimensional torsion in three dimensional space. (1994: 189)

Grosz's argument is one that complements Fuss' suggestion that maybe what is assumed to be fixed and unchanging – that is, nature – and what is assumed to be flexible and changeable – that is, sociality – may not be so. She suggests that the body might better be approached via a model such as a Möbius strip, which would enable one to explore the sense in which there are not simply two sides – the inner (biological, psychical, body) and the outer (environment, culture, power) – but there are what Grosz terms 'surfaces' that can meet, twist, accommodate and delimit. Her model aims to get beyond those accounts of the body which concentrate either on the 'inner' or the 'outer', such that feminists can begin the task of exploring how 'fixed and unchangeable elements of facticity, biologically given factors, are amenable to wide historical vicissitudes and transformations' (1994: 190); to see how 'our ideas and attitudes seep into the functioning of the body itself, making up the realm of its possibilities or impossibilities' (1994: 190). There are, Grosz argues, interventions and limits that both genetics and the environment pose; biology

> cannot be regarded as a form whose contents are historically provided, nor as a base on which cultural constructs are founded, nor indeed as a container for a mixture of culturally or individually specific ingredients. It is *an open materiality*, a set of (possibly infinite) tendencies and potentialities which may be developed, yet whose development will necessarily hinder or induce other developments and other trajectories. (1994: 191, emphasis added)

Thus Grosz's intention here is to complicate dominant models of thinking of the body, and to free feminist work from the debates around essentialism, through a notion of 'open materiality'. Her use of Foucault and Deleuze has been echoed by other theorists – such as Elspeth Probyn (1993) or Susan Bordo (1993) – and with these same intentions. The task is to explore the twists and turns of the 'Möbius strip', to see how inner and outer are misleading terms, and how the divisions that enable them to make sense are themselves in need of interrogation. Probyn's work is particularly close to Grosz's in her use of Deleuze, and her intention is close to mine insofar as she states that 'I do want to insist upon the necessity of bringing together a recognition of the ontological affectivity of being gendered and an epistemological critique of the production of that affectivity' (1993: 168). This is the crux of the matter. That is, how to respond to the need to acknowledge felt embodiment as central to identity, while simultaneously placing that sense within a critique that refuses to replicate the divisions feminist theory has managed so well to question. *The affect – Levinas' sense of the proximity of embodiment – needs to be recognised at the same time as the production of that affect – the 'mediation' of Fanon's historicity – is subjected to critique.*

Furthermore, contemporary feminist explorations have been made in a way that enables the question of racism to be raised as central to these enquiries. The work of Nancy Caraway in her chapter 'Coded bodies, femininity and black womanhood' in *Segregated Sisterhood* (1991), is an example of this, and can be read within the concerns of this chapter, as in a trajectory with Fanon's concerns but as challenging certain of his perspectives, insofar as she explores the 'technologies of gender' – a phrase she borrows from Teresa de Lauretis' (1987) influential work – that code bodies in both gendered and racialised ways.

Caraway discusses the power of historical discourses on black women's sense of embodiment in the United States, the 'deadly discursive mechanisms' (1991: 91), as she terms them, drawing on the historical work of Gerda Lerner, that reiterate, amongst other things, the myth of the 'bad' black woman, the discourse that associated black women with 'loose' morals, that spoke of her body as if it were always sexually available and as if she were filthy and contagious.[11] Such discourses have affected black women's everyday sense of embodiment, she suggests, in a similar way to Fanon's argument that colonial racism results in a struggle to make sense of one's own feelings of being embodied. As one perhaps slight but significant example of this, Caraway discusses the writings of bell hooks and Alice Walker, who have both written about their relationship to their hair, the

11 Lerner wrote (of US context): 'A wide range of practices reinforced this myth: the laws against intermarriage; the denial of the title Miss or Mrs to any black woman; the taboos against respectable social mixing of the races; the refusal to let any black woman try on clothing in stores before making a purchase; the assigning of single toilet facilities to both sexes of blacks; the different legal sanctions against rape, abuse of minors and other sex crimes when committed against white or black women' (quoted in Caraway, 1991: 92).

way that different conceptions of expectations – of beauty, of authenticity, of radicalism – have meant their sense of themselves has altered through time and space. Writes Caraway, 'the world of racist gender signs – cultural messages and images "always already" defining the Black woman's physical worth – can penetrate even the strongest psychological barriers' (1991: 97). The discourses are powerful – but resistance is not simply 'rejection': the Möbius strip is turning and twisting. Attempting to resist these discursive mechanisms cannot return to or reassert the authentic body, for this too is a form of political strategy that can result in problematic relations being set up. In her feminist class discussions, Caraway reports, radical white feminist students have urged a black student not to 'deny or invalidate her "Blackness", her "special beauty"' (1991: 111) by straightening her hair or wearing blue contact lenses, or choosing 'preppy' over 'ethnic' clothing. The 'authenticity' that the white students praise and crave is that which Trinh Minh-ha discusses when she speaks of feeling the need before certain audiences to paint herself 'thick with authenticity' (1991: 113). The rhetoric of authenticity, Caraway argues, must itself be subject to critique, which- ever direction the phrase is thrown. Like essentialist modes of thought, the discourse of authenticity has had radical, but can also have conservative and restricting, effects; it is, for Caraway, another sort of image to which bodies are asked to conform. Relatedly, Spivak argues that teachers should guard against a mode of teaching that offers a simple 'authority of mar- ginality'; rather than evoking a notion of multiplicity that makes students 'representative' in various ways (and thereby authorised to speak 'on behalf of', or to tell others to conform, as Caraway is suggesting), she advocates a mode of reflection on the way in which subject speaking positions have been coded to allow and disallow certain authorities (Spivak, 1993: 18–19). That coding, Spivak explains elsewhere, involves the speaker in a peculiar relation to her multifaceted self and also may involve placing those listening in a hegemonic, homogenising position.[12]

Spivak's work is useful here as a reminder that the questions of 'race', sexuality and gender do not exhaust the dimensions by which one can think of the coding and constitution of the female body. In accord with other theorists, she has been concerned to emphasise the import of other entwining aspects of embodiment – language, accent, tone, skin colour,

12 In an interview in *The Post-Colonial Critic*, Spivak describes this in relation to her own speaking position. She says 'A hundred years ago it was impossible for me to speak, for exactly the reason that makes it only too possible for me to speak in certain circles now. I see in that a kind of reversal which is again a little suspicious . . . The question of "speaking as" involves a distancing from oneself . . . There are many subject positions one may inhabit; one is not just one thing. That is when political consciousness comes in. So that in fact, for the person who does the "speaking as" something, it is a problem of distancing oneself from oneself whatever that self might be. But when cardcarrying listeners, the hegemonic people . . . want to hear some one "speaking as", then there is a problem.' The problem is that the 'listeners' are then allowed to possess ignorance, and they are allowed to homogenise those who they believe the speaker 'represents' (1990: 60).

age, height, class-status – their government by various regimes, administrative and academic, and their negotiation over time and space (see, e.g., 1990: 80–93).

Caraway's chapter ends in a rather peculiar way, one that brings me back to some of the concerns that have been mine. She implies that in critiquing images and the politics of bodily appearance, feminist critics need to avoid becoming too overinvested in symbolic politics, too fixated on imagery, for this may result in the 'aestheticisation of politics' which she argues, Walter Benjamin had warned as a 'step toward fascism' (Caraway, 1991: 115). The fascist elevation of style, where political activity or agents are evaluated in terms of the visual impact or 'beauty' is dangerous, she argues, and feminists must take care not to substitute 'style, imagery or aesthetics for concrete political engagement' (1991: 115). In this way, Caraway illustrates the recurrence of the guarding against fascism in feminist theory, but also the entwinement of the issue of embodiment, her primary concern in the chapter, with fascism, even while she is, my argument would suggest, making a false opposition between the feminist interest in challenging those aesthetic ideals that constitute a discourse of femininities, and some notion of concrete political engagement, insofar as she implies that one mimics the fascist obsession with style when one adopts aesthetics as the site for political critique. My argument here has been that it is exactly for these latter reasons that there is a need to continue critiquing and thinking through appeals to the body, and to continue feminist theorising on processes of embodiment. How people understand themselves to be merely bodies is a discursively constituted understanding that carries with it the sense in which bodies are the embodiment of historical movement.

Conclusion

There is at present, it seems, a rush to find an adequate theory of embodiment, with feminist theorists reaching out to several different philosophies in order to find a route away from discredited and discriminatory legacies and away from the negativity that was beginning to mire the abstract debate on the issue of anti-essentialism. I have only touched on the contributors to these debates, and have attempted not to enter into them so much as to notice and applaud the general sense of movement within it. But I have wanted to suggest that there is a further dimension to these debates, one that is highlighted by thinking about feminist theory against a different backdrop from the one in which it is usually placed, a backdrop into which I have placed the thought of Emmanuel Levinas and Frantz Fanon, for whom the affective relationship of the body to 'self' is to be explored, crucially, within specific historico-discursive deployments. Although essentialism has been repeatedly refuted in feminist theory, it is worth recalling the reasons why this is so: not because the explorations of embodiment would necessarily change their theoretical foci as a result, but because monitoring the deployment of essentialist modes of thought, and countering the claims of those who would use them in conservative or hierarchically discriminating ways, is a task that feminism shares with other political commitments, where we might fruitfully explore the connections that feminist politics has outside its apparent boundaries.

Feminist theory need not be paranoid about essentialism if it takes a cue from Fuss' and Spivak's work and treats essentialism as a deployment. This would in turn bring the question of the connections and the wider strategies associated with various articulations of the body into the frame. The politics behind the paranoia, in other words, may be fruitfully aired, and its accuracy debated, rather than continuing to allow the paranoia to act as the unaddressed but driving sentiment of a wide-reaching debate. I have been arguing in this chapter that the theoretical exploration of embodiment that feminist theory and philosophy is currently engaged in is to be welcomed, for feminists need to continue the exploration of embodiment as a retort and a defence against those who would monopolise appeals to the body as genealogically given and politically destined.

7

CONCLUSION: TRAUMA AND TEMPORALITY IN GENEALOGICAL FEMINIST CRITIQUE

Criticism is no longer going to be practiced in the pursuit of formal structures with universal value, but rather as a historical investigation into the events that have led us to constitute ourselves and recognise ourselves as subjects of what we do, think and say. (Michel Foucault, in Rabinow, 1984: 46)

In this book I have argued that the way in which feminist theory imagines the political landscape is not only a political issue but also a philosophical and an affective concern. I have explored (some of) the ramifications of this argument by seeking to connect the debates that take place under the sign 'feminism' with certain political horizons and figures. Each of the chapters stands on its own, and takes its own look at particular authors and arguments; taken together, they suggest that the way in which feminist debate is conducted is not a purely 'internal' conversation, but is also about the political horizons and limits that have been the changing political landscape of this century. In particular, I have been concerned to explore how racism and anti-Semitism are, in various ways, related to key feminist concepts, to feminist modes of argumentation and to the shape of feminist debates. Several more explorations, it goes without saying, remain. Nevertheless, I wish to conclude the book with a reflection upon the style of analysis that I have conducted.

Feminism has flourished in this century, it is true, but it has also been witness to it. In various ways, feminist theory bears the marks of its journeys. These are not all wounds, and I would not go so far as to argue that feminist theory is somehow 'traumatised' by the period of its development. Nevertheless, feminist theory resonates with the traumas that are the 'proof' of the twentieth century (probably in many more ways than I have explored here), and there is something about the temporality of trauma that intrigues me, and that serves me here, if only heuristically, as a route to discussing the concept of genealogy and the possibilities for genealogical feminist critique.

Trauma – as a response to an experience of sudden or catastrophic events that often manifests in the delayed, uncontrolled and repetitive appearance of intrusive phenomena (such as hallucinations) – has a peculiar temporality.[1] In her discussion of Freud's *Moses and Monotheism*, Cathy Caruth (1996) explains how trauma has, by his definition, a period of *latency*. Freud writes:

> [I]t may happen that someone gets away, apparently unharmed, from the spot where he has suffered a shocking accident, for instance a train collision. In the course of the following weeks, however, he develops a series of grave psychical and motor symptoms, which can be ascribed only to his shock or whatever else happened at the time of the accident. He has developed a 'traumatic neurosis.' (quoted in Caruth, 1996: 16)

It is only in the development of the neurosis that one learns of the event, or the quality of the event, perhaps. Whichever, there is a period in which the event is not forgotten, but in which the victim is 'apparently unharmed', such that, one might say, there is a time lapse between the accident and the experience of the accident. Freud uses his discussion of trauma to explain and defend the thesis of *Moses and Monotheism* but I wish to move, with Caruth, to the more general argument that she draws from his discussion. She writes: 'for history to be a history of trauma means that it is referential precisely to the extent that it is not fully perceived as it occurs; or to put it somewhat differently, that a history can be grasped only in the very inaccessibility of its occurrence' (1996: 18). The point I wish to make is not nearly as fantastic nor as ambitious as Freud's, but the more straightforward point that one can read so-called 'second wave' feminist theory in the context of a political and theoretical landscape haunted by ghostly figures of past, shocking experiences that have shaped the way in which political landscapes are imagined, even as they are not grasped. In feminist thought, their traces are left. In this way, political thought carries with it the unacknowledged marks of previous inaccessible events, events which have made talk of the suffering of women that has constituted 'second wave feminism' also talk of the suffering of others.

I want to be clear that I am not imposing a repressive hypothesis on feminist thought by utilising this notion of trauma. It is feminist political imagination – the figures and horizons of the landscape and the modes of argumentation – that I am focussing upon. It is these that have been shaped by the politics and events of the twentieth century; and it is with these that feminist imagination is entangled. Caruth makes several provocative remarks in her discussion of the implications of the temporality of trauma, one of which concerns the implication of others in trauma. She argues that 'it is in the constitutive bond of latency, in history, that Freud discovers the indissoluble bond to other histories. To put it somewhat differently, we can say that the traumatic nature of history means that *events are only historical to the extent that they implicate others*' (1996: 18, emphasis added). The shocking accident does not have to have

---

1 I am guided in my discussion by the work of Cathy Caruth (1996), whose discussion of trauma in relation to history initiated this train of thought.

happened to oneself. Just as the man who walks away may be walking away from 'merely' *witnessing* a shocking accident, so the Jews in Freud's argument did not themselves commit the murder, the traumas of which they suffer. Implication does not necessarily imply responsibility. I have argued in this book that the feminist political imagination implies other histories as well as that which it explicitly addresses, that in the content of its argument, in the histories of the concepts it employs, in the affects that animate it, and in the fears and connections it displays, it 'speaks' of fascism, anti-Semitism, racism. Putting feminism 'into' the twentieth century, into historical context, could mean simply telling a story of *a* social movement, whereas pursuing it through the notion of the political imagination has meant peopling the feminist political imagination with others (with those 'outside' feminist theory, with other 'others'). Feminist theory is bound to other and to others' histories. To relate this back to the quotation from Foucault that heads this chapter, one could say that the constitution of oneself as 'feminist' is related to historical events that give a force and a vision to that subject position. For, as I am not the first to say, not only is 'making feminism historic' about the successes of feminist struggle, and the hope for the eventual redundancy of feminist argument, but also it is about implicating others and implicating feminism in other histories.

The temporality of trauma, then, interests me here because it provides a vehicle by which to argue that the exposures of suffering that this century has witnessed are 'at work' within feminist political imagination. The fact that feminism is invested in the exposure of sufferings, moreover, and that it is indebted to and connected with other twentieth-century movements – most significantly here, civil rights, labour and peace movements – makes these stress-lines, and their entanglement with feminism, more than understandable. However, the implications of the term 'trauma' may be slightly misleading given the Foucauldian framework that I am, broadly speaking, writing within. It seems more plausible to me to retain some sense of the temporal argument that emerges through a discussion of trauma, but to move away from implications that risk the reductionism apparent in treating a large and diverse body of praxis as if it suffered trauma in the manner of one psyche.

I am aided in such a manoeuvre by a discussion that bridges the topics of traumatic memory and of genealogy. In his exploration of what he terms 'memoro-politics', Ian Hacking (1994) sketches the beginnings of a genealogical approach to contemporary discussions on 'the politics of memory', those surrounding the notion of false memory syndrome, for example. Hacking argues that it was through the late-nineteenth-century establishment of sciences of memory that the notion of trauma moved from meaning a physical wound or lesion caused by accident or malice to meaning 'a spiritual wound working secretly in the soul' (1994: 34). His arguments have many interesting dimensions, but it is his approach that is of concern here, for it is in the work of Foucault that Hacking finds a way to frame his arguments, to tell the intriguing historical movements of memoro-politics. In Foucault, Hacking finds both a way to adopt an attitude to the collection of documents and texts he has collected on memory, and a way of organising his thoughts on the politics of the movements and changes in their articulation and deployment: a genealogical attitude displaying the detached and 'patiently documentary' working of apparently insignificant truths into a history of power/knowledge relations, forming and entwining into clusters of varying densities, constituting new ways of casting and governing the question of memory. But what of the temporality of genealogy, the attitude to time that Hacking, following Foucault, employs? How does genealogy think temporality? And how, consequently, does the approach that I have adopted in the preceding essays think the temporality of feminist thought and of feminism?

While I believe they share a concern for recognising the unobvious, non-teleological impact of the past on the present, there is something rather different about the approach that might stem from the concept of trauma and that which arises from the concept of genealogy. For trauma, the past experience is treated as that secret 'working on the soul', as Hacking suggests, that the therapist is to discern and reveal. Genealogical investigation, on the other hand, attempts to get away from the idea of an originary event or an originary experience that 'continues secretly to animate the present, having imposed a predetermined form on all its vicissitudes' (Foucault, 1984a: 81).

As I mentioned in Chapter 1, Foucault's use of the term 'genealogy' is indebted to Nietzsche, who, Foucault tells us, wished to challenge the pursuit of origin, 'at least on those occasions when he is truly a genealogist' (1984a: 78). In *The Genealogy of Morals*, certainly, Nietzsche was concerned to argue that the genealogy of morality was about finding the correct approach, about learning how to ask questions:

> [W]hoever sticks with it and learns how to ask questions here will experience what I experienced – a tremendous prospect opens up for him, a new possibility comes over him like a vertigo . . . finally a new demand becomes audible. Let us articulate this *new demand*: we need a *critique* of moral values, *the value of these values themselves must first be called into question* – and for that there is needed a knowledge of the conditions and circumstances in which they evolved and changed. (1967: 20)

Genealogy refuses to search for origins because it feels that such a search is misconceived. Such a search, Foucault argues, assumes 'the existence of immobile forms that precede the external world of accident and succession' (1984a: 78). Refusing faith in this assumption, refusing to see the identity of forms with their origins, the genealogist assumes instead a non-teleological history, and the genealogist listens to history, finding 'something "altogether different" behind things: not a timeless and essential secret, but the secret that they have no essence or that their essence was fabricated in a piecemeal fashion from alien forms' (1984a: 78). Recognising the lowly and disparate beginnings of contemporary truths, the genealogist cultivates the 'detail and accidents that accompany every beginning'; she will recognise 'the events of history, its jolts, its surprises, its unsteady victories and unpalatable defeats' (1984a: 80). The movements, contingencies, unexpected connections, these are what interests the genealogist in Foucault's vision. While genealogy is 'patiently documentary', and is therefore a 'grey' occupation, genealogy is also a diagnostics, and, especially if we allow the Nietzschean influence on Foucault to shine through, that involves judgement. The diagnosis judges its subject as a living, present, body.

What I have attempted to do in this book is to consider what I would regard as *specific* genealogies; exploring certain contemporary feminist theoretical work and certain specific concepts has led me to argue that feminist theoretical argument is, in the sense of genealogy, *non-identical*; the movements of historical change have drawn the feminist political imagination towards other figures and modes of argument, and have placed feminist voices within political horizons and concerns that are not essentially 'feminist' while simultaneously being of fundamental importance to the mode of argumentation presently understood as feminist. The book does not form one complete and united history, and nor should it, for feminist thought has indeed a disparate past, and certainly its 'origins' can be correctly found in a myriad of different times and places. Nor has my point been to argue that there are secrets animating the feminist political imagination; there is nothing secret about the relationships I have pursued. But I have wanted to express a certain way of viewing contemporary feminist debate, to comment on the 'living body' of feminist thought by becoming alive to the other histories, rhetorics and debates that are simultaneously implicated.

If the attitude to the past is one that refuses to see it as containing 'the origins', the attitude to the present refuses to regard it as a special time, as destined by the past or as the completion of it. The present is treated respectfully – in all its contradictions – but without elevating it, totalising it or even pretending to 'know' it. I enjoy Foucault's attitude, as I had reason to quote in Chapter 1, which was that today 'is a day like any other, or much more, a day which is never like another' (Lotringer, 1989: 251). Thus, in distancing myself from debates that see the demise of feminist thought in its intermingling with 'post-structuralism', I would wish to refuse the 'apocalyptic tone' that resounds not only in philosophy but also in other forms of theorising. Doing genealogical feminist criticism is about being apocalyptic only in the sense of a hoping for the end of masculinist privilege and patriarchal attitudes (as Lee Quinby (1994) argues); otherwise, genealogy is anti-apocalyptic since it is too interested in the past and present to become so obsessive about the future. Feminism should avoid, I believe, being drawn into the apocalyptic tones of theorising the 'ends' of things. The possibility of ends might be real, terrifying, dramatic, and in this era of nuclear power, Nancy may be correct that, unlike good, evil retains its positivity in the present. But too much of social theory has become caught up in the attraction of the suffix 'post'.[2] There is reason to be interested, but I would rather that feminist interest were less about the declaration of 'ends' than in considering how we conceive of ends and what the threat of ends makes us do in the present. There is, of course, a tension in feminism in the sense that it wants the end of its own necessity – it is 'suicidal' – and is therefore directed at a future 'beyond' the present, but it must stay alive as long as its task is incomplete. Suicide is an affirmation of the present (see Critchley on Blanchot, 1997: 69), and feminism cannot afford to affirm this present. Not yet. 'No apocalypse, not now.' There is a peculiarity to genealogical critique, to which I will return, in this sense: it may extend from certain impulses, interests, desires, but its work is focussed on the present, calling the present – or at least certain aspects of it – into question, without worrying apocalyptically about the 'ends' and getting too embroiled in sketching visions of what the 'beyond' will be.

For the genealogist, therefore, being attentive and alert to the present is, first and foremost, about being interested in the past; genealogy as 'effective history' attends to the present by tracing the present's heritage in the messy 'unstable assemblage of faults, fissures and heterogeneous layers that threaten the fragile inheritor from within or from underneath' (Foucault, 1984a: 82). But it also, I would argue, has a purpose, and involves critical judgement in such a way that it has implications for understanding the present as the beginning of the future. As Wendy Brown has emphasised in her discussion of genealogical politics, the purpose is a disruptive one – to find the fracture lines, the fragility of the present – not in order to push a preformulated political programme, but to make one reflect differently on the present, to dislodge truth effects in such a way that the layers of historical weight become seen and felt. She writes,

> [R]ather than promising a certain future, as progressive history does, genealogy is deployed to incite possible futures. Openings along fault lines, and incitements from destabilised (because denaturalised) configurations of the present comprise the stage of political possibility. But in so doing, these openings and incitements dictate neither the terms nor the direction of political possibility, both of which are matters of imagination and invention, themselves limited by what Foucault terms the 'political ontology of the present'. (1998: 37)

For feminist genealogical criticism, therefore, there will be present con-figurations that are investigated for their fragility, and particular truths that feminists will wish to interrogate for their fault lines, but these investigations need to take place without the prelaid path of a directional feminist politics being simultaneously laid over them. Genealogy means the future is embraced as unknown, even as the present contains the archive of the future genealogist. One must be at peace with the fact that there are

---

2 It is remarkable how the term 'post-feminism' has become 'domesticated' within feminist theory as a way of speaking about the relationship of feminist to post-structuralist theory (see Brooks, 1997). But post-feminism, as a term of the mass media, is about the end of feminism, the exhaustion of its necessity.

more ideas than those contained within academic feminist theory, that there are more ways of arguing than the ones we believe are 'appropriate', and that there will be more struggles than we predict, with different concerns.

But none of this means that feminist imagination should or could remove its futural dimensions. For while genealogy regards political programmes as attempts to direct and 'still' future events, as political rationalities that themselves are subject to genealogical scrutiny, that is not to say that genealogy is disinterested or *unconcerned* for the future; it is rather that when the dual notions propounded by modernist versions of history – that history unfolds, and that change is totalising – are removed, any statements about the future are always presented in the knowledge that they are provisional, that they will be revised, and that what in our present appears progressive – even feminist ventures themselves – *may* need to be radically revised in the future. Such a stance need not be thought weak, or make genealogical feminist critique automatically a liberal enterprise. The impact of the emblem of the cyborg, for example, that Donna Haraway's (1991) 'A cyborg manifesto' introduced with such finesse, has the status of a futural emblem that works exactly on the interstices of the debates concerning the possibility of a feminist engagement which both welcomes the future for all the potentially advantageous changes it may bring – particularly those scientific and technological – while simultaneously being sceptical that 'modern' concerns that have mobilised resistance – particularly socialist–feminist – may be forgotten or rejected in the rush to embrace new possibilities. Haraway's cyborg manifesto has been widely discussed and critiqued; as Linda Howell has noted, it is a 'post-humanist' manifesto, maintaining a politics and vision for the position of women and feminists after the crisis in humanism, and it continues to enliven debate in several intersecting areas of feminist and cultural studies (1995: 199–200). Haraway's cyborg is a feminist emblem that both encompasses diversity and enjoys change, that is beyond the debate on modern and postmodern, and that has an anti-totalising politics that concerns itself, at its most broad, with boundaries. 'Our time', Haraway writes, echoing Kristeva, in which ontology has become cyborg ontology, where boundaries have become 'leaky', is one where she advocates 'pleasure in the confusion of boundaries and . . . responsibility in their construction' (1991: 150). The cyborg is without innocence, and in that sense intervention becomes envisioned as without claims of victimisation, and the purpose of intervention is to disrupt the circuits 'of the super-savers of the new right' (1991: 181).

While the emblem of the cyborg may not be an attractive one to all feminists – it does seem to dovetail with futuristic imagery that has a decidely non-feminist and non-socialist history – it has to my mind certain attractive aspects for the genealogical feminist: the impulse to continue approaching the future but without teleological thinking; to give up innocent claims in the name of directed interventions; to be observant of the boundaries that are being erected, defended and deployed around one and within one's own life and discourse. All these aspects of the cyborg manifesto are in the spirit of Foucault, for despite the fact that commentators are fond of quoting Foucault's refusals to direct or to predict, his position was less a refusal to engage with such questions, and more an attitude of humility that refused to believe that one person or group of people could have the ability to predict. In an interview he remarked:

> I do not believe in the old dirges about decadence . . . the sterility of thought, the bleak and foreboding horizons ahead of us. I believe, on the contrary, that our problem is one of overabundance; not that we are suffering from an emptiness, but that *we lack adequate means to think all that is happening*. (quoted in Gordon, 1993: 31, emphasis added)

As genealogists, we may interrogate some small aspects of this present, and, in particular, as I have attempted in this book, to interrogate boundaries that make up the order of things in this present. One cannot think of all that happens in the present: but the purpose is not to understand all, so that one might 'go to the source' and effect a totalised change. Instead, the purpose is to follow those 'lines of fragility in the present' so as to 'grasp why and how that-which-is might no longer be that-which-is' (Foucault, 1988: 36).

Genealogy doesn't gaze too far into the distance; it shortens its vision to those things nearest to it; but, if genealogy studies that which is closest, it does so 'in an abrupt dispossession, so as to seize it at a distance' (in Rabinow, 1984: 89). It is with the same sentiments that I have presented the essays that form this book, writing as I am about feminist theory, which has so often been my 'home base' ground for other investigations, in order to regard it at a distance. Attempting to avoid the arrogance and sterility of the survey, the book has instead been an attempt to give some serious attention to some aspects of some feminist thought, and to find a different way into the debates that make up contemporary feminist theory. Perhaps what I have written will be received as addressing the debate about 'difference' within feminist theory, which it does, although from an unusual angle. This debate occupies much of contemporary feminist theory. The most pressing, the most difficult and the most hopeful question: how is feminist theory to adequately theorise the diversity amongst women – their differences – while retaining a defining interest in the category 'women'? In terms of 'race', ethnicity, sexuality, religion, location and age, to name only the main aspects debated, 'women' are a diverse group with a diverse range of affiliations and attachments. Care is needed in making connections, in drawing parallels, and in reaching for adequate 'representations'; sometimes, one might be wiser to accept the partial and ambivalent nature of identity politics. As Rita Felski has recently argued in the context of debating 'difference' within feminist theory:

> Any oppositional politics, surely, operates by means of a complex array of identifications, partial self recognitions, and critical refusals, whereby subordinate social groups negotiate their ambivalent relationships to the representations that define them. Women both are and are not 'women'. A vision of femininity as pure

otherness cannot speak to this messy blend of tradition and inoculation, of recuperation and recreation, of borrowing from the past and imagining the future, that shapes feminist practice. (1997: 7)

In this book I have attempted to contribute to this discussion without being straightforwardly 'within' it. I have argued that in the few examples I have chosen feminist theory is internally connected in other histories, ones that shape its political imagination – especially its imagination of who its 'enemies' and what its fears are – and ones that shape its allegiances and its theoretical choices. The feminist theorists I have discussed are involved in histories that are about other histories than those that a steady focus on 'women' or 'the history of feminism' might reveal. I have not been comprehensive in my task, but, in the essays that I have presented here, I have deliberately wanted my mind's eye to wander away from the logic of the arguments in order to consider some of the details of what was argued, of how the argument was articulated, and some aspects of the histories of these ways of arguing. Rather reluctantly, given the proliferation of ways of (re)naming the model of subjectivity best suited to feminist enquiry, I would plump for that of Teresa de Lauretis, to suggest that this has been a study of the 'eccentric subject' of feminism, for I feel a certain allegiance to her position that feminist theory's discursive and epistemological character lies in 'its being at once inside its own social and discursive determinations, and yet also outside and excessive to them' (1990: 116). De Lauretis welcomes the critical awareness of recent feminist theoretical work, arguing that reconceptualising feminism involves not merely reconceptualising the subject of feminism as purely constituted along one axis – that of gender – but also a shifting or displacing of 'any notion of feminism as an all encompassing home' (1990: 136). Here she is drawing upon the arguments of Biddy Martin and Chandra Mohanty (1986), who are drawing, in turn, upon the work of Minnie Bruce Pratt (1984), in her articulation of a new way of seeing feminist consciousness necessarily set in relation to new ways of seeing feminism beyond a unidimensional gender perspective and beyond a feminist subject reliant upon 'the opposition of woman to man on the axis of gender and purely constituted by the oppression, repression or negation of its sexual difference' (de Lauretis, 1990: 137).[3] Moreover, to see feminism as a 'home' that contains discrete, coherent and absolutely separate identities does not deal with the complexities of difference; these complexities require that one's conceptualisation of what feminism *is* becomes able to deal with a 'leaving home' that means a displacing of any feminism which articulates an ideology of the same and the bounded. Her notion of eccentricity owes much to her reading of Monique Wittig (1980, 1981), for whom the term 'lesbian' exists outside (is excessive to) the terms

3 De Lauretis writes, 'The understanding feminism as a community whose boundaries shift and whose differences can be expressed and renegotiated through connections both interpersonal and political goes hand in hand with a particular understanding of individual experience as the result of a complex bundle of determinations and struggles, a process of continuing renegotiation of external pressures and internal resistances' (1990: 137).

of gender since a lesbian is not defined in relation to a man and is therefore *not a woman*, whose definition is her socio-economic relation to men.[4] Wittig's arguments inspire de Lauretis to suggest that one might develop a feminist consciousness which is eccentric, which is 'a form of feminist consciousness that can only exist historically, in the here and now, as the consciousness of a "something else"' (1990: 145).

Thus have I attempted to think feminist theory from both within and without, to be at once intimately concerned with it, while my attention was drawn to the places where the boundaries are necessarily blurred, where the concerns with and of feminism take one outside the boundaries of what is thought to constitute it. When de Beauvoir reaches out to make a connection with a character from her friend's novel, what does it mean for feminist theorising that this character is a black man? When feminist theorists use Hannah Arendt in order to think through contemporary feminist politics, what happens to her controversial racial politics in relation to desegregation? What questions are raised about the relation of gender and ethnicity if one reads Judith Butler's use of the term 'mimesis' as an echo of theoretical work on anti-Semitism? When feminists argue a need to theorise embodiment without essentialism, is it simply in the name of a better theory, or is there a motivation that concerns the historical deployment of essentialism, concerns of embodiment and history that have occupied those attempting to comprehend other sorts of bodies than those constituted along the gender axes? Pushing at questions such as these I have wanted to make some contribution to feminist theory while I am not sure that I would wish any of it to be concluded in absolutist terms. I have wanted to suggest that feminist argument has a complex and non-obvious relation to the history of this century, in particular to the impact that fascistic politics has had on the way in which the political landscape is imagined, and the struggles of the civil rights movement in America. Such arguments are 'real' in the sense that someone better qualified than I could do a conventional history of these relations, but there are also traces of these relations in the mode and shape of contemporary feminist theoretical debate, in the discursive tactics, conceptual armoury and imaginative landscapes that feminist theory presently employs. That should not mean that I advocate a feminist theory that is always seeking to locate itself in relation to these miserable markers of the twentieth century. It is no doubt

4 Wittig's argument has been enormously influential as an attempt to rethink a materialist feminist analysis. Here she is important in that she argues that feminism should lose women as the focus of feminism, and should conceive the social subject in terms that exceed the categories of gender – such as 'lesbian' (de Lauretis, 1990: 143).

De Lauretis is attracted by the notion that Wittig's lesbian is not simply an individual with a personal 'sexual preference' or a social subject with a simply 'political' priority, but an eccentric subject constituted in a process of struggle and interpretation, a rewriting of self – as Martin and Mohanty say – in relation to a new understanding of community, of history, of culture. See Phelan, 1997 for a sympathetic but more recent take on these questions in the context of thinking 'lesbian politics'.

the case that viewed from elsewhere the contours of the twentieth-century political landscape would be rather different. It is *not* my argument that these *are* and *should forever* be the markers of thinking feminist politics. Rather, in support of those who would argue that feminist theories are located and require a politics of location (Rich, 1986; Mohanty, 1993), the implication is that there are genealogical investigations that are not about declaring one's location as an obvious and explicit fact, but about exploring the complexities of one's temporal and spatial location as it effects one's very mode of argumentation.

An eccentric feminist consciousness – like the 'ecstatic' in Jean-Luc Nancy's notion of 'community' – is one that does not seek a common identity that is expressed in the political interventions of feminism. It is one that can explore and make present its eccentricity without losing the exposition of the 'being together with' that retreats from the idea of common substance or identity that is constituted similarly for each and every existence that it purportedly 'represents'. It is with this eccentric consciousness that feminist genealogical thought operates; it is this which is performed and which constitutes its appearance.

The status of the future is somewhat complicated in genealogy because the questioning of one's hopes has turned, much to the chagrin of several commentators, even to the basic good and goal of freedom, arguing both that freedom is in the present and that it is best understood as a practice, as opposed to a timeless positivity. Freedom is not given a location, a place which political movements might aim toward, but freedom is seen as already within the present – we are, Foucault once argued, possibly much freer than we think we are. The status of critique, then, is not so much about designing models for the future, but about conduct in the present; it is an active engagement with the modes of freedom practised in the present, with their contingencies and consequences. Such a critique is

> genealogical in the sense that it will not deduce from the form of what we are, what it is possible for us to do and to know; but it will separate out, from the contingency that has made us what we are, the possibility of no longer being, doing or thinking what we are, or do, or think. It is not seeking to make possible a metaphysics that has finally become a science; it is seeking to give new impetus, as far and as wide as possible, to the undefined work of freedom. (Foucault, 1984a: 46)

Just as Haraway's cyborg manifesto frustrates in its refusal to state categorically which boundaries are the target, which changes should be demanded (although Haraway gives us a sense of which are prioritised for her), so a genealogical feminist politics has a general remit which does not direct the nature of feminist enquiry so much as offer an attitude. Genealogical feminism entails both 'a genealogy of the forces that subject us and an exercise in transforming them into forces of freedom' (Quinby, 1997: 165). But the 'undefined work of freedom' is not complacent; rather, it is open to the future, refusing to act as if feminism has the political chart drawn up that will guide critique through any possible future event.

Genealogical feminism has to resist the tendency to see always the same patterns, has always instead to begin again, in order to make the present strange, in order to consider being otherwise.

Caruth reminds us that there is an act of leaving at the core of trauma, one echoed in Freud's own departure from the city of Vienna, which he regarded as a movement to freedom. In a letter to his son, Freud speaks of the freedom that being forced to leave gave him; he was concerned both to be free to publish his text, and to be allowed to die in freedom (Caruth, 1996: 23). The last four words of Freud's text 'to die in freedom' were written in English in the original, leading Caruth to suggest that the leaving that is required to reach freedom is rehearsed in the form of departure that is required for the reader who reads a movement from German to English. Moreover, Caruth suggests, we need to comprehend that departure in relation to the central argument of *Moses and Monotheism*, that history is never simply one's own, that history is precisely the way we are implicated in each other's traumas. The act of departure that is Nietzsche's 'leaving town', and the genealogist's mimicry of that movement in her approach to the present, is also, in itself, a movement within the undefined work of freedom and, as I have argued, a movement that connects genealogical feminist critique with other histories of the present.

In the preceding chapters I have been concerned with the question of *how* that connection is articulated. I have chosen to approach particular writers in a way that attends to their mode of argumentation, such that the task becomes almost akin to a study of rhetoric. This, too, is how Denise Riley explained her approach to feminist discourse, as I have mentioned, when she wrote that 'the question of the politics of identity could be rephrased as a question of rhetoric', and that that would be concerned with 'what the proliferations of addresses, descriptions, and attributions were doing' (1992: 122). This work has considered the voices of some privileged feminist figures, and I have posed my questions so as to enquire into the connections that have been made or refused, to trace them not in order to judge them in a futile exercise of individual assessment, but to think about what these modes of argument are doing. Collectively, I have wanted to suggest that there is a reaching out that one can find within the exclusive practice that is feminism. Such an approach is concerned with the past of present feminist arguments, and it is concerned to trace the other histories and moments of connections outside the sculpting of feminist enunciative positions. When one speaks 'as a feminist', one need not necessarily understand that speech as a mode of closure, as a mode of *ressentiment*, although one must be alert to those tendencies. Nor need the connections that are made involve the measuring of respective sufferings; rather, the conceptual and historical investigations that I have engaged in this book are intended to intervene by arguing that the implication of other histories in feminism can be a resource for the difficult work of thinking through the history of feminist rhetoric, and the genealogy of the feminist political imagination. I have hoped to allow feminist theory to show itself in (some of) its historical complexity, by showing how these specific genealogies point to the complexity of the sculpting of feminist political imagination. In an earlier chapter I had reason to quote Judith Butler on the phantasmatic nature of the feminist 'we':

> The tenuous or phantasmatic status of the 'we' however, is not a cause for despair, or not *only* a cause for despair. The radical instability of the category sets into question the *foundational* restrictions on feminist political theorizing and opens up other configurations, not only of genders and bodies, but of politics itself. (1990: 142)

It is with this hope that I would wish to end; that exploring the edges of feminist thought – those moments where feminism blurs into other connections, where its affections and worries are revealed, where one can trace constitutional manoeuvres in the feminist political landscape – may be received as a contribution to the task of holding open the possibilities for a non-foundational configuration of eccentric feminist politics.

REFERENCES

Adorno, T. (1973) *Negative Dialectics*. London: Routledge.

Adorno, T. and Horkheimer, M. (1986) *Dialectic of Enlightenment*. London: Verso. (First published 1944.)

Ansell-Pearson, K. (1994) *An Introduction to Nietzsche as Political Thinker*. Cambridge: Cambridge University Press.

Anzaldua, G. (ed.) (1990) *Making Faces, Making Soul/Haciendo Caras*. San Francisco: Aunt Lute Foundation.

Arendt, H. (1959a) 'Reflections on Little Rock', *Dissent*, Vol. 6.

Arendt, H. (1959b) *The Human Condition: A Study of the Central Dilemmas Facing Modern Man*. New York: Doubleday Anchor.

Arendt, H. (1963a) 'The crisis of education', in H. Arendt (ed.), *Between Past and Future: Six Exercises in Political Thought*. New York: Meridian.

Arendt, H. (1963b) 'What is freedom?', in H. Arendt (ed.), *Between Past and Future: Six Exercises in Political Thought*. New York: Meridian.

Arendt, H. (1973) *The Origins of Totalitarianism*. San Diego, CA: Harvest, Harcourt, Brace and Co.

Arendt, H. (1977) *Eichmann in Jerusalem: A Report on the Banality of Evil*. New York: Penguin. (First published 1963.)

Arendt, H. (1978a) *The Life of the Mind*. New York: Harcourt Brace Jovanovich.

Arendt, H. (1978b) 'Martin Heidegger at eighty', in M. Murray (ed.), *Heidegger and Modern Philosophy*. New Haven, CT: Yale University Press. (First published 1971.)

Arendt, H. (1984) 'Thinking and moral considerations', *Social Research*, Fiftieth Anniversary Issue, Vol. 38 (Spring/Summer).

Aschheim, S. (1992) *Nietzsche's Legacy in Germany 1890–1990*. Berkeley, CA: University of California Press.

Austin, J.L. (1962) *How to do Things with Words*. Cambridge, MA: Harvard University Press.

Baeumler, A. (1966) 'Nietzsche and National Socialism', in G. Mosse (ed.), *Nazi Culture*. London: W.H. Allen. (First published 1937.)

Bair, D. (1990) *Simone de Beauvoir: A Biography*. London: Vintage.

Baker, Houston, Jr (1991) *Workings of the Spirit: The Poetics of Afro-American Women's Writing*. Chicago: University of Chicago Press.

Bar On, Bat-Ami (1996) 'Women in dark times: Rahel Varnhagen, Rosa Luxemborg, Hannah Arendt and Me', in L. May and J. Kohn (eds), *Hannah Arendt: Twenty Years Later*. Cambridge, MA: MIT.

Bartky, S. (1988) 'Foucault, feminism and the modernisation of patriarchal power', in I. Diamond and L. Quinby (eds), *Feminism and Foucault: Reflections on Resistance*. Boston: Northeastern University Press.

Bauman, Z. (1989) *Modernity and the Holocaust*. Cambridge: Polity Press.

Beiner, R. (1983) *Political Judgement*. London: Methuen.

Bell, V. (1994) 'Dreaming and time in Foucault's philosophy', *Theory, Culture & Society*, 11: 2.

Bell, V. (1995) 'On metaphors of suffering', *Economy & Society*, 24: 4.

Bell, V. (1996) 'Show and tell: passing and narrative in Toni Morrison's *Jazz*', *Social Identities*, 2: 2.

Bellour, R. (1992) 'Towards fiction', in T. Armstrong (ed.), *Michel Foucault: Philosopher*. Hemel Hempstead: Harvester Wheatsheaf.

Benhabib, S. (1995) 'The pariah and her shadow: Hannah Arendt's biography of Rahel Varnhagen', in B. Honig (ed.), *Feminist Interpretations of Hannah Arendt*. Philadelphia: Pennsylvania State University Press.

Benhabib, S. (1996) *The Reluctant Modernism of Hannah Arendt*. Thousand Oaks, CA: Sage.

Benjamin, A. (1997) *Present Hope: Philosophy, Architecture, Judaism*. London: Routledge.

Benjamin, W. (1992) *Illuminations* (with an introduction by H. Arendt). London: Fontana Press.

Bennington, G. and Derrida, J. (1993) *Jacques Derrida* (trans. G. Bennington). Chicago: University of Chicago Press.

Bergner, G. (1995) 'The role of gender in Fanon's *Black Skin, White Masks*', *PMLA*, Vol. 110.

Bernauer, J. (1995) 'Beyond life and death: on Foucault's post-Auschwitz ethic', in T. Armstrong (ed.), *Michel Foucault: Philosopher*. Hemel Hempstead: Harvester Wheatsheaf.

Bhabha, H. (1986) 'Foreword: remembering Fanon', in F. Fanon (ed.), *Black Skin, White Masks*. London: Pluto Press.

Bhabha, H. (1994) *The Location of Culture*. London: Routledge.

Bickford, S. (1995) 'In the presence of others: Arendt and Anzaldua on the paradox of public appearance', in B. Honig (ed.), *Feminist Interpretations of Hannah Arendt*. Philadelphia: Pennsylvania State University Press.

Binswanger, L. (1986) 'Dream and Existence' (trans. J. Needleman), in K. Hoeller (ed.), *Dream and Existence* (special issue of *Review of Existential Psychology and Psychiatry*), first published 1930. Seattle: REPP.

Blanchot, M. (1986) *The Writing of the Disaster* (trans. A. Smock), Lincoln, NE/London: University of Nebraska Press.

Bohman, J. (1996) 'The moral costs of political pluralism: the dilemmas of difference and equality in Arendt's "Reflections on Little Rock"', in L. May and J. Kohn (eds), *Hannah Arendt: Twenty Years Later*. Cambridge, MA: MIT.

Bone, R. (1986) 'Wright and the Chicago Renaissance', *Calalloo*, 9: 3.

Bordo, S. (1993) *Unbearable Weight: Feminism, Western Culture and the Body*. Berkeley, CA: University of California Press.

Bourdieu, P. (1991) *Language and Symbolic Power* (trans. G. Raymond and M. Adamson). Cambridge, MA: Harvard University Press.

Boyarin, D. and Boyarin, J. (1993) 'Diaspora: generation and the ground of Jewish identity', *Critical Inquiry*, Vol. 19 (Summer).

Boyarin, J. (1995) 'Before the law, there stands a woman: in *Re Taylor v. Butler* (with court-appointed Yiddish translator)', *Cardozo Law Review*, Vol. 16.

Boyarin, J. (1996) *Thinking in Jewish*. Chicago: University of Chicago Press.

Boyarin, J. and Boyarin, D. (1995) 'Self-exposure as theory: the double mark of the male Jew', in D. Battaglia (ed.), *Rhetorics of Self-Making*. Berkeley/Los Angeles: University of California Press.

Bradshaw, L. (1989) *Acting and Thinking: The Political Thought of Hannah Arendt*. Toronto: University of Toronto Press.

Brah, A. (1996) *Cartographies of Diaspora*. London: Routledge.

Brooks, A. (1997) *Postfeminisms: Feminism, Cultural Theory and Cultural Forms*. London: Routledge.

Brown, W. (1995) *States of Injury: Power and Freedom in Late Modernity*. Princeton, NJ: Princeton University Press.

Brown, W. (1998) 'Genealogical politics', in J. Moss (ed.), *The Later Foucault*. London: Sage.

Butler, J. (1987) *Subjects of Desire: Hegelian Reflections in Twentieth Century France*. New York: Columbia University Press.

Butler, J. (1990) *Gender Trouble: Feminism and the Subversion of Identity*. New York: Routledge.

Butler, J. (1991) 'Imitation and gender insubordination', in D. Fuss (ed.), *Inside/Out: Lesbian and Gay Theories*. New York: Routledge.

Butler, J. (1993a) *Bodies that Matter: On the Discursive Limits of 'Sex'*. New York: Routledge.

Butler, J. (1993b) 'Endangered/endangering: schematic racism and white paranoia', in R.

Gooding-Williams (ed.), *Reading Rodney King: Reading Urban Uprising*. New York: Routledge.

Butler, J. (1995) 'For a careful reading', in S. Benhabib et al. (eds), *Feminist Contentions*. New York: Routledge.

Butler, J. (1997a) *Excitable Speech*. New York: Routledge.

Butler, J. (1997b) *The Psychic Life of Power: Theories in Subjection*. Stanford, CA: Stanford University Press.

Butler, J. (1998) 'Merely cultural', *New Left Review*, January/February.

Caraway, N. (1991) *Segregated Sisterhood: Racism and the Politics of American Feminism*. Knoxville: University of Tennessee Press.

Caruth, C. (1996) *Unclaimed Experience: Trauma, Narrative and History*. Baltimore, MD: Johns Hopkins University Press.

Chanter, T. (1995) *Ethics of Eros: Irigaray's Rewriting of the Philosophers*. London: Routledge.

Cheyette, B. (1995) 'Jews and Jewishness in the writings of George Eliot and Frantz Fanon', *Patterns of Prejudice*, 29: 4.

Cixous, H. (1993) 'We who are free, are we free?', in B. Johnson (ed.), *Freedom and Interpretation: The Oxford Amnesty Lectures 1992*. New York: Basic Books.

Clifford, J. (1997) *Routes*. Cambridge, MA: Harvard University Press.

Cornell, D. (1997) 'Gender hierarchy, equality and the possibility of democracy', in J. Dean (ed.), *Feminism and the New Democracy: Resiting the Political*. New York: Sage.

Critchley, S. (1997) *Very Little, Almost Nothing: Death, Philosophy, Literature*. London: Routledge.

De Beauvoir, S. (1991) *Letters to Sartre* (translated and edited by Quintin Hoare). London: Radius.

De Beauvoir, S. (1993) *The Second Sex*. London: Everyman. (First published 1949.)

Decosta-Willis, M. (1986) 'Avenging angels and mute mothers: Black Southern women in Wright's fictional world', *Calalloo*, 9: 3.

De Lauretis, T. (1987) *Technologies of Gender*. Basingstoke: Macmillan.

De Lauretis, T. (1990) 'Eccentric subjects: feminist theory and historical consciousness', *Feminist Studies*, 16: 1 (Spring).

Deleuze, G. and Guattari, F. (1984) *Anti-Oedipus: Capitalism and Schizophrenia*. London: Athlone Press.

Dellamora, R. (ed.) (1995) *Postmodern Apocalypse: Theory and Cultural Practice at the End*. Philadelphia: University of Pennsylvania Press.

De Man, P. (1986) *Allegories of Reading*. New Haven, CT: Yale University Press.

Derrida, J. (1988) *Limited, Inc.* (trans. S. Weber and J. Mehlman). Evanston, IL: Northwestern University Press.

Dietz, M. (1994) 'Hannah Arendt and feminist politics', in L. Hinchman and S. Hinchman (eds), *Hannah Arendt: Critical Essays*. Albany: State University of New York Press.

Drake, St. Clair and Cayton, H.R. (1945) *Black Metropolis: A Study of Negro Life in a Northern City*. New York: Harcourt, Brace and Co.

Durham, M. (1998) *Women and Fascism*. London: Routledge.

Elshtain, J. (1995) 'Political children', in B. Honig (ed.), *Feminist Interpretations of Hannah Arendt*. Philadelphia: Pennsylvania State University Press.

Eribon, D. (1991) *Michel Foucault* (trans. B. Wing). Cambridge, MA: Harvard University Press.

Ettinger, E. (1995) *Hannah Arendt: Martin Heidegger*. New Haven, CT: Yale University Press.

Fabre, M. (1985) *The World of Richard Wright*. Jackson: University Press of Mississipi.

Fanon, F. (1969) *The Wretched of the Earth*. Harmondsworth: Penguin. (First published 1961 in French.)

Fanon, F. (1986) *Black Skin, White Masks*. London: Pluto Press. (First published 1952 in French.)

Fanon, F. (1989) *Studies in a Dying Colonialism*. London: Earthscan. (First published 1959.)

Felski, R. (1989) 'Feminism, postmodernism and the critique of modernity', *Cultural Critique*, Vol. 13.

Felski, R. (1997) 'The doxa of difference', *Signs*, 23: 1.

Fergusson, K. (1993) *The Man Question: Visions of Subjectivity in Feminist Theory*. Berkeley/ Los Angeles: University of California Press.

Flax, J. (1993) *Disputed Subjects: Essays on Psychoanalysis, Politics and Philosophy*. New York: Routledge.

Foucault, M. (1970) *The Order of Things: An Archaeology of the Human Sciences*. London: Tavistock.

Foucault, M. (1981) *The History of Sexuality Volume One*. Harmondsworth: Penguin.

Foucault, M. (1984a) 'Nietzsche, genealogy, history', in P. Rabinow (ed.), *The Foucault Reader*. New York: Pantheon Books.

Foucault, M. (1984b) 'Preface', in G. Deleuze and F. Guattari (eds), *Anti-Oedipus: Capitalism and Schizophrenia*. London: Athlone Press.

Foucault, M. (1986) 'Dream, imagination and existence', in K. Hoeller (ed.), *Dream and Existence* (special issue of *Review of Existential Psychology and Psychiatry*), first published 1930. Seattle: REPP.

Foucault, M. (1988) 'Critical theory/intellectual history', in L. Kritzman (ed.), *Michel Foucault: Politics, Philosophy, Culture: Interviews and Other Writings 1977–1984*. New York: Routledge.

Foucault, M. (1996) 'Paris–Berlin', in S. Lotringer (ed.), *Foucault Live: Collected Interviews 1961–1984* (trans. L. Hochroth and J. Johnston). New York: Semiotext(e).

Fraser, M. (1999) 'Classing queer: politics in competition', *Theory, Culture & Society*, 16: 2.

Fraser, N. (1991) 'Rethinking the public sphere: a contribution to the critique of actually existing democracy', in C. Calhoun (ed.), *Habermas and the Public Sphere*. Cambridge, MA: MIT Press.

Fraser, N. (1997) *Justice Interruptus: Critical Reflections on the 'Post-Socialist' Condition*. New York: Routledge.

Fraser, N. (1998) 'Heterosexism, misrecognition and capitalism: a response to Judith Butler', *New Left Review* (March/April).

Fuss, D. (1989) *Essentially Speaking: Feminism, Nature and Difference*. New York: Routledge.

Fuss, D. (1994) 'Interior colonies: Frantz Fanon and the politics of identification', *Diacritics*, 24: 2–3.

Gatens, M. (1996) *Imaginary Bodies: Ethics, Power and Corporeality*. London: Routledge.

Gayle, A. (1980) *Richard Wright: Ordeal of a Native Son*. New York: Anchor Press/ Doubleday.

Gilroy, P. (1993) *The Black Atlantic: Modernity and Double Consciousness*. London: Verso.

Gilroy, P. (1994) 'After the love has gone: biopolitics and ethnopoetics in the Black public sphere', *Third Text*, Vol. 38.

Gilroy, P. (1996) 'Introduction' to R. Wright, *Eight Men*. New York: Harper Perennial.

Girard, R. (1978) 'Interview', *Diacritics* (March).

Gordon, C. (1993) 'Question, ethos, event: Foucault on Kant and enlightenment', in M. Gane and T. Johnson (eds), *Foucault's New Domains*. London: Routledge.

Gordon, L., Sharpley-Whiting, T. and White, R. (eds) (1996) *Fanon: A Critical Reader*. Oxford: Blackwell.

Grewal, I. and Kaplan, C. (1994) *Scattered Hegemonies: Postmodernity and Transnational Feminist Practices*. Minneapolis: University of Minnesota Press.

Grosz, E. (1990) 'Conclusion: a note on essentialism and difference', in S. Gunew (ed.), *Feminist Knowledge: Critique and Construct*. New York: Routledge.

Grosz, E. (1994) *Volatile Bodies: Toward a Corporeal Feminism*. Cambridge: Polity.

Hacking, I. (1994) 'Memoro-politics, trauma and the soul', *History of the Human Sciences*, 7: 2.

Haraway, D. (1991) 'A cyborg manifesto: science, technology and socialist-feminism in the late twentieth century', in *Simians, Cyborgs and Women: The Reinvention of Nature*. London: Free Association Books.

Havas, R. (1995) *Nietzsche's Genealogy: Nihilism and the Will to Knowledge*. Ithaca, NY: Cornell University Press.

Heath, S. (1978) 'Difference', *Screen*, 19: 3 (Autumn).

Heidegger, M. (1993a) 'On the essence of truth', in *Martin Heidegger: Basic Writings*. London: Routledge.

Heidegger, M. (1993b) 'Letter on humanism', in *Martin Heidegger: Basic Writings*. London: Routledge.

Hekman, S. (ed.) (1996) *Feminist Interpretations of Michel Foucault*. Philadelphia: Pennsylvania State University Press.

Helie-Lucas, M.-A. (1990) 'Women, nationalism and religion in the Algerian liberation struggle', in M. Badran and M. Cooke (eds), *Opening the Gates: A Century of Arab Feminist Writing*. London: Virago.

Heller, A. (1993) *A Philosophy of History in Fragments*. Oxford: Blackwell.

Hemenway, R. (1986) *Zora Neale Hurston: a literary biography*. London: Camden Press.

Hennessey, R. (1995) 'Queer visibility in commodity culture', in L. Nicholson and S. Seidman (eds), *Social Postmodernism: Beyond Identity Politics*. Cambridge: Cambridge University Press.

Hewitt, A. (1994) 'A feminine dialectic of enlightenment? Horkheimer and Adorno revisited', *New German Critique*, Vol. 28.

Hewitt, A. (1995) 'Coitus interruptus: fascism and the deaths of history', in R. Dolamore (ed.), *Postmodern Apocalypse*. Philadelphia: University of Pennsylvania Press.

Honig, B. (1995) 'Toward an agonistic feminism: Hannah Arendt and the politics of identity', in B. Honig (ed.), *Feminist Interpretations of Hannah Arendt*. University Park: Pennsylvania State University Press

hooks, b. (1982) *Ain't I a Woman? Black Women and Feminism*. London: Pluto Press.

hooks, b. (1984) *Feminist Theory: From Margin to Centre*. Boston: South End Press.

hooks, b. (1991) *Yearning: Race, Gender and Cultural Politics*. London: Turnaround.

Howell, L. (1995) 'The cyborg manifesto revisited: issues and methods for technocultural feminism', in R. Dellamora (ed.), *Postmodern Apocalypse: Theory and Cultural Practice at the End*. Philadelphia: University of Pennsylvania Press.

Hutchings, K. (1996) *Kant, Critique and Politics*. London: Routledge.

Huyssen, A. (1990) 'Mapping the postmodern', in L. Nicholson (ed.), *Feminism/ Postmodernism*. New York: Routledge.

Irigaray, L. (1985) *This Sex Which is Not One* (trans. C. Porter with C. Burke). Ithaca, NY: Cornell University Press.

Irigaray, L. (1986) 'The fecundity of the caress', in R. Cohen (ed.), *Face to Face with Levinas*. Albany: State University of New York.

Irigaray, L. (1991) 'Questions to Emmanuel Levinas', in R. Bernasconi and S. Critchley (eds), *Re-Reading Levinas*. Bloomington: Indiana University Press.

Jayawardena, K. (1995) *The White Woman's Other Burden: Western Women and South Asia During British Rule*. New York: Routledge.

Kaplan, M. (1995) 'Refiguring the Jewish question: Arendt, Proust and the politics of sexuality', in B. Honig (ed.), *Feminist Interpretations of Hannah Arendt*. University Park: Pennsylvania State University Press.

Kinnamon, K. and Fabre, M. (1993) *Conversations with Richard Wright*. Jackson: University Press of Mississippi.

Kristeva, J. (1986) 'Women's time', in T. Moi (ed.), *The Kristeva Reader*. New York: Columbia University Press. (First published 1979 in French.)

Laclau, E. (1996) *Emancipation(s)*. London: Verso.

Lacoue-Labarthe, P. and Nancy, J.-L. (1990) 'The Nazi myth', *Critical Inquiry*, Vol. 16.

Levinas, E. (1969) *Totality and Infinity* (trans. A. Lingis). Pittsburgh: Duquesne University Press.

Levinas, E. (1985) *Ethics and Infinity: Conversations with Philippe Nemo* (trans. R. Cohen). Pittsburgh: Duquesne University Press.

Levinas, E. (1987) *Time & the Other* (trans. R. Cohen). Pittsburgh: Duquesne University Press.

Levinas, E. (1988) 'Useless suffering', in L. Bernasconi and D. Wood (eds), *The Provocation of Levinas*. London: Routledge.

Levinas, E. (1990) 'The politics of Hitlerism', *Critical Inquiry*, Vol. 17 (first published 1933).

Lotringer, S. (ed.) (1989) *Foucault Live* (trans. Mia Foret and Marion Martius). New York: Semiotext(e).

Lundgren-Gothlin, E. (1996) *Sex and Existence: Simone de Beauvoir's 'The Second Sex'*. London: Athlone Press.

MacIntyre, A. (1990) *Three Rival Versions of Moral Enquiry*. London: Duckworth.

MacNay, L. (1992) *Foucault and Feminism*. Cambridge: Polity.

MacNay, L. (1999) 'Subject, psyche and agency: the work of Judith Butler', *Theory, Culture & Society*, 16: 2.

Martin, B. and Mohanty, C. (1986) 'Feminist politics: what's home got to do with it?', in T. de Lauretis (ed.), *Feminist Studies/Critical Studies*. Bloomington: Indiana University Press.

May, L. and Kohn, J. (eds) (1996) *Hannah Arendt: Twenty Years Later*. Cambridge, MA: MIT Press.

McCall, D. (1988) 'The bad nigger', in H. Bloom (ed.), *Modern Critical Interpretations: Native Son*. New York: Chelsea House.

Michaud, E. (1993) 'National Socialist architecture as an acceleration of time', *Critical Inquiry*, Vol. 19 (Winter).

Modleski, T. (1991) *Feminism Without Women: Culture and Criticism in a 'Postfeminist' Age*. New York: Routledge.

Mohanty, C. (1993) 'Under Western eyes: feminist scholarship and colonial discourses', in P. Williams and L. Chrisman (eds), *Colonial Discourse and Post-Colonial Theory*. Hemel Hempstead: Harvester Wheatsheaf.

Moi, T. (1994) *Simone de Beauvoir: The Making of an Intellectual Woman*. Oxford: Blackwell.

Moraga, C. and Anzaldua, G. (eds) (1983) *This Bridge Called My Back*. New York: Women of Colour Press.

Mosse, G. (ed.) (1966) *Nazi Culture*. London: W.H. Allen.

Nancy, J.-L. (1991) *The Inoperative Community* (trans. P. Connor, L. Garbus, M. Holland and S. Sawhney). Minneapolis: University of Minnesota Press.

Nancy, J.-L. (1992) 'La comparution/the compearance: from the existence of "Communism" to the Community of "Existence"' (trans. T. Strong). *Political Theory*, 20: 3 (August).

Nancy, J.-L. (1993a) *The Birth To Presence* (trans. B. Holmes et al.). Stanford, CA: Stanford University Press.

Nancy, J.-L. (1993b) *The Experience of Freedom*. Stanford, CA: Stanford University Press.

Nietzsche, F. (1909) 'The will to power', in O. Levy (ed.), *The Complete Works of Friedrich Nietzsche*. Edinburgh: T.N. Folis.

Nietzsche, F. (1967) *The Genealogy of Morals and Ecce Homo* (trans. W. Kaufmann). New York: Vintage. (First published 1887.)

Nietzsche, F. (1969) *Thus Spoke Zarathustra*. Harmondsworth: Penguin.

Nietzsche, F. (1974) *The Gay Science* (trans. W. Kaufmann). New York: Random House. (First published 1887.)

Nietzsche, F. (1986) *Human, All Too Human: A Book for Free Spirits* (trans. R.J. Hollingdale). Cambridge: Cambridge University Press.

Nietzsche, F. (1989) *Beyond Good and Evil: Prelude to a Philosophy of the Future* (trans. W. Kaufmann). New York: Vintage. (First published 1886.)

Nilson, H. (1998) *Michel Foucault and the Games of Truth* (trans. R. Clark). Basingstoke: Macmillan.

Phelan, S. (1997) '(Be)Coming out: lesbian identity and politics', in J. Dean (ed.), *Feminism and the New Democracy: Resiting the Political*. London: Sage.

Plato (1974) *Plato: The Republic* (trans. D. Lee). Harmondsworth: Penguin.

Pratt, M. (1984) 'Identity: skin, blood, heart', in E. Bulkin, M. Pratt and B. Smith (eds), *Yours in Struggle: Three Feminist Perspectives on Anti-Semitism and Racism*. Brooklyn, NY: Long Haul Press.

Probyn, E. (1993) *Sexing the Self: Gendered Positions in Cultural Studies*. London: Routledge.

Quinby, L. (1994) *Anti-Apocalypse: Exercises in Genealogical Criticism.* Minneapolis: University of Minnesota Press.

Quinby, L. (1997) 'Genealogical feminism: a politics way of looking', in J. Dean (ed.), *Feminism and the New Democracy: Re-siting the Political.* Thousand Oaks, CA: Sage.

Rabinow, P. (1984) *The Foucault Reader.* New York: Pantheon Books.

Ramazanoglu, C. (ed.) (1993) *Up Against Foucault.* London: Routledge.

Rich, A. (1986) *Blood, Bread and Poetry: Selected Prose 1979–85.* New York: W.W. Norton and Co.

Riley, D. (1988) *Am I that Name?: Feminism and the Category of 'Women' in History.* Basingstoke: Macmillan.

Riley, D. (1992) 'A history of some preoccupations', in J. Scott and J. Butler (eds), *Feminists Theorise the Political.* New York: Routledge.

Rose, G. (1993) *Judaism and Modernity: Philosophical Essays.* Oxford: Blackwell.

Rose, G. (1996) *Mourning Becomes the Law: Philosophy and Representation.* Cambridge: Cambridge University Press.

Rose, J. (1993) *Why War? Psychoanalysis, Politics and the Return to Melanie Klein.* Cambridge, MA: Blackwell.

Said, E. (1994) *Culture & Imperialism.* London: Vintage.

Sanchez-Eppeler, K. (1988) 'Bodily bonds: the intersecting rhetorics of feminism and abolition', *Representations*, Vol. 21.

Sartre, J.-P. (1963) *Black Orpheus* (trans. S.W. Allen). Paris: Presence Africaine. (First published as 'Preface' to *Anthologie de la Nouvelle Poesie Negre et Malgache*, 1948.)

Sartre, J.-P. (1965) *Anti-Semite and Jew.* New York: Schoken. (First published 1946.)

Schor, N. (1989) 'This essentialism which is not one: coming to grips with Irigaray', *Differences: A Journal of Feminist Cultural Studies*, 1: 1.

Schott, R.M. (1997) *Feminist Interpretations of Immanuel Kant.* University Park: Pennsylvania State University Press.

Speer, A. (1970) *Inside the Third Reich: Memoirs* (trans. R. Winston and C. Winston). London: Weidenfeld & Nicolson.

Spelman, E. (1988) *Inessential Woman: Problems of Exclusion in Feminist Thought.* Boston: Beacon Press.

Spivak, G. (1988) 'Can the subaltern speak?', in C. Nelson and L. Grossberg (eds), *Marxism and the Interpretation of Culture.* Basingstoke: Macmillan Education.

Spivak, G. (1990) *The Post-Colonial Critic.* London: Routledge.

Spivak, G. (1993) *Outside in the Teaching Machine.* New York: Routledge.

Stoekl, A. (1995) 'Blanchot, violence and the disaster', in L. Kritzman (ed.), *Auschwitz and After: Race, Culture and 'the Jewish Question' in France.* New York: Routledge.

Tapper, M. (1993) 'Ressentiment and power: reflections on feminist practice', in P. Patton (ed.), *Nietzsche, Feminism and Political Theory.* London: Routledge.

Thiele, L.P. (1990) 'The agony of politics: the Nietzschean roots of Foucault's thought', *American Political Science Review*, Vol. 84 (September).

Thiele, L.P. (1995) *Timely Meditations: Martin Heidegger and Postmodern Politics.* Princeton, NJ: Princeton University Press.

Trinh, Minh-ha (1991) *When the Moon Waxes Red: Representation, Gender and Cultural Politics.* New York: Routledge.

Villa, D. (1996a) *Arendt and Heidegger: The Fate of the Political.* Princeton, NJ: Princeton University Press.

Villa, D. (1996b) 'The banality of philosophy: Arendt on Heidegger and Eichmann', in L. May and J. Kohn (eds), *Hannah Arendt: Twenty Years Later.* Cambridge, MA: MIT.

Ware, V. (1992) *Beyond the Pale: White Women, Racism and History.* London: Verso.

Warren, R. (1966) *Who Speaks for the Negro?* New York: Vintage Books.

Williams, J. (1988) *Eyes on the Prize: America's Civil Rights Years 1954–1965.* New York: Penguin.

Wittig, M. (1980) 'The straight mind', *Feminist Issues*, Vol. 1 (Summer).

Wittig, M. (1981) 'One is not born a woman', *Feminist Issues*, Vol. 2 (Winter).

Wright, R. (1945) *Black Boy* (with introduction by D. Fisher). New York: Harper & Brothers. (First published 1937.)

Wright, R. (1953) *The Outsider*. New York: Harper & Brothers.

Wright, R. (1977) *American Hunger*, New York: Harper & Row. (First published 1944.)

Wright, R. (1978a) Twelve Million Black Voices, in *The Richard Wright Reader*. New York: Harper & Row. (First published 1941.)

Wright, R. (1978b) 'Long black song', in *The Richard Wright Reader*. New York: Harper & Row.

Wright, R. (1987) 'Introduction: how Bigger was born', in R. Wright (ed.), *Native Son*. Harmondsworth: Penguin.

Wright, R. (1991) *Native Son*. New York: The Library of America. (First published 1940.)

Young, I.M. (1990) *Throwing Like a Girl and Other Essays in Feminist Philosophy*. Bloomington, IN: Indiana University Press.

Young, L. (1996) 'Missing persons: fantasising black women in *Black Skin, White Masks*', in A. Read (ed.), *The Fact of Blackness*. London: ICA.

Young-Bruehl, E. (1982) *Hannah Arendt: For Love of the World*. New Haven, CT: Yale University Press.

INDEX

Adorno, T., 15, 22, 57, 86, 93–7, 102–3, 105, 106, 108, 111, 120
aesthetic practices, 28, 32, 137
Algerian women, embodiment of, 130–1
Algren, N., 42
alterity, 76
  of black people, 47, 49
  and mimesis, 95–6, 107, 108
  of women, 45–7, 48–9
  see also difference
Ansell-Pearson, K., 67
anti-essentialism, 27, 29, 59, 85, 115
  and embodiment, 123, 132–3, 148
  and identity, 122–3
  see also essentialism
anti-Semitism, 128
  community in, 97
  and mimesis, 94, 95–9, 108, 148
  and Nazism, 99
  and reflection, 97–8
  see also Holocaust; Jewish people
Anzaldua, G., 29
appearance, 62–3, 128
  and natality, 71–5
  in the political realm, 67–71, 75–6, 77, 79–80, 82
  and visibility, 68–9, 70–1, 75–6, 77, 78–9
Arendt, H., 11, 15, 84, 128, 148
  on appearance, 62–3, 67–76
  on desegregation, 63–7, 70
  on difference, 75–80
  on feminism, 83
  on thinking, 81–3
Aristotle, 116
Arnold, E., 13
Aschheim, S., 34
Austin, J.L., 88
authenticity, 76
  in black women, 136
  in Jewish people, 98–9
  in women, 58

Baeumler, A., 33
Bair, D., 42, 43

Bar On, B.-A., 80
Bartky, S.L., 104–5
Bauman, Z., 22
Beauvoir, S. de *see* de Beauvoir, S.
becoming *see* recreation
Beiner, R., 82
Being, 67–8, 82
Bell, V., 37, 44, 71, 127
Bellour, R., 37
Benhabib, S., 75, 76, 80, 91
Benjamin, A., 1, 107
Benjamin, W., 24, 137
Bennington, G., 6
Bergner, G., 124, 127, 132
Bernauer, J., 1
Bhabha, H., 93, 125
Bickford, S., 79, 128
Bigger Thomas *see* Wright, R., *Native Son*
Binswanger, L., 38
birth *see* natality
black people,
  alterity of, 47, 49
  celebration of, 74–5
  historicity of, 125, 129
  living conditions, 55–6
  music, 53–4
  objectification of, 57–8, 127, 128
  passivity of, 58
  and sacrifice, 74
  visibility of, 68–9, 70–1, 75–6, 77, 78–9
  see also racism
black women, authenticity in, 136
blackness *see* racial epidermal schema; visibility
Blanchot, M., 19, 22, 23, 144
body,
  concept of, 117–18, 119–20
  and identity, 120–1, 126–7, 131, 135–6
  and Nazism, 119, 120, 121
  and recreation, 126
  see also embodiment
Bohman, J., 76, 79
Bone, R., 56
Bordo, S., 113, 114, 116, 135

boundaries,
  of feminism, 53
  of the political realm, 62–3, 64, 65, 69, 70,
    80
  of the private realm, 66
  of the social realm, 65–6, 70
Bourdieu, P., 133
Boyarin, D., 7, 92–3, 94, 95, 97, 99–102,
    103–4, 105–6, 107, 109–10, 111
Boyarin, J., 7, 86, 92–3, 94, 95, 97, 99–102,
    103–4, 105–6, 107, 109–10, 111
Bradshaw, L., 81, 82
Brah, A., 110
Brooks, A., 144
Brown, W., 9, 40, 41, 144
Bruehl, E. Young- see Young-Bruehl, E.
Burdi, G., 33–4
Butler, J., 1, 11, 15, 28, 36, 38, 43, 63, 85–6,
    94, 97, 100, 101, 102, 127, 133, 151
  on citation, 106, 107–9, 110
  on cultural constructions of gender, 86–9
  on cultural survival, 102, 105, 106, 109,
    111
  on encrypting, 90, 106–7
  on gender performativity, 87–9, 90–1, 92,
    106, 107, 108–9
  on heterosexual mimesis, 89–92, 103, 104,
    106–7
  on mimesis, 102–3, 148

capitalism, 57
Caraway, N., 8, 135–6, 137
Caruth, C., 140, 150
categorisation, sexual, 27–9, 35, 36
Cayton, H.R., 56
celebration, of black people, 74–5
Chanter, T., 44, 119
Cheyette, B., 129
Chicago School, 56, 57, 60
children, and the political realm, 65, 71–2,
    73
Christianity,
  and Jewish cultural survival, 100–1
  see also morality; Pauline theology
citation, and identity, 106, 107–9, 110
cities, sociology of, 55–8
Cixous, H., 17, 21, 34
class structures, 57
Clifford, J., 110
colonialism, 124–7, 129–30, 131
communism see Marxism
communities, and violence, 7
community,
  in anti-Semitism, 97
  concept of, 19–20, 121

  of feminism, 7, 19, 20, 147
  identity in, 19, 108
  and temporality, 20
  see also Jewish community
concealment, 68
connectivity, 53–4, 58, 59, 60, 61
consciousness, historical, 4
constructionism, 115, 116
  see also cultural constructions
Cornell, D., 78
counterpublic spheres, 76–7, 78, 79, 80
creativity, 58
  see also music
Critchley, S., 144
cross dressing, 90, 106–7
cultural constructions, of gender, 86–9
cultural survival,
  and gender, 103, 104, 105, 106, 109
  of Jewish people, 97, 102, 104, 105–6, 111
    and Christianity, 100–1
    and diaspora, 92–3, 105, 110–11
    and faithfulness, 98–9
cyborg manifesto, 29, 145–6, 149

de Beauvoir, S., 11, 14–15, 86–7, 124, 127,
    148
  on alterity, 45–7
  friendship with Richard Wright, 41–3
  on racism, 43
    and gender oppression, 44, 47–61
Decosta-Willis, M., 43
de Lauretis, T., 135, 147, 148
Deleuze, G., 39, 134, 135
Dellamora, R., 34
de Man, P., 88
Derrida, J., 6, 35, 38, 88, 115
Descartes, R., 113, 114, 116
desegregation, in schools, 63–7, 70, 73–4, 75
dialectic, Hegelian, 125
diaspora,
  and cultural survival, 92–3, 105, 110–11
  and gender, 110
Dietz, M., 62, 84
difference, 75–80, 146–7
  ethnic, 109–10
  modes of, 101, 102
  see also alterity
disclosive theory, 68
discrimination see class structures; exclusion;
    gender oppression; racism; social
    discrimination
Dollard, J., 43
drag, 90, 106–7
Drake, St. C., 56
Durham, M., 11

education, desegregation in, 63–7, 70, 73–4,
    75
Eichmann, A., 81, 82
Ellis, R., 23
Ellison, R., 48, 74, 81
Elshtain, J., 73
embodiment,
    and anti-essentialism, 123, 132–3, 148
    concept of, 117–19, 121, 134–5, 136–7
    and essentialism, 132–3, 148
    experience of, 126–7, 128
    and fascism, 137
    and history, 131–2, 133, 134
    and Jewish people, 104
    and liberalism, 120–2
    in the political realm, 77–8, 121–2
    and racism, 126–9, 135–7
    and recreation, 126
    and spatiality, 128
    of women, 130–1
    see also body; visibility
encrypting, 90, 106–7
Eppeler, K. Sanchez- see Sanchez-Eppeler, K.
equality, 69–70
Eribon, D., 4
erotic relationships, 46, 61
essentialism, 8, 35, 85, 115–16, 117, 123,
    137–8
    and embodiment, 132–3, 148
    and Nazism, 122
    and paranoia, 114–15, 116, 117, 122
    and race, 116–17
    and racism, 117
    see also anti-essentialism
ethical relationships, 46
    see also morality
ethnicity see Algerian women; black people;
    Jewish people; race; racial difference;
    racism
Ettinger, E., 82
exclusion,
    in feminism, 7–8, 36
    see also social discrimination

Fabre, M., 42, 43, 44, 54
faith,
    of feminism, 27, 35
    see also ideology; religion
faithfulness see authenticity
Fanon, F., 16, 70, 71, 93, 114, 118, 123–32,
    135, 137
fascism, 11, 12, 34
    and embodiment, 137
    and feminism, 23–4, 137
    see also anti-Semitism; Nazism; racism

fear,
    of essentialism, 114–15, 116, 117, 122
    of the future, 39
Felski, R., 77, 102, 146–7
feminism,
    boundaries, 53
    commitment to, 6
    as a community, 7, 19, 20, 147
    concept of, 147–8
    concepts of the future, 35–6, 144–6
    exclusion in, 7–8, 36
    faith of, 27, 35
    and fascism, 23–4, 137
    genealogical understanding, 5–7, 143,
        149–50
    generational tensions, 25
    historical nature, 6–7, 9, 11, 141
    and ideology, 8
    inclusion in, 7–8
    and the nation-state, 24, 25
    nature of, 1–2, 8–9, 11, 19, 36, 83–4, 149
    and postmodernism, 27–9, 32–3
    and religion, 26–7, 28
    ressentiment in, 40–1, 53
    and sexual categorisation, 36
    and spatiality, 20–1, 24, 35, 149
    and suffering, 35, 141
    and temporality, 20–1, 24, 25–8, 35,
        148–9
    trauma in, 140
    violence in, 27
    see also gender oppression; post-feminism;
        woman; women
feminist identity, 19, 36
feminist political imagination, 10–12
Fergusson, K., 8
Flax, J., 8–9, 82
Foucault, M., 1, 2, 3–4, 9, 11, 17, 18, 21, 30,
    34, 35, 36, 37–8, 39, 63, 87, 104, 105, 122,
    123, 134, 135, 139, 141–3, 144, 146,
    149
France, racism in, 59
Fraser, M., 78
Fraser, N., 34, 77, 79, 102, 103
freedom, nature of, 149, 150
Fremont, G., 36
Freud, S., 38, 106, 128, 140, 141, 150
Fuss, D., 8, 16, 113, 124, 131
    on constructionism, 116
    on embodiment, 121–2, 134
    on essentialism, 114–16, 117, 123, 138
future,
    concepts of, 35–6, 144–6
    fear of, 39
    see also temporality

Gatens, M., 122–3, 133
gay sexuality *see* homosexuality; lesbian sexuality
Gayle, A., 42, 43
gender,
    concept of, 85
    cultural constructions, 86–9
    and cultural survival, 103, 104, 105, 106, 109
    and diaspora, 110
    and identity, 109–11
    and Judaism, 105
    and lesbian sexuality, 147–8
    and mimesis, 94, 103, 104–5
    performativity of, 87–9, 90–1, 92, 106, 107, 108–9
    and race, 109
    see also man; sexual identity; woman; women
gender oppression, and racism, 44, 47–61, 131
genealogy,
    characteristics, 4, 142–3, 144–5, 146
    definition, 2
    in feminism, 5–7, 143, 149–50
    and freedom, 149
    and identity, 100–1
    and the politics of memory, 141–2
    purpose, 144
    and temporality, 38–9, 142–4
    see also history
generational tensions, in feminism, 25
Gilroy, P., 43, 44, 50, 77, 79, 110
Girard, R., 90
Gordon, C., 146
Gordon, L., 131
Gothlin, E. Lundgren- *see* Lundgren-Gothlin, E.
Grewal, I., 8
Grosz, E., 133–5
Guattari, F., 39, 134

Hacking, I., 141–2
Haraway, D., 9, 29, 36, 145, 149
hate speech, 108–9
Havas, R., 2
Heath, S., 115
Hegelian dialectic, 125
Heidegger, M., 63, 67–8, 81–2
Hekman, S., 37
Helie-Lucas, M.-A., 131
Heller, A., 4
Hemenway, R., 74–5
Hennessey, R., 78
heroism, 32, 33

heterosexuality, as mimesis, 89–92, 103, 104–5, 106–7
Hewitt, A., 21, 94, 105
historical consciousness, 4
historical nature, of feminism, 6–7, 9, 11, 141
historicity,
    of black people, 125, 129
    concept of, 18–19, 71
    see also temporality
history,
    and embodiment, 131–2, 133, 134
    and trauma, 140–1, 142
    see also genealogy; temporality
Hitlerism *see* Nazism
Holocaust,
    representation of, 22–3
    see also anti-Semitism; Jewish people
homosexuality,
    encrypting of, 90, 106–7
    repression of, 90, 91
    see also lesbian sexuality
Honig, B., 62, 83
hooks, b., 7, 8, 73, 135–6
Horkheimer, M., 15, 57, 86, 93–7, 102–3, 105, 106, 108, 111, 120
Howell, L., 145
Hurston, Z.N., 74–5
Hutchings, K., 82
Huyssen, A., 8

ideas, power of, 3–4
identity, 34
    and anti-essentialism, 122–3
    and body, 120–1, 126–7, 131, 135–6
    and citation, 106, 107–9, 110
    in community, 19, 108
    concept of, 85, 146–7
    feminist, 19, 36
    and gender, 109–11
    and genealogy, 100–1
    non-hegemonic, 92–3, 100, 103
    political, 40–1
    and racism, 108, 109
    sexual, 27, 35, 45
ideology,
    and feminism, 8
    see also faith
imperialism *see* colonialism
inclusion, in feminism, 7–8
Irigaray, L., 90–1, 119

Jayawardena, K., 8
Jewish community, nature of, 98, 99, 100–1, 103–4, 110

Jewish people,
  authenticity in, 98–9
  cultural survival *see* cultural survival, of
    Jewish people
  and diaspora, 92–3, 105, 110–11
  and embodiment, 104
  and encrypting, 107
  and mimesis, 92–3, 95, 98–9, 103–4, 107
  see also anti-Semitism; Holocaust
Joyce, J., 54
Judaism,
  faithfulness to, 98–9
  and gender, 105
judgement, 82

Kant, I., 82
Kaplan, C., 8
Kaplan, M., 80
Kinnamon, K., 42, 44, 54
Klein, M., 90
Kohn, J., 83
Kreis, W., 22
Kristeva, J., 11, 14, 17, 18, 23, 24, 25–9, 30,
  36, 145

Labarthe, P. Lacoue- *see* Lacoue-Labarthe,
  P.
Lacan, J., 35
Laclau, E., 10
Lacoue-Labarthe, P., 22
land, sense of *see* diaspora
Lauretis, T. de *see* de Lauretis, T.
Lazare, B., 76
Lerna, G., 135
lesbian sexuality, 107
  and gender, 147–8
  as mimesis, 89
  see also homosexuality
Levinas, E., 16, 45–7, 61, 99, 114, 118,
  119–22, 123, 126, 131, 132, 135, 137
liberalism, and embodiment, 120–2
liberation, from colonialism, 125–6, 129–30,
  131
limits *see* boundaries
linguistics, and gender performativity, 88,
  90–1
Little Rock, desegregation in, 63–7, 70,
  75
living conditions, of black people, 55–8
Lotringer, S., 17, 143
Lucas, M.-A. Helie- *see* Helie-Lucas, M.-A.
Lundgren-Gothlin, E., 44

MacIntyre, A., 122
MacNay, L., 37, 133

man,
  dichotomy with woman, 27–9, 35,
    45
  see also gender
Man, P. de *see* de Man, P.
Martin, B., 147, 148
Marxism, 119
May, L., 83
McCall, D., 56
melancholia, 90, 92, 106, 107
memoro-politics, 141–2
  see also remembering
metaphysics, 27, 30, 32, 34, 35
Michaud, E., 22
mimesis,
  and alterity, 95–6, 107, 108
  and anti-Semitism, 94, 95–9, 108, 148
  and citation, 107–9
  concept of, 94–5, 102–3
  and gender, 94, 103, 104–5
  in heterosexuality, 89–92, 103, 104–5,
    106–7
  and Jewish people, 92–3, 95, 98–9, 103–4,
    107
  in lesbian sexuality, 89
  and Pauline theology, 100–1
  and power relations, 103
  and racism, 93, 108, 127, 128–30
  repressed, 96–7, 106–7, 108
  and repression, 89–90, 91
  and speech, 108
  by women, 94, 104–5, 130
Modleski, T., 29
Mohanty, C., 7, 147, 148, 149
Moi, T., 44, 124
Moraga, C., 29
morality, 26, 28, 30, 31–2
  see also ethical relationships; religion
Mosse, G., 33
music,
  of black people, 53–4
  connectivity in, 61

Nancy, J.-L., 6, 7, 10, 18–20, 22, 38, 101, 109,
  143, 149
natality, 71–5
nation-state,
  and feminism, 24, 25
  and the politics of resistance, 23
Native Son (Wright), 44, 47–9, 50–3, 54–5,
  56–7
Nazism, 21–2, 33, 56–7, 76, 80–2
  and anti-Semitism, 99
  and the body, 119, 120, 121
  and essentialism, 122

Nietzsche, F., 2, 9, 26–7, 30–4, 37, 39, 40, 51, 63, 67, 86, 87, 88, 122, 142, 143, 150
nihilism, 30, 31, 35
Nilson, H., 2
non-hegemonic identity, 92–3, 100, 103

objectification,
  of black people, 57–8, 127, 128
  of women, 47, 48–9, 52–3
On, B.-A. Bar see Bar On, B.-A.
oppression, 122–3
  concepts of, 54–5
  connectivity in, 58, 60, 61
  see also class structures; exclusion; gender oppression; living conditions; racism; social discrimination
origins, and genealogy, 142–3
otherness see alterity

paranoia, and essentialism, 114–15, 116, 117, 122
pariahs, 76
Park, R., 56
participation, and visibility, 78–9
parvenus, 73, 76
passivity, 53, 58
Pauline theology, 100–1
Pearson, K. Ansell- see Ansell-Pearson, K.
performativity, of gender, 87–9, 90–1, 92, 106, 107, 108–9
Phelan, S., 148
Plato, 25, 101, 116
plurality see social plurality
political affiliations, critical assessment of, 4–5
political identity, 40–1
political imagination, feminist, 10–12
political realm,
  appearance in, 67–71, 75–6, 77, 79–80, 82
  boundaries of, 62–3, 64, 65, 69, 70, 80
  and children, 65, 71–2, 73
  concept of, 77
  and counterpublic spheres, 76–7, 78, 79, 80
  embodiment in, 77–8, 121–2
  and natality, 71–5
  and social plurality, 75–6
  thinking in, 81–3
  see also liberalism; Marxism; Nazism; totalitarianism
politics,
  of memory, 141–2
  of resistance, 4–5, 7, 8, 9, 37
    and the nation-state, 23

sentiment in, 9
  and suffering, 58
post-feminism, 144
postmodernism, 8
  and feminism, 27–9, 32–3
  see also temporality
post-structuralism, 8, 24, 28, 143
power, will to, 2, 33
power relations, and mimesis, 103
Pratt, M.B., 147
private realm, boundaries of, 66
Probyn, E., 135
promised land see diaspora
public realm see political realm

Quinby, L., 34, 38, 143, 149

Rabinow, P., 139, 146
race,
  and essentialism, 116–17
  and gender, 109
racial difference, 109–10
racial epidermal schema, 127–9, 131, 135–6
racism, 12, 33–4, 60
  de Beauvoir's interest in, 43
  and embodiment, 126–9, 135–7
  and essentialism, 117
  in France, 59
  and gender oppression, 44, 47–61, 131
  and identity, 108, 109
  and mimesis, 93, 108, 127, 128–30
  ressentiment in, 48, 50–1
  see also anti-Semitism; black people; desegregation
racist speech, 108–9
Ramazanoglu, C., 37
recreation, 124–6
reflection, and anti-Semitism, 97–8
relationships, theory of, 45–7, 61
religion,
  and the body, 119
  and feminism, 26–7, 28
  and mimesis, 107
  and social discrimination, 65
  and temporality, 27
  see also Christianity; faith; ideology; Judaism; morality; Pauline theology
remembering, 122–3
  see also memoro-politics
repressed mimesis, 96–7, 106–7, 108
repression, and mimesis, 89–90, 91
resistance, politics of see politics, of resistance

ressentiment,
  in feminism, 40–1, 53
  in racism, 48, 50–1
Rich, A., 149
Riley, D., 5, 7, 28, 150
Rose, G., 2, 22, 34
Rose, J., 23

sacrifice,
  and black people, 74
  see also suffering
Said, E., 8
Sanchez-Eppeler, K., 8
Sartre, J.-P., 15, 42, 43, 86, 96, 97–8, 99, 101,
  102, 106, 108, 111, 124, 125, 128
schools, desegregation in, 63–7, 70, 73–4,
  75
Schor, N., 91, 116, 117
Schott, R.M., 82
sentiment, in politics, 9
sex see gender
sexual categorisation, 27–9, 35, 36
sexual discrimination see gender oppression
sexual identity, 27, 35, 45
Sharpley-Whiting, T., 131
skin colour see racial epidermal schema;
  visibility
social discrimination, 65–6, 76–7, 78
social plurality, and the political realm,
  75–6
social realm,
  boundaries of, 65–6, 70
  and political concerns, 78
sociology, of cities, 55–8
Socrates, 81
soul, concept of, 119
spatiality,
  and colonialism, 129–30
  and embodiment, 128
  and feminism, 20–1, 24, 35, 149
  of Nazism, 22
speech,
  and mimesis, 108
  racist, 108–9
Speer, A., 22
Spelman, E., 8, 116
Spivak, G., 3, 8, 35, 131, 132, 133, 136–7,
  138
state see nation-state
Stoekl, A., 22
subaltern woman, 35
suffering, 46
  connectivity in, 61
  and feminism, 35, 141
  gendered, 44, 47–61, 131

and political identity, 40–1
and politics, 58
shared, 53
see also oppression; sacrifice

Tapper, M., 40, 53
temporality,
  and community, 20
  and feminism, 20–1, 24, 25–8, 35,
    148–9
  and genealogy, 38–9, 142–4
  of Nazism, 21–2
  and religion, 27
  and trauma, 139–41
  see also future; historicity; history;
    post-feminism; postmodernism;
    post-structuralism
Thatcher, M., 23
theology, Pauline, 100–1
Thiele, L.P., 30, 32, 33, 37, 39
thinking, in the political realm, 81–3
time, concept of, 18
totalitarianism, 70, 72, 73, 76, 81
tradition, 110
  see also cultural survival
trauma,
  in feminism, 140
  and history, 140–1, 142
  and temporality, 139–41
Trinh, Minh-ha, 36, 136

Ubermensch, 32, 34
urban deprivation, 55–8

Villa, D., 68, 69, 70, 81, 82
violence,
  and communities, 7
  in feminism, 27
visibility, 68–9, 70–1, 75–6, 77, 78–9
  see also appearance; embodiment

Walker, A., 135–6
Ware, V., 8
Warren, R., 74
White, R., 131
Whiting, T. Sharpley- see Sharpley-Whiting,
  T.
will to power, 2, 33
Willis, M. Decosta- see Decosta-Willis, M.
Wittig, M., 85, 90, 107, 147–8
woman,
  concept of, 7, 8, 9, 26
  dichotomy with man, 27–9, 35, 45
  subaltern, 35
  see also gender

women,
  alterity of, 45–7, 48–9
  authenticity in, 58, 136
  embodiment of, 130–1
  mimesis by, 94, 104–5, 130
  objectification of, 47, 48–9, 52–3
  passivity of, 58
  Wright's attitude to, 43–4, 60
Wright, E., 42, 43

Wright, R., 14–15, 53–4, 55–6, 57–8, 59,
    60–1, 75
  attitude to women, 43–4, 60
  friendship with Simone de Beauvoir, 41–3
  Native Son, 44, 47–9, 50–3, 54–5, 56–7

Young, I.M., 133
Young, L., 124, 127
Young-Bruehl, E., 73, 74, 83